The
Oxford Book
Of Modern Verse

1892–1935

The
Oxford Book
Of Modern Verse

1892–1935

Chosen by
W. B. Yeats

New York
Oxford University Press
1937

PRINTED IN THE UNITED STATES OF AMERICA

INTRODUCTION

I

I HAVE tried to include in this book all good poets who have lived or died from three years before the death of Tennyson to the present moment, except some two or three who belong through the character of their work to an earlier period. Even a long-lived man has the right to call his own contemporaries modern. To the generation which began to think and read in the late eighties of the last century the four poets whose work begins this book were unknown, or, if known, of an earlier generation that did not stir its sympathy. Gerard Hopkins remained unpublished for thirty years. Fifty-odd years ago I met him in my father's studio on different occasions, but remember almost nothing. A boy of seventeen, Walt Whitman in his pocket, had little interest in a querulous, sensitive scholar. Thomas Hardy's poems were unwritten or unpublished. Robert Bridges seemed a small Victorian poet whose poetry, published in expensive hand-printed books, one could find behind glass doors in the houses of wealthy friends. I will consider the genius of these three when the development of schools gives them great influence. Wilfred Blunt one

knew through the report of friends as a fashion-
able amateur who had sacrificed a capacity for
literature and the visible arts to personal ad-
venture. Some ten years had to pass before
anybody understood that certain sonnets, lyrics,
stanzas of his were permanent in our literature.
A young man, London bred or just arrived
there, would have felt himself repelled by the
hard, cold energy of Henley's verse, called it
rhetoric, or associated it in some way with that
propaganda whereby Henley, through the vehi-
cle of a weekly review and a magazine that were
financial failures, had turned the young men at
Oxford and Cambridge into imperialists. 'Why
should I respect Henley?' said to me Clement
Shorter. 'I sell two hundred thousand copies
a week of *The Sphere*; the circulation of *The
National Observer* fell to two hundred at the
end.' Henley lay upon the sofa, crippled by
his incautious youth, dragged his body, crutch-
supported, between two rooms, imagining im-
perial might. For a young man, struggling for
expression, despairing of achievement, he re-
mained hidden behind his too obvious effective-
ness. Nor would that young man have felt
anything but contempt for the poetry of Oscar
Wilde, considering it an exaggeration of every
Victorian fault, nor, except in the case of one
poem not then written, has time corrected the

verdict. Wilde, a man of action, a born drama-
tist, finding himself overshadowed by old fa-
mous men he could not attack, for he was of
their time and shared its admirations, tricked
and clowned to draw attention to himself. Even
when disaster struck him down it could not
wholly clear his soul. Now that I have plucked
from the *Ballad of Reading Gaol* its foreign
feathers it shows a stark realism akin to that of
Thomas Hardy, the contrary to all its author
deliberately sought. I plucked out even famous
lines because, effective in themselves, put into
the Ballad they become artificial, trivial, arbi-
trary; a work of art can have but one subject.

> Yet each man kills the thing he loves,
>   By each let this be heard,
> Some do it with a bitter look,
>   Some with a flattering word.
> The coward does it with a kiss,
>   The brave man with a sword!
>
> Some kill their love when they are young,
>   And some when they are old;
> Some strangle with the hands of Lust,
>   Some with the hands of Gold:
> The kindest use a knife, because
>   The dead so soon grow cold.

I have stood in judgement upon Wilde, bring-
ing into the light a great, or almost great poem,

as he himself had done had he lived; my work gave me that privilege.

II

All these writers were, in the eye of the new generation, in so far as they were known, Victorian, and the new generation was in revolt. But one writer, almost unknown to the general public — I remember somebody saying at his death ' no newspaper has given him an obituary notice ' — had its entire uncritical admiration, Walter Pater. That is why I begin this book with the famous passage from his essay on Leonardo da Vinci. Only by printing it in *vers libre* can one show its revolutionary importance. Pater was accustomed to give each sentence a separate page of manuscript, isolating and analysing its rhythm; Henley wrote certain 'hospital poems,' not included in this book, in *vers libre*, thinking of his dramatic, everyday material, in that an innovator, but did not permit a poem to arise out of its own rhythm as do Turner and Pound at their best and as, I contend, Pater did. I shall presently discuss the meaning of this passage which dominated a generation, a domination so great that all over Europe from that day to this men shrink from Leonardo's masterpiece as from an over-flattered woman.

For the moment I am content to recall one later writer:

> O wha's been here afore me, lass,
> And hoo did he get in?

The revolt against Victorianism meant to the young poet a revolt against irrelevant descriptions of nature, the scientific and moral discursiveness of *In Memoriam* — ' When he should have been broken-hearted ', said Verlaine, ' he had many reminiscences ' — the political eloquence of Swinburne, the psychological curiosity of Browning, and the poetical diction of everybody. Poets said to one another over their black coffee — a recently imported fashion — ' We must purify poetry of all that is not poetry ', and by poetry they meant poetry as it had been written by Catullus, a great name at that time, by the Jacobean writers, by Verlaine, by Baudelaire. Poetry was a tradition like religion and liable to corruption, and it seemed that they could best restore it by writing lyrics technically perfect, their emotion pitched high, and as Pater offered instead of moral earnestness life lived as ' a pure gem-like flame ' all accepted him for master.

But every light has its shadow, we tumble out of one pickle into another, the ' pure gem-like flame ' was an insufficient motive; the sons of

men who had admired Garibaldi or applauded
the speeches of John Bright, picked Ophelias
out of the gutter, who knew exactly what they
wanted and had no intention of committing
suicide. My father gave these young men their
right name. When I had described a supper
with Count Stenbock, scholar, connoisseur,
drunkard, poet, pervert, most charming of men,
he said ' they are the Hamlets of our age'.
Some of these Hamlets went mad, some drank,
drinking not as happy men drink but in solitude,
all had courage, all suffered public opprobrium
— generally for their virtues or for sins they did
not commit — all had good manners. Good
manners in written and spoken word were an
essential part of their tradition — ' Life', said
Lionel Johnson, ' must be a ritual'; all in the
presence of women or even with one another put
aside their perplexities; all had gaiety, some had
wit:

> Unto us they belong,
> To us the bitter and gay,
> Wine and woman and song.

Some turned Catholic — that too was a tradition.
I read out at a meeting of The Rhymers' Club a
letter describing Meynell's discovery of Francis
Thompson, at that time still bedded under his
railway arch, then his still unpublished *Ode to
the Setting Sun*. But Francis Thompson had

been born a Catholic; Lionel Johnson was the first convert; Dowson adopted a Catholic point of view without, I think, joining that church, an act requiring energy and decision.

Occasionally at some evening party some young woman asked a poet what he thought of strikes, or declared that to paint pictures or write poetry at such a moment was to resemble the fiddler Nero, for great meetings of revolutionary Socialists were disturbing Trafalgar Square on Sunday afternoons; a young man known to most of us told some such party that he had stood before a desk in an office not far from Southampton Row resolved to protect it with his life because it contained documents that would hang William Morris, and wound up by promising a revolution in six months. Shelley must have had some such immediate circle when he wrote to friends urging them to withdraw their money from the Funds. We poets continued to write verse and read it out at ' The Cheshire Cheese ', convinced that to take part in such movements would be only less disgraceful than to write for the newspapers.

III

Then in 1900 everybody got down off his stilts; henceforth nobody drank absinthe with his black coffee; nobody went mad; nobody committed suicide; nobody joined the Catholic church; or if they did I have forgotten.

Victorianism had been defeated, though two writers dominated the movement who had never heard of that defeat or did not believe in it; Rudyard Kipling and William Watson. Indian residence and associations had isolated the first, he was full of opinions, of politics, of impurities — to use our word — and the word must have been right, for he interests a critical audience to-day by the grotesque tragedy of ' Danny Deever ', the matter but not the form of old street ballads, and by songs traditional in matter and form like the ' *St. Helena Lullaby* '. The second had reached maturity before the revolt began, his first book had been published in the early eighties. ' Wring the neck of rhetoric ' Verlaine had said, and the public soon turned against William Watson, forgetting that at his best he had not rhetoric but noble eloquence. As I turn his pages I find verse after verse read long ago and still unforgettable, this to some journalist who, intoxicated perhaps by William Archer's translations from Ibsen, had described, it may be, some lyric elaborating or deepening its own tradition as of ' no importance to the age ':

> Great Heaven! When these with clamour shrill
>   Drift out to Lethe's harbour bar

> A verse of Lovelace shall be still
> As vivid as a pulsing star:

this, received from some Miltonic cliff that had
it from a Roman voice:

> The august, inhospitable, inhuman night
> Glittering magnificently unperturbed.

IV

Conflict bequeathed its bias. Folk-song, un-
known to the Victorians as their attempts to
imitate it show, must, because never declama-
tory or eloquent, fill the scene. If anybody will
turn these pages attending to poets born in the
'fifties, 'sixties, and 'seventies, he will find how
successful are their folk-songs and their imita-
tions. In Ireland, where still lives almost undis-
turbed the last folk tradition of western Europe,
the songs of Campbell and Colum draw from
that tradition their themes, return to it, and are
sung to Irish airs by boys and girls who have
never heard the names of the authors; but the
reaction from rhetoric, from all that was pre-
pense and artificial, has forced upon these writers
now and again, as upon my own early work, a
facile charm, a too soft simplicity. In England
came like temptations. The *Shropshire Lad* is
worthy of its fame, but a mile further and all had

been marsh. Thomas Hardy, though his work lacked technical accomplishment, made the necessary correction through his mastery of the impersonal objective scene. John Synge brought back masculinity to Irish verse with his harsh disillusionment, and later, when the folk movement seemed to support vague political mass excitement, certain poets began to create passionate masterful personality.

V

We remembered the Gaelic poets of the seventeenth and early eighteenth centuries wandering, after the flight of the Catholic nobility, among the boorish and the ignorant, singing their loneliness and their rage; James Stephens, Frank O'Connor made them symbols of our pride:

> The periwinkle, and the tough dog-fish
> At eventide have got into my dish!
> The great, where are they now! the great had
>   said —
> This is not seemly, bring to him instead
> That which serves his and serves our dignity —
> And that was done.

> I am O'Rahilly:
> Here in a distant place I hold my tongue,
> Who once said all his say, when he was young!

I showed Lady Gregory a few weeks before her death a book by Day Lewis. 'I prefer', she said, 'those poems translated by Frank O'Connor because they come out of original sin.' A distinguished Irish poet said a month back — I had read him a poem by Turner — 'We cannot become philosophic like the English, our lives are too exciting.' He was not thinking of such passing episodes as civil war, his own imprisonment, but of an always inflamed public opinion that made sonnet or play almost equally perilous; yet civil war has had its effect. Twelve years ago Oliver Gogarty was captured by his enemies, imprisoned in a deserted house on the edge of the Liffey with every prospect of death. Pleading a natural necessity he got into the garden, plunged under a shower of revolver bullets and as he swam the ice-cold December stream promised it, should it land him in safety, two swans. I was present when he fulfilled that vow. His poetry fits the incident, a gay, stoical — no, I will not withhold the word — heroic song. Irish by tradition and many ancestors, I love, though I have nothing to offer but the philosophy they deride, swashbucklers, horsemen, swift indifferent men; yet I do not think that is the sole reason, good reason though it is, why I gave him considerable space, and think him one of the great lyric poets of our age.

VI

We have more affinity with Henley and Blunt than with other modern English poets, but have not felt their influence; we are what we are because almost without exception we have had some part in public life in a country where public life is simple and exciting. We are not many; Ireland has had few poets of any kind outside Gaelic. I think England has had more good poets from 1900 to the present day than during any period of the same length since the early seventeenth century. There are no predominant figures, no Browning, no Tennyson, no Swinburne, but more than I have found room for have written two, three, or half a dozen lyrics that may be permanent.

During the first years of the century the best known were celebrators of the country-side or of the life of ships; I think of Davies and of Masefield; some few wrote in the manner of the traditional country ballad. Others, descended not from Homer but from Virgil, wrote what the young communist scornfully calls 'Belles-lettres': Binyon when at his best, as I think, of Tristram and Isoult: Sturge Moore of centaurs, amazons, gazelles copied from a Persian picture: De la Mare short lyrics that carry us back through *Christabel* or *Kubla Khan*.

Through what wild centuries
Roves back the rose?

The younger of the two ladies who wrote under the name of ' Michael Field ' made personal lyrics in the manner of Walter Savage Landor and the Greek anthology.

None of these were innovators; they preferred to keep all the past their rival; their fame will increase with time. They have been joined of late years by Sacheverell Sitwell with his *Canons of Giant Art*, written in the recently rediscovered 'sprung verse', his main theme changes of colour, or historical phase, in Greece, Crete, India. *Agamemnon's Tomb*, however, describes our horror at the presence and circumstance of death and rises to great intensity.

VII

Robert Bridges seemed for a time, through his influence on Laurence Binyon and others less known, the patron saint of the movement. His influence — practice, not theory — was never deadening; he gave to lyric poetry a new cadence, a distinction as deliberate as that of Whistler's painting, an impulse moulded and checked like that in certain poems of Landor, but different, more in the nerves, less in the blood, more birdlike, less human; words often

commonplace made unforgettable by some trick
of speeding and slowing,

> A glitter of pleasure
> And a dark tomb,

or by some trick of simplicity, not the impulsive
simplicity of youth but that of age, much im-
pulse examined and rejected:

> I heard a linnet courting
>   His lady in the spring!
> His mates were idly sporting,
>   Nor stayed to hear him sing
>   His song of love. —
> I fear my speech distorting
>   His tender love.

Every metaphor, every thought a commonplace,
emptiness everywhere, the whole magnificent.

VIII

A modern writer is beset by what Rossetti
called 'the soulless self-reflections of man's
skill'; the more vivid his nature, the greater his
boredom, a boredom no Greek, no Elizabethan,
knew in like degree, if at all. He may escape
to the classics with the writers I have just de-
scribed, or with much loss of self-control and
coherence force language against its will into a
powerful, artificial vividness. Edith Sitwell has

a temperament of a strangeness so high-pitched
that only through this artifice could it find ex-
pression. One cannot think of her in any other
age or country. She has transformed with her
metrical virtuosity traditional metres reborn not
to be read but spoken, exaggerated metaphors
into mythology, carrying them from poem to
poem, compelling us to go backward to some
first usage for the birth of the myth; if the storm
suggest the bellowing of elephants, some later
poem will display ' The elephant trunks of the
sea '. Nature appears before us in a hashish-
eater's dream. This dream is double; in its
first half, through separated metaphor, through
mythology, she creates, amid crowds and scen-
ery that suggest the Russian Ballet and Aubrey
Beardsley's final phase, a perpetual metamor-
phosis that seems an elegant, artificial child-
hood; in the other half, driven by a necessity of
contrast, a nightmare vision like that of Web-
ster, of the emblems of mortality. A group of
writers have often a persistent image. There
are ' stars ' in poem after poem of certain writers
of the 'nineties as though to symbolize an aspira-
tion towards what is inviolate and fixed; and
now in poem after poem by Edith Sitwell or
later writers are ' bones ' — ' the anguish of the
skeleton ', ' the terrible Gehenna of the bone ';
Eliot has:

> No contact possible to flesh
> Allayed the fever of the bone.

and Eleanor Wylie, an American whose exquisite work is slighter than that of her English
contemporaries because she has not their full
receptivity to the profound hereditary sadness
of English genius:

> Live like the velvet mole:
> Go burrow underground,
>
> And there hold intercourse
> With roots of trees and stones,
> With rivers at their source
> And disembodied bones.

Laurence Binyon, Sturge Moore, knew nothing
of this image; it seems most persistent among
those who, throwing aside tradition, seek something somebody has called ' essential form ' in
the theme itself.   A fairly well-known woman
painter in September drew my house, at that
season almost hidden in foliage; she reduced the
trees to skeletons as though it were mid-winter,
in pursuit of ' essential form.'   Does not intellectual analysis in one of its moods identify man
with that which is most persistent in his body?
The poets are haunted once again by the Elizabethan image, but there is a difference.   Since
Poincaré said ' space is the creation of our ances-

tors', we have found it more and more difficult to separate ourselves from the dead when we commit them to the grave; the bones are not dead but accursed, accursed because unchanging.

> The small bones built in the womb
> The womb that loathed the bones
> And cast out the soul.

Perhaps in this new, profound poetry, the symbol itself is contradictory, horror of life, horror of death.

IX

Eliot has produced his great effect upon his generation because he has described men and women that get out of bed or into it from mere habit; in describing this life that has lost heart his own art seems grey, cold, dry. He is an Alexander Pope, working without apparent imagination, producing his effects by a rejection of all rhythms and metaphors used by the more popular romantics rather than by the discovery of his own, this rejection giving his work an unexaggerated plainness that has the effect of novelty. He has the rhythmical flatness of The *Essay on Man* — despite Miss Sitwell's advocacy I see Pope as Blake and Keats saw him — later, in *The Waste Land*, amid much that is moving in symbol and imagery there is much monotony of accent:

> When lovely woman stoops to folly and
> Paces about her room again, alone,
> She smooths her hair with automatic hand,
> And puts a record on the gramophone.

I was affected, as I am by these lines, when I saw
for the first time a painting by Manet. I longed
for the vivid colour and light of Rousseau and
Courbet, I could not endure the grey middle-
tint — and even to-day Manet gives me an in-
complete pleasure; he had left the procession.
Nor can I put the Eliot of these poems among
those that descend from Shakespeare and the
translators of the Bible. I think of him as satir-
ist rather than poet. Once only does that early
work speak in the great manner:

> The host with someone indistinct
> Converses at the door apart,
> The nightingales are singing near
> The Convent of the Sacred Heart,
>
> And sang within the bloody wood
> When Agamemnon cried aloud,
> And let their liquid siftings fall
> To stain the stiff dishonoured shroud.

Not until *The Hollow Men* and *Ash-Wednes-
day*, where he is helped by the short lines, and in
the dramatic poems where his remarkable sense
of actor, chanter, scene, sweeps him away, is
there rhythmical animation. Two or three of

my friends attribute the change to an emotional enrichment from religion, but his religion compared to that of John Gray, Francis Thompson, Lionel Johnson in *The Dark Angel*, lacks all strong emotion; a New England Protestant by descent, there is little self-surrender in his personal relation to God and the soul. *Murder in the Cathedral* is a powerful stage play because the actor, the monkish habit, certain repeated words, symbolize what we know, not what the author knows. Nowhere has the author explained how Becket and the King differ in aim; Becket's people have been robbed and persecuted in his absence; like the King he demands strong government. Speaking through Becket's mouth Eliot confronts a world growing always more terrible with a religion like that of some great statesman, a pity not less poignant because it tempers the prayer book with the results of mathematical philosophy.

Peace. And let them be, in their exaltation.
They speak better than they know, and beyond your
    understanding,
They know and do not know, that acting is suffering
And suffering is action. Neither does the actor suffer
Nor the patient act. But both are fixed
In an eternal action, an eternal patience
To which all must consent that it may be willed
And which all must suffer that they may will it,

That the pattern may subsist, for the pattern is the
    action
And the suffering, that the wheel may turn and still
Be forever still.

X

Ezra Pound has made flux his theme; plot,
characterization, logical discourse, seem to him
abstractions unsuitable to a man of his genera-
tion. He is mid-way in an immense poem in
vers libre called for the moment *The Cantos*,
where the metamorphosis of Dionysus, the
descent of Odysseus into Hades, repeat them-
selves in various disguises, always in association
with some third that is not repeated. Hades
may become the hell where whatever modern
men he most disapproves of suffer damnation,
the metamorphosis petty frauds practised by
Jews at Gibraltar. The relation of all the ele-
ments to one another, repeated or unrepeated, is
to become apparent when the whole is finished.
There is no transmission through time, we pass
without comment from ancient Greece to
modern England, from modern England to
medieval China; the symphony, the pattern, is
timeless, flux eternal and therefore without
movement. Like other readers I discover at
present merely exquisite or grotesque frag-
ments. He hopes to give the impression that
all is living, that there are no edges, no convexi-

ties, nothing to check the flow; but can such a poem have a mathematical structure? Can impressions that are in part visual, in part metrical, be related like the notes of a symphony; has the author been carried beyond reason by a theoretical conception? His belief in his own conception is so great that since the appearance of the first Canto I have tried to suspend judgement.

When I consider his work as a whole I find more style than form; at moments more style, more deliberate nobility and the means to convey it than in any contemporary poet known to me, but it is constantly interrupted, broken, twisted into nothing by its direct opposite, nervous obsession, nightmare, stammering confusion; he is an economist, poet, politician, raging at malignants with inexplicable characters and motives, grotesque figures out of a child's book of beasts. This loss of self-control, common among uneducated revolutionists, is rare — Shelley had it in some degree — among men of Ezra Pound's culture and erudition. Style and its opposite can alternate, but form must be full, sphere-like, single. Even where there is no interruption he is often content, if certain verses and lines have style, to leave unbridged transitions, unexplained ejaculations, that make his meaning unintelligible. He has great influence, more perhaps than any contemporary except Eliot, is probably the source of that lack of form and consequent obscurity which is the main defect of Auden, Day Lewis, and their school, a school which, as will presently be seen, I greatly admire. Even where the style is sustained throughout one gets an impression, especially when he is writing in *vers libre*, that he has not got all the wine into the bowl, that he is a brilliant improvisator translating at sight from an unknown Greek masterpiece:

> See, they return; ah, see the tentative
> Movements, and the slow feet,
> The trouble in the pace and the uncertain
> Wavering!
>
> See, they return, one, and by one,
> With fear, as half-awakened;
> As if the snow should hesitate
> And murmur in the wind,
> and half turn back;
>
> These were the Wing'd-with-awe,
> Inviolable.
> Gods of the winged shoe!
> With them the silver hounds,
> sniffing the trace of air!

XI

When my generation denounced scientific humanitarian pre-occupation, psychological curiosity, rhetoric, we had not found what ailed Victorian literature. The Elizabethans had all these things, especially rhetoric. A friend writes ' all bravado went out of English literature when Falstaff turned into Oliver Cromwell, into England's bad conscience '; but he is wrong. Dryden's plays are full of it. The mischief began at the end of the seventeenth century when man became passive before a mechanized nature; that lasted to our own day with the exception of a brief period between Smart's *Song to David* and the death of Byron, wherein imprisoned man beat upon the door. Or I may dismiss all that ancient history and say it began when Stendhal described a masterpiece as a ' mirror dawdling down a lane '. There are only two long poems in Victorian literature that caught public attention; *The Ring and the Book* where great intellect analyses the suffering of one passive soul, weighs the persecutor's guilt, and *The Idylls of the King* where a poetry in itself an exquisite passivity is built about an allegory where a characterless king represents the soul. I read few modern novels, but I think I am right in saying that in every novel that has created

INTRODUCTION

an intellectual fashion from Huysmans's *La Cathédrale* to Ernest Hemingway's *Farewell to Arms*, the chief character is a mirror. It has sometimes seemed of late years, though not in the poems I have selected for this book, as if the poet could at any moment write a poem by recording the fortuitous scene or thought, perhaps it might be enough to put into some fashionable rhythm — ' I am sitting in a chair, there are three dead flies on a corner of the ceiling '.

Change has come suddenly, the despair of my friends in the 'nineties part of its preparation. Nature, steel-bound or stone-built in the nineteenth century, became a flux where man drowned or swam; the moment had come for some poet to cry ' the flux is in my own mind '.

XII

It was Turner who raised that cry, to gain upon the instant a control of plastic material, a power of emotional construction, Pound has always lacked. At his rare best he competes with Eliot in precision, but Eliot's genius is human, mundane, impeccable, it seems to say ' this man will never disappoint, never be out of character. He moves among objects for which he accepts no responsibility, among the mapped and measured.' Generations must pass before man recovers control of event and circumstance; mind has recognized its responsibility, that is all; Turner himself seems the symbol of an incomplete discovery. After clearing up some metaphysical obscurity he leaves obscure what a moment's thought would have cleared; author of a suave, sophisticated comedy he can talk about 'snivelling majorities'; a rich-natured friendly man he has in his satirical platonic dialogue *The Aesthetes* shot upon forbidden ground. The first romantic poets, Blake, Coleridge, Shelley, dazed by new suddenly opening vistas, had equal though different inconsistencies. I think of him as the first poet to read a mathematical equation, a musical score, a book of verse, with an equal understanding; he seems to ride in an observation balloon, blue heaven above, earth beneath an abstract pattern.

We know nothing but abstract patterns, generalizations, mathematical equations, though such the havoc wrought by newspaper articles and government statistics, two abstractions may sit down to lunch. But what about the imagery we call nature, the sensual scene? Perhaps we are always awake and asleep at the same time; after all going to bed is but a habit; is not sleep by the testimony of the poets our common mother? In *The Seven Days of the Sun*, where there is much exciting thought, I find:

But to me the landscape is like a sea
The waves of the hills
And the bubbles of bush and flower
And the springtide breaking into white foam!

It is a slow sea,
Mare tranquillum,
And a thousand years of wind
Cannot raise a dwarf billow to the moonlight.

But the bosom of the landscape lifts and falls
With its own leaden tide,
That tide whose sparkles are the lilliputian stars.

It is that slow sea
That sea of adamantine languor,
Sleep!

I recall Pater's description of the Mona Lisa; had the individual soul of da Vinci's sitter gone down with the pearl divers or trafficked for strange webs? or did Pater foreshadow a poetry, a philosophy, where the individual is nothing, the flux of *The Cantos* of Ezra Pound, objects without contour as in *Le Chef-d'œuvre Inconnu,* human experience no longer shut into brief lives, cut off into this place and that place, the flux of Turner's poetry that within our minds enriches itself, re-dreams itself, yet only in seeming — for time cannot be divided? Yet one theme perplexes Turner, whether in comedy, dialogue, poem. Somewhere in the middle of it all da Vinci's sitter had private reality like that of

the Dark Lady among the women Shakespeare
had imagined, but because that private soul is
always behind our knowledge, though always
hidden it must be the sole source of pain, stupe-
faction, evil. A musician, he imagines Heaven
as a musical composition, a mathematician, as a
relation of curves, a poet, as a dark, inhuman sea.

> The sea carves innumerable shells
> Rolling itself into crystalline curves
> The cressets of its faintest sighs
> Flickering into filagreed whorls,
> Its lustre into mother-of-pearl
> Its mystery into fishes' eyes
> Its billowing abundance into whales
> Around and under the Poles.

XIII

In *The Mutations of the Phoenix* Herbert
Read discovers that the flux is in the mind, not
of it perhaps, but in it. The Phoenix is finite
mind rising in a nest of light from the sea or in-
finite; the discovery of Berkeley in ' Siris ' where
light is ' perception ', of Grosseteste, twelfth-
century philosopher, who defines it as ' corpore-
ality, or that of which corporeality is made '.

> All existence
>   past, present and to be
>   is in this sea fringe.
> There is no other temporal scene.

INTRODUCTION

The Phoenix burns spiritually
   among the fierce stars
   and in the docile brain's recesses.
Its ultimate spark
you cannot trace . . .

Light burns the world in the focus of an eye.

XIV

To Dorothy Wellesley nature is a womb, a
darkness; its surface is sleep, upon sleep we
walk, into sleep drive the plough, and there lie
the happy, the wise, the unconceived;

   They lie in the loam
   Laid backward by slice of the plough;
   They sit in the rock;
   In a matrix of amethyst crouches a man . .

but unlike Turner or Read she need not prove or
define, that was all done before she began to
write and think. As though it were the tale of
Mother Hubbard or the results of the last gen-
eral election, she accepts what Turner and Read
accept, sings her joy or sorrow in its presence, at
times facile and clumsy, at times magnificent in
her masculine rhythm, in the precision of her
style. Eliot and Edith Sitwell have much of
their intensity from a deliberate re-moulding or
checking of past impulse, Turner much of his
from a deliberate rejection of current belief, but
here is no criticism at all. A new positive belief

xxxii

has given to her, as it gave to Shelley, an un-checkable impulse, and this belief is all the more positive because found, not sought; like certain characters in William Morris she has ' lucky eyes ', her sail is full.

I knew nothing of her until a few months ago I read the opening passage in *Horses*, delighted by its changes in pace, abrupt assertion, then a long sweeping line, by its vocabulary modern and precise;

Who, in the garden-pony carrying skeps
Of grass or fallen leaves, his knees gone slack,
Round belly, hollow back,
Sees the Mongolian Tarpan of the Steppes?
Or, in the Shire with plaits and feathered feet,
The war-horse like the wind the Tartar knew?
Or, in the Suffolk Punch, spells out anew
The wild grey asses fleet
With stripe from head to tail, and moderate ears?

The swing away from Stendhal has passed Turner; the individual soul, the betrayal of the unconceived at birth, are among her principal themes, it must go further still; that soul must become its own betrayer, its own deliverer, the one activity, the mirror turn lamp. Not that the old conception is untrue, new literature better than old. In the greater nations every phase has characteristic beauty — has not Nicholas of Cusa said reality is expressed through contradiction?

Yet for me, a man of my time, through my poetical faculty living its history, after much meat fish seems the only possible diet. I have indeed read certain poems by Turner, by Dorothy Wellesley, with more than all the excitement that came upon me when, a very young man, I heard somebody read out in a London tavern the poems of Ernest Dowson's despair — that too living history.

XV

I have a distaste for certain poems written in the midst of the great war; they are in all anthologies, but I have substituted Herbert Read's *End of a War* written long after. The writers of these poems were invariably officers of exceptional courage and capacity, one a man constantly selected for dangerous work, all, I think, had the Military Cross; their letters are vivid and humorous, they were not without joy — for all skill is joyful — but felt bound, in the words of the best known, to plead the suffering of their men. In poems that had for a time considerable fame, written in the first person, they made that suffering their own. I have rejected these poems for the same reason that made Arnold withdraw his *Empedocles on Etna* from circulation; passive suffering is not a theme for poetry. In all the great tragedies, tragedy is a joy to the man who dies; in Greece the tragic chorus danced. When man has withdrawn into the quicksilver at the back of the mirror no great event becomes luminous in his mind; it is no longer possible to write *The Persians, Agincourt, Chevy Chase:* some blunderer has driven his car on to the wrong side of the road — that is all.

If war is necessary, or necessary in our time and place, it is best to forget its suffering as we do the discomfort of fever, remembering our comfort at midnight when our temperature fell, or as we forget the worst moments of more painful disease. Florence Farr returning third class from Ireland found herself among Connaught Rangers just returned from the Boer War who described an incident over and over, and always with loud laughter: an unpopular sergeant struck by a shell turned round and round like a dancer wound in his own entrails. That too may be a right way of seeing war, if war is necessary; the way of the Cockney slums, of Patrick Street, of the *Kilmainham Minut,* of *Johnny I hardly knew ye,* of the medieval *Dance of Death.*

XVI

Ten years after the war certain poets combined the modern vocabulary, the accurate record of the relevant facts learnt from Eliot, with the sense of suffering of the war poets, that sense of suffering no longer passive, no longer an obsession of the nerves; philosophy had made it part of all the mind. Edith Sitwell with her Russian Ballet, Turner with his *Mare Tranquillum*, Dorothy Wellesley with her ancient names — 'Heraclitus added fire ' — her moths, horses and serpents, Pound with his descent into Hades, his Chinese classics, are too romantic to seem modern. Browning, that he might seem modern, created an ejaculating man-of-the-world good humour; but Day Lewis, Madge, MacNeice, are modern through the character of their intellectual passion. We have been gradually approaching this art through that cult of sincerity, that refusal to multiply personality which is characteristic of our time. They may seem obscure, confused, because of their concentrated passion, their interest in associations hitherto untravelled; it is as though their words and rhythms remained gummed to one another instead of separating and falling into order. I can seldom find more than half a dozen lyrics that I like, yet in this moment of sympathy I prefer them to Eliot, to myself — I too have tried to be modern. They have pulled off the mask, the manner writers hitherto assumed, Shelley in relation to his dream, Byron, Henley, to their adventure, their action. Here stands not this or that man but man's naked mind.

Although I have preferred, and shall again, constrained by a different nationality, a man so many years old, fixed to some one place, known to friends and enemies, full of mortal frailty, expressing all things not made mysterious by nature with impatient clarity, I have read with some excitement poets I had approached with distaste, delighted in their pure spiritual objectivity as in something long foretold.

Much of the war poetry was pacificist, revolutionary; it was easier to look at suffering if you had somebody to blame for it, or some remedy in mind. Many of these poets have called themselves communists, though I find in their work no trace of the recognized communist philosophy and the practising communist rejects them. The Russian government in 1930 silenced its Mechanists, put Spinoza on his head and claimed him for grandfather; but the men who created the communism of the masses had Stendhal's mirror for a contemporary, believed that religion, art, philosophy, expressed economic change, that the shell secreted the fish. Perhaps all that the masses accept is obsolete — the Orangeman beats his drum every Twelfth of July — perhaps fringes, wigs, furbelows, hoops, patches, stocks, Wellington boots, start up as armed men; but were a poet sensitive to the best thought of his time to accept that belief, when time is restoring the soul's autonomy, it would be as though he had swallowed a stone and kept it in his bowels. None of these men have accepted it, communism is their *Deus ex Machina*, their Santa Claus, their happy ending, but speaking as a poet I prefer tragedy to tragi-comedy. No matter how great a reformer's energy a still greater is required to face, all activities expended in vain, the unreformed. 'God,' said an old country-woman, 'smiles alike when regarding the good and condemning the lost.' MacNeice, the anti-communist, expecting some descent of barbarism next turn of the wheel, contemplates the modern world with even greater horror than the communist Day Lewis, although with less lyrical beauty. More often I cannot tell whether the poet is communist or anti-communist. On what side is Madge? Indeed I know of no school where the poets so closely resemble each other. Spender has said that the poetry of belief must supersede that of personality, and it is perhaps a belief shared that has created their intensity, their resemblance; but this belief is not political. If I understand aright this difficult art the contemplation of suffering has compelled them to seek beyond the flux something unchanging, inviolate, that country where no ghost haunts, no beloved lures because it has neither past nor future.

This lunar beauty
Has no history
Is complete and early;
If beauty later
Bear any feature
It had a lover
And is another.

XVII

I read Gerard Hopkins with great difficulty,
I cannot keep my attention fixed for more than a
few minutes; I suspect a bias born when I began
to think. He is typical of his generation where
most opposed to mine. His meaning is like some
faint sound that strains the ear, comes out of
words, passes to and fro between them, goes back
into words, his manner a last development of
poetical diction. My generation began that
search for hard positive subject-matter, still a
predominant purpose. Yet the publication of his
work in 1918 made ' sprung verse ' the fashion,
and now his influence has replaced that of Hardy
and Bridges. In sprung verse a foot may have
one or many syllables without altering the metre,
we count stress not syllable, it is the metre of the
Samson Agonistes chorus and has given new
vitality to much contemporary verse. It enables
a poet to employ words taken over from science
or the newspaper without stressing the more un-
musical syllables, or to suggest hurried conver-

sation where only one or two words in a sentence are important, to bring about a change in poetical writing like that in the modern speech of the stage where only those words which affect the situation are important. In syllabic verse, lyric, narrative, dramatic, all syllables are important. Hopkins would have disliked increase of realism; this stoppage and sudden onrush of syllables were to him a necessary expression of his slight constant excitement. The defect or limitation of ' sprung verse ', especially in five-stress lines, is that it may not be certain at a first glance where the stress falls. I have to read lines in *The End of a War* as in *Samson Agonistes* several times before I am certain.

XVIII

That I might follow a theme I have given but a bare mention or none at all to writers I greatly admire. There have, for instance, been notable translators. Ezra Pound's *Cathay* created the manner followed with more learning but with less sublety of rhythm by Arthur Waley in many volumes; Tagore's translation from his own Bengali I have praised elsewhere. Æ (George Russell) found in Vedantic philosophy the emotional satisfaction found by Lionel Johnson, John Gray, Francis Thompson in Catholicism and seems despite this identity of aim, and the

originality and beauty of his best work, to stand
among the translators, so little has he in common
with his time. He went to the *Upanishads*, both
for imagery and belief. I have been able to say
but little of translations and interpretations of
modern and medieval Gaelic literature by Lady
Gregory, James Stephens, Frank O'Connor.
Then again there are certain poets I have left
aside because they stand between two or more
schools and might have confused the story
— Richard Hughes, Robert Nichols, Hugh
M'Diarmid. I would, if I could, have dealt at
some length with George Barker, who like Mac-
Neice, Auden, Day Lewis, handled the tradi-
tional metres with a new freedom — *vers libre*
lost much of its vogue some five years ago —
but has not their social passion, their sense of
suffering. There are one or two writers who are
not in my story because they seem to be born out
of time. When I was young there were almost
as many religious poets as love poets and no
philosophers. After a search for religious
poetry, among the new poets I have found a
poem by Force Stead, until lately chaplain
of Worcester, and half a dozen little poems,
which remind me of Emily Brontë, by Margot
Ruddock, a young actress well known on the
provincial stage. I have said nothing of my own
work, not from modesty, but because writing

through fifty years I have been now of the same school with John Synge and James Stephens, now in that of Sturge Moore and the younger ' Michael Field ': and though the concentration of philosophy and social passion of the school of Day Lewis and in MacNeice lay beyond my desire, I would, but for a failure of talent have been in that of Turner and Dorothy Wellesley.

A distinguished American poet urged me not to attempt a representative selection of American poetry; he pointed out that I could not hope to acquire the necessary knowledge: ' If your selection looks representative you will commit acts of injustice.' I have therefore, though with a sense of loss, confined my selections to those American poets who by subject, or by long residence in Europe, seem to English readers a part of their own literature.

Certain authors are absent from this selection through circumstances beyond my control. Robert Graves, Laura Riding, and the executors of Canon John Gray and Sir William Watson have refused permission. Two others, Rudyard Kipling and Ezra Pound, are inadequately represented because too expensive even for an anthologist with the ample means the Oxford University Press puts at his disposal.

W. B. YEATS

September, 1936

ACKNOWLEDGMENTS

I MUST gratefully acknowledge the kindness of authors (or their executors) and of publishers in granting me permission to include copyright poems in this book. I name them here: Mr. Lascelles Abercrombie, Mr. W. H. Auden, Mr. George Barker, Mr. Julian Bell, Mr. Hilaire Belloc, Mr. Laurence Binyon, Mr. Edmund Blunden, Mr. Gordon Bottomley; the executors of the late Mr. Robert Bridges for permission to reprint seven poems; the executors of the late Wilfrid Scawen Blunt for four poems and extracts from a fifth; the literary executors of Rupert Brooke; Mr. Joseph Campbell, Mr. Roy Campbell, Mr. Richard Church, Mr. Padraic Colum, Mr. A. E. Coppard, Mrs. Frances Cornford, Mr. W. H. Davies, Mr. Walter de la Mare; Lady Desborough for the poem by Julian Grenfell; Mr. John Drinkwater, Mr. T. S. Eliot, Mr. William Empson; Mrs. Flecker for permission to include two poems by James Elroy Flecker; Mrs. Freeman for poems by John Freeman; Mr. Wilfrid Gibson; the executors of the late Lady Gregory; Dr. Oliver St. John Gogarty, Mr. F. R. Higgins, Mr. Ralph Hodgson; Captain Vyvyan Beresford Holland for the poem by Oscar Wilde; Mr. Laurence Housman for permission to use the five poems by his brother the late A. E. Housman; Mr. Richard Hughes, Mr. James Joyce; Mrs. Frieda Lawrence for poems by the late D. H. Lawrence; Mr. C. Day Lewis, Mr. Hugh M'Diarmid, Mr. Louis MacNeice, Mr. Charles

ACKNOWLEDGMENTS

Madge; The Poet Laureate, Mr. John Masefield, for permission to reprint six poems from *Collected Poems* (Messrs. Heinemann); Mr. Thomas McGreevy, Mr. Edward Powys Mathers; Mr. Wilfrid Meynell for three poems by Alice Meynell and for the poems by Francis Thompson; Mrs. Harold Monro for the poems by the late Harold Monro and for permission to omit stanzas in *Midnight Lamentation* and *Natural History;* Mr. Thomas Sturge Moore for his own poems and those of 'Michael Field'; Sir Henry Newbolt for his poem and for the poem by Mary Coleridge; Mr. Robert Nichols; V. Sackville-West, Mr. Frank O'Connor; The Marchese Origo for the poems by the late Geoffrey Scott; Professor Vivian de Sola Pinto, Mr. William Plomer, Mr. Ezra Pound; the executors of F. York Powell for two poems; Mr. Herbert Read, Mr. Ernest Rhys, Mr. Michael Roberts, Miss Margot Ruddock, Mr. Diarmuid Russell for poems; G. W. Russell, Mr. Siegfried Sassoon, Mr. Edward Shanks, Miss Edith Sitwell, Mr. Sacheverell Sitwell, Mr. Stephen Spender, Sir John Squire, Mr. William Force Stead, Mr. James Stephens, Mr. L. A. G. Strong, Mr. Frank Pearce Sturm, Shri Purohit Swami, Mr. Arthur Symons; Mr. Edward Synge for permission to use the poems and translations by John Millington Synge; Mr. D. Trench for the poem by his father the late Herbert Trench; Mrs. Thomas for a poem by the late Edward Thomas; Mr. W. J. Turner for twelve poems; Mr. Arthur Waley for the title poem from his book *The Temple* (Messrs. George Allen and Unwin); Mrs. Sylvia Townsend Warner, Lady Gerald Wellesley.

My obligations to publishers are great, and I have to

thank Messrs. Dodd, Mead and Co. for two poems by
Edmund Blunden, one by Rupert Brooke, and two by
G. K. Chesterton; Messrs. Doubleday, Doran and Co.
for *The Looking-Glass* and *A St. Helena Lullaby* by
Rudyard Kipling; Messrs. Harper and Brothers for a
poem by Edward Davison; Messrs. Houghton, Mifflin
and Co. for two poems by John Drinkwater; A. A.
Knopf, Inc. for two poems by James Elroy Flecker;
The Macmillan Co. for poems by George Russell
(Æ), Wilfrid Gibson, Thomas Hardy, Rabindranath
Tagore, John Masefield, and for my own poems; The
Modern Library Inc. for poems by John Millington
Synge; Messrs. Charles Scribner's Sons for poems by
W. E. Henley; The Viking Press for poems by Thomas
McGreevy.

In two cases it has been impossible to trace the author
or his executor and I must therefore apologize for seem-
ing negligence to Thomas Boyd, and to the executors
of Edwin J. Ellis.

W. B. Y.

WALTER PATER

1839–1894

I   *Mona Lisa*

SHE is older than the rocks among which she sits;
Like the Vampire,
She has been dead many times,
And learned the secrets of the grave;
And has been a diver in deep seas,
And keeps their fallen day about her;
And trafficked for strange webs with Eastern merchants;
And, as Leda,
Was the mother of Helen of Troy,
And, as St Anne,
Was the mother of Mary;
And all this has been to her but as the sound of lyres and
      flutes,
And lives
Only in the delicacy
With which it has moulded the changing lineaments,
And tinged the eyelids and the hands.

WILFRID SCAWEN BLUNT

1840–1922

2   *Esther* (*i*)

HE who has once been happy is for aye
   Out of destruction's reach. His fortune then
Holds nothing secret, and Eternity,
   Which is a mystery to other men,
Has like a woman given him its joy.
   Time is his conquest. Life, if it should fret,
Has paid him tribute. He can bear to die.
   He who has once been happy! When I set
The world before me and survey its range,
   Its mean ambitions, its scant fantasies,
The shreds of pleasure which for lack of change
   Men wrap around them and call happiness,
The poor delights which are the tale and sum
Of the world's courage in its martyrdom;

3   (*ii*)

WHEN I hear laughter from a tavern door,
   When I see crowds agape and in the rain
Watching on tiptoe and with stifled roar
   To see a rocket fired or a bull slain,
When misers handle gold, when orators
   Touch strong men's hearts with glory till they weep,
When cities deck their streets for barren wars
   Which have laid waste their youth, and when I keep
Calmly the count of my own life and see
   On what poor stuff my manhood's dreams were fed
Till I too learned what dole of vanity
   Will serve a human soul for daily bread,
— Then I remember that I once was young
And lived with Esther the world's gods among.

4   *Depreciating her Beauty*

I LOVE not thy perfections.   When I hear
  Thy beauty blazoned, and the common tongue
Cheapening with vulgar praise a lip, an ear,
A cheek that I have prayed to; — when among
The loud world's gods my god is noised and sung,
Her wit applauded, even her taste, her dress,
Her each dear hidden marvel lightly flung
At the world's feet and stripped to nakedness —
Then I despise thy beauty utterly,
Crying, ' Be these your gods, O Israel! '
And I remember that on such a day
I found thee with eyes bleared and cheeks all pale,
And lips that trembled to a voiceless cry,
And that thy bosom in my bosom lay.

5   *Honour Dishonoured*

('Written in an Irish Prison 1888')

HONOURED I lived e'erwhile with honoured men
  In opulent state.   My table nightly spread
Found guests of worth, peer, priest and citizen,
  And poet crowned, and beauty garlanded.
  Nor these alone, for hunger too I fed,
And many a lean tramp and sad Magdalen
  Passed from my doors less hard for sake of bread.
Whom grudged I ever purse or hand or pen?

To-night, unwelcomed at these gates of woe
  I stand with churls, and there is none to greet
My weariness with smile or courtly show
  Nor, though I hunger long, to bring me meat.
God! what a little accident of gold
Fences our weakness from the wolves of old!

3

WILFRID SCAWEN BLUNT

6 *A Nocturne*

THE Moon has gone to her rest,
   A full hour ago.
The Pleiads have found a nest
   In the waves below.
Slow, the Hours one by one
   In Midnight's footsteps creep.
Lovers who lie alone
   Soon wake to weep.
Slow-footed tortoise Hours, will ye not hasten on,
   Till from his prison
   In the golden East
  A new day shall have risen,
And the last stars be gone,
   Like guests belated from a bridal feast?
    When the long night is done
    Then shall ye sleep.

7 *From 'The Wisdom of Merlyn'*

WOULDST thou be wise, O Man? At the knees of a
   woman begin.
  Her eyes shall teach thee thy road, the worth of the thing
    called pleasure, the joy of the thing called sin.
Else shalt thou go to thy grave in pain for the folly that
    might have been.

For know, the knowledge of women the beginning of wis-
   dom is.
  Who had seven hundred wives and concubines hundreds
    three, as we read in the book of bliss?
Solomon, wisest of men and kings, and 'all of them prin-
   cesses.'

4

WILFRID SCAWEN BLUNT

Yet, be thou stronger than they. To be ruled of a woman
is ill.
  Life hath an hundred ways, beside the way of her arms,
  to give thee of joy thy fill.
Only is love of thy life the flower. Be thine the ultimate
will.

What is the motto of youth? There is only one. Be thou
strong.
  Do thy work and achieve, with thy brain, with thy hands,
  with thy heart, the deeds which to strength belong.
Strike each day thy blow for the right, or failing strike for
the wrong.

Love is of body and body, the physical passion of joy;
  The desire of the man for the maid, her nakedness
  strained to his own; the mother's who suckles her boy
With the passionate flow of her naked breast. All else is a
fraudulent toy.

Experience all is of use, save one, to have angered a friend.
  Break thy heart for a maid; another shall love thee anon.
  The gold shall return thou didst spend,
Ay, and thy beaten back grow whole. But friendship's
grave is the end.

Why do I love thee, brother? We have shared what things
in our youth,
  Battle and siege and triumph, together, always together,
  in wanderings North and South.
But one thing shared binds nearer than all, the kisses of one
sweet mouth.

He that hath loved the mother shall love the daughter no less,
   Sister the younger sister. There are tones how sweet to his ear, gestures that plead and press,
Echoes fraught with remembered things that cry in the silences.

Friendship is fostered with gifts. Be it so; little presents? Yes.
   Friendship! But ah, not Love, since love is itself Love's gift and it angereth him to have less.
Woe to the lover who dares to bring more wealth than his tenderness.

Whence is our fountain of tears? We weep in childhood for pain,
   Anon for triumph in manhood, the sudden glory of praise, the giant mastered and slain.
Age weeps only for love renewed and pleasure come back again.

I have tried all pleasures but one, the last and sweetest; it waits.
   Childhood, the childhood of age, to totter again on the lawns, to have done with the loves and the hates,
To gather the daisies, and drop them, and sleep on the nursing knees of the Fates.

6

THOMAS HARDY

1840–1928

Weathers

(*i*)

THIS is the weather the cuckoo likes,
    And so do I;
When showers betumble the chestnut spikes,
    And nestlings fly:
And the little brown nightingale bills his best,
And they sit outside at ' The Travellers' Rest,'
And maids come forth sprig-muslin drest,
And citizens dream of the south and west,
    And so do I.

(*ii*)

This is the weather the shepherd shuns,
    And so do I;
When beeches drip in browns and duns,
    And thresh, and ply;
And hill-hid tides throb, throe on throe,
And meadow rivulets overflow,
And drops on gate-bars hang in a row,
And rooks in families homeward go,
    And so do I.

Snow in the Suburbs

EVERY branch big with it,
    Bent every twig with it;
Every fork like a white web-foot;
Every street and pavement mute:

Some flakes have lost their way, and grope back upward, when
Meeting those meandering down they turn and descend again.
　　The palings are glued together like a wall,
　　And there is no waft of wind with the fleecy fall.

　　　　A sparrow enters the tree,
　　　　Whereon immediately
　　A snow-lump thrice his own slight size
　　Descends on him and showers his head and eyes.
　　　　　And overturns him,
　　　　　And near inurns him,
　　　　And lights on a nether twig, when its brush
Starts off a volley of other lodging lumps with a rush.

　　　　The steps are a blanched slope,
　　　　Up which, with feeble hope,
　　A black cat comes, wide-eyed and thin;
　　　　And we take him in.

10　　　　*The Night of Trafalgar (i)*

IN the wild October night-time, when the wind raved
　　round the land,
And the Back-sea [1] met the Front-sea, and our doors were
　　blocked with sand,
And we heard the drub of Dead-man's Bay, where bones of
　　thousands are,
We knew not what the day had done for us at Trafalgár.
　　　　(*All*)　Had done,
　　　　　　Had done,
　　　　For us at Trafalgár!

　　[1] In those days the hind-part of the harbour adjoining this
scene was so named, and at high tides the waves washed across
the isthmus at a point called ' The Narrows.'

(*ii*)

' Pull hard, and make the Nothe, or down we go! ' one says,
   says he.
We pulled; and bedtime brought the storm; but snug at
   home slept we.
Yet all the while our gallants after fighting through the day,
Were beating up and down the dark, sou'-west of Cadiz
   Bay.
          The dark,
          The dark,
   Sou'-west of Cadiz Bay!

(*iii*)

The victors and the vanquished then the storm it tossed and tore,
As hard they strove, those worn-out men, upon that surly shore;
Dead Nelson and his half-dead crew, his foes from near and far,
Were rolled together on the deep that night at Trafalgár!
          The deep,
          The deep,
   That night at Trafalgár!

11   *Former Beauties*

THESE market-dames, mid-aged, with lips thin-drawn,
      And tissues sere,
Are they the ones we loved in years agone,
      And courted here?

9

THOMAS HARDY

Are these the muslined pink young things to whom
    We vowed and swore
In nooks on summer Sundays by the Froom,
    Or Budmouth shore?

Do they remember those gay tunes we trod
    Clasped on the green;
Aye; trod till moonlight set on the beaten sod
    A satin sheen?

They must forget, forget!   They cannot know
    What once they were,
Or memory would transfigure them, and show
    Them always fair.

ROBERT BRIDGES

1844–1930

12   *Muse and Poet*

Muse.

WILL Love again awake,
   That lies asleep so long?

Poet.

O hush! ye tongues that shake
The drowsy night with song.

Muse.

  It is a lady fair
Whom once he deigned to praise,
That at the door doth dare
Her sad complaint to raise.

10

ROBERT BRIDGES

Poet.

She must be fair of face,
As bold of heart she seems,
If she would match her grace
With the delight of dreams.

Muse.

Her beauty would surprise
Gazers on Autumn eves,
Who watched the broad moon rise
Upon the scattered sheaves.

Poet.

O sweet must be the voice
He shall descend to hear,
Who doth in Heaven rejoice
His most enchanted ear.

Muse.

The smile, that rests to play
Upon her lip, foretells
What musical array
Tricks her sweet syllables.

Poet.

And yet her smiles have danced
In vain, if her discourse
Win not the soul entranced
In divine intercourse.

Muse.

She will encounter all
This trial without shame,
Her eyes men Beauty call,
And Wisdom is her name.

Poet.

Throw back the portals then,
Ye guards, your watch that keep,
Love will awake again
That lay so long asleep.

13   *On a Dead Child*

PERFECT little body, without fault or stain on thee,
   With promise of strength and manhood full and fair!
         Though cold and stark and bare,
The bloom and the charm of life doth awhile remain on
      thee.

Thy mother's treasure wert thou; — alas! no longer
   To visit her heart with wondrous joy; to be
         Thy father's pride; — ah, he
Must gather his faith together, and his strength make
      stronger.

To me, as I move thee now in the last duty,
   Dost thou with a turn or gesture anon respond;
         Startling my fancy fond
With a chance attitude of the head, a freak of beauty.

Thy hand clasps, as 'twas wont, my finger, and holds it:
  But the grasp is the clasp of Death, heartbreaking and
      stiff;
          Yet feels to my hand as if
'Twas still thy will, thy pleasure and trust that enfolds it.

So I lay thee there, thy sunken eyelids closing, —
  Go lie thou there in thy coffin, thy last little bed! —
          Propping thy wise, sad head,
Thy firm, pale hands across thy chest disposing.

So quiet! doth the change content thee? — Death, whither
      hath he taken thee?
  To a world, do I think, that rights the disaster of this?
          The vision of which I miss,
Who weep for the body, and wish but to warm thee and
      awaken thee?

Ah! little at best can all our hopes avail us
  To lift this sorrow, or cheer us, when in the dark,
          Unwilling, alone we embark,
And the things we have seen and have known and have
      heard of, fail us.

14   *The Storm is over*

THE storm is over, the land hushes to rest:
  The tyrannous wind, its strength fordone,
Is fallen back in the west
To couch with the sinking sun.
The last clouds fare
With fainting speed, and their thin streamers fly
In melting drifts of the sky.
Already the birds in the air

13

Appear again; the rooks return to their haunt,
And one by one,
Proclaiming aloud their care,
Renew their peaceful chant.

Torn and shattered the trees their branches again reset,
They trim afresh the fair
Few green and golden leaves withheld from the storm,
And awhile will be handsome yet.
To-morrow's sun shall caress
Their remnant of loveliness:
In quiet days for a time
Sad Autumn lingering warm
Shall humour their faded prime.

But ah! the leaves of summer that lie on the ground!
What havoc! The laughing timbrels of June,
That curtained the birds' cradles, and screened their song,
That sheltered the cooing doves at noon,
Of airy fans the delicate throng, —
Torn and scattered around:
Far out afield they lie,
In the watery furrows die,
In grassy pools of the flood they sink and drown,
Green-golden, orange, vermilion, golden and brown,
The high year's flaunting crown
Shattered and trampled down.

The day is done: the tired land looks for night:
She prays to the night to keep
In peace her nerves of delight:
While silver mist upstealeth silently,
And the broad cloud-driving moon in the clear sky
Lifts o'er the firs her shining shield,

And in her tranquil light
Sleep falls on forest and field.
Sée! sléep hath fallen: the trees are asleep:
The night is come.   The land is wrapt in sleep.

15   *Weep not To-day*

WEEP not to-day: why should this sadness be?
    Learn in present fears
      To o'ermaster those tears
      That unhindered conquer thee.

Think on thy past valour, thy future praise:
      Up, sad heart, nor faint
      In ungracious complaint,
      Or a prayer for better days.

Daily thy life shortens, the grave's dark peace
      Draweth surely nigh,
      When good-night is good-bye;
      For the sleeping shall not cease.

Fight, to be found fighting: nor far away
      Deem, nor strange thy doom.
      Like this sorrow 'twill come,
      And the day will be to-day.

16   *I heard a Linnet courting*

I HEARD a linnet courting
  His lady in the spring:
His mates were idly sporting,
    Nor stayed to hear him sing
      His song of love. —
I fear my speech distorting
      His tender love.

The phrases of his pleading
   Were full of young delight;
And she that gave him heeding
   Interpreted aright
      His gay, sweet notes, —
So sadly marred in the reading, —
      His tender notes.

And when he ceased, the hearer
   Awaited the refrain,
Till swiftly perching nearer
   He sang his song again,
      His pretty song:
Would that my verse spake clearer
      His tender song!

Ye happy, airy creatures!
   That in the merry spring
Think not of what misfeatures
   Or cares the year may bring;
      But unto love
Resign your simple natures,
      To tender love.

17   *Nightingales*

BEAUTIFUL must be the mountains whence ye come,
   And bright in the fruitful valleys the streams, wherefrom
      Ye learn your song:
Where are those starry woods? O might I wander there,
Among the flowers, which in that heavenly air
      Bloom the year long!

Nay, barren are those mountains and spent the streams:
Our song is the voice of desire, that haunts our dreams,
   A throe of the heart,
Whose pining visions dim, forbidden hopes profound,
 No dying cadence nor long sigh can sound,
   For all our art.

 Alone, aloud in the raptured ear of men
 We pour our dark nocturnal secret; and then,
   As night is withdrawn
From these sweet-springing meads and bursting boughs of
  May,
  Dream, while the innumerable choir of day
   Welcome the dawn.

GERARD MANLEY HOPKINS

1844–1889

18   *The Habit of Perfection*

E LECTED Silence, sing to me
 And beat upon my whorlèd ear,
Pipe me to pastures still and be
The music that I care to hear.

Shape nothing, lips; be lovely-dumb:
It is the shut, the curfew sent
From there where all surrenders come
Which only makes you eloquent.

Be shellèd, eyes, with double dark
And find the uncreated light:
This ruck and reel which you remark
Coils, keeps, and teases simple sight.

Palate, the hutch of tasty lust,
Desire not to be rinsed with wine:
The can must be so sweet, the crust
So fresh that come in fasts divine!

Nostrils, your careless breath that spend
Upon the stir and keep of pride,
What relish shall the censers send
Along the sanctuary side!

O feel-of-primrose hands, O feet
That want the yield of plushy sward,
But you shall walk the golden street
And you unhouse and house the Lord.

And, Poverty, be thou the bride
And now the marriage feast begun,
And lily-coloured clothes provide
Your spouse not laboured-at nor spun.

19   *Pied Beauty*

GLORY be to God for dappled things —
For skies of couple-colour as a brinded cow;
    For rose-moles all in stipple upon trout that swim;

Fresh fire-coal chestnut-falls; finches' wings;
  Landscape plotted and pieced — fold, fallow, and plough;
    And áll trádes, their gear and tackle and trim.

All things counter, original, spare, strange;
  Whatever is fickle, freckled (who knows how?)
    With swift, slow; sweet, sour; adazzle, dim;
He fathers-forth whose beauty is past change:
        Praise him.

20 *Spring*

NOTHING is so beautiful as spring —
  When weeds, in wheels, shoot long and lovely and
     lush;
  Thrush's eggs look little low heavens, and thrush
Through the echoing timber does so rinse and wring
The ear, it strikes like lightnings to hear him sing;
  The glassy peartree leaves and blooms, they brush
  The descending blue; that blue is all in a rush
With richness; the racing lambs too have fair their fling.

What is all this juice and all this joy?
  A strain of the earth's sweet being in the beginning
In Eden garden. — Have, get, before it cloy,
  Before it cloud, Christ, lord, and sour with sinning,
Innocent mind and Mayday in girl and boy,
  Most, O maid's child, thy choice and worthy the winning.

21 *The Caged Skylark*

AS a dare-gale skylark scanted in a dull cage
  Man's mounting spirit in his bone-house, mean house,
     dwells —
  That bird beyond the remembering his free fells;
This in drudgery, day-labouring-out life's age.

Though aloft on turf or perch or poor low stage,
  Both sing sometimes the sweetest, sweetest spells,
  Yet both droop deadly sómetimes in their cells
Or wring their barriers in bursts of fear or rage.

Not that the sweet-fowl, song-fowl, needs no rest —
Why, hear him, hear him babble and drop down to his nest,
    But his own nest, wild nest, no prison.

Man's spirit will be flesh-bound when found at best,
But uncumbered: meadow-down is not distressed
    For a rainbow footing it nor he for his bónes rísen.

22   *The Sea and the Skylark*

ON ear and ear two noises too old to end
    Trench — right, the tide that ramps against the
      shore;
  With a flood or a fall, low lull-off or all roar,
Frequenting there while moon shall wear and wend.

Left hand, off land, I hear the lark ascend,
    His rash-fresh re-winded new-skeinèd score
    In crisps of curl off wild winch whirl, and pour
And pelt music, till none 's to spill nor spend.

How these two shame this shallow and frail town!
    How ring right out our sordid turbid time,
Being pure! We, life's pride and cared-for crown,

    Have lost that cheer and charm of earth's past prime:
Our make and making break, are breaking, down
    To man's last dust, drain fast towards man's first slime.

23   *Duns Scotus's Oxford*

TOWERY city and branchy between towers;
 Cuckoo-echoing, bell-swarmèd, lark-charmèd, rook-
  racked, river-rounded;
The dappled-eared lily below thee; that country and town
 did
Once encounter in, here coped and poisèd powers.

Thou hast a base and brickish skirt there, sours
That neighbour-nature thy grey beauty is grounded
Best in; graceless growth, thou hast confounded
Rural rural keeping — folk, flocks, and flowers.

Yet ah! this air I gather and I release
He lived on; these weeds and waters, these walls are what
He haunted who of all men most sways my spirits to peace;

Of realty the rarest-veinèd unraveller; a not
Rivalled insight, be rival Italy or Greece;
Who fired France for Mary without spot.

24   *The Leaden Echo and the Golden
Echo*

(*Maidens' song from St. Winefred's Well*)
THE LEADEN ECHO

HOW to kéep — is there ány any, is there none such,
 nowhere known some, bow or brooch or braid or
  brace, láce, latch or catch or key to keep
Back beauty, keep it, beauty, beauty, beauty, . . . from
 vanishing away?
Ó is there no frowning of these wrinkles, rankèd wrinkles
 deep,

21

Dówn? no waving off of these most mournful messengers,
    still messengers, sad and stealing messengers of grey?
No there 's none, there 's none, O no there 's none,
Nor can you long be, what you now are, called fair,
Do what you may do, what, do what you may,
And wisdom is early to despair:
Be beginning; since, no, nothing can be done
To keep at bay
Age and age's evils, hoar hair,
Ruck and wrinkle, drooping, dying, death's worst, winding
    sheets, tombs and worms and tumbling to decay;
So be beginning, be beginning to despair.
O there 's none; no no no there 's none:
Be beginning to despair, to despair,
Despair, despair, despair, despair.

THE GOLDEN ECHO

    Spare!
There ís one, yes I have one (Hush there!);
Only not within seeing of the sun,
Not within the singeing of the strong sun,
Tall sun's tingeing, or treacherous the tainting of the earth's
    air,
Somewhere elsewhere there is ah well where! one,
One. Yes I can tell such a key, I do know such a place,
Where whatever 's prized and passes of us, everything that 's
    fresh and fast flying of us, seems to us sweet of us and
    swiftly away with, done away with, undone,
Undone, done with, soon done with, and yet dearly and
    dangerously sweet
Of us, the wimpled-water-dimpled, not-by-morning-
    matchèd face,

22

The flower of beauty, fleece of beauty, too too apt to, ah! to
    fleet,
Never fleets móre, fastened with the tenderest truth
To its own best being and its loveliness of youth: it is an
    everlastingness of, O it is an all youth!
Come then, your ways and airs and looks, locks, maiden
    gear, gallantry and gaiety and grace,
Winning ways, airs innocent, maiden manners, sweet looks,
    loose locks, long locks, lovelocks, gaygear, going gallant,
    girlgrace —
Resign them, sign them, seal them, send them, motion them
    with breath,
And with sighs soaring, soaring síghs deliver
Them; beauty-in-the-ghost, deliver it, early now, long be-
    fore death
Give beauty back, beauty, beauty, beauty, back to God,
    beauty's self and beauty's giver.
See; not a hair is, not an eyelash, not the least lash lost;
    every hair
Is, hair of the head, numbered.
Nay, what we had lighthanded left in surly the mere mould
Will have waked and have waxed and have walked with the
    wind what while we slept,
This side, that side hurling a heavyheaded hundredfold
What while we, while we slumbered.
O then, weary then whý should we tread?   O why are we
    so haggard at the heart, so care-coiled, care-killed, so
    fagged, so fashed, so cogged, so cumbered,
When the thing we freely fórfeit is kept with fonder a care,
Fonder a care kept than we could have kept it, kept
Far with fonder a care (and we, we should have lost it)
    finer, fonder

A care kept. — Where kept?   Do but tell us where kept,
    where. —
Yonder. — What high as that!   We follow, now we fol-
    low. — Yonder, yes yonder, yonder,
Yonder.

WILLIAM ERNEST HENLEY

1849–1903

25   *Ballade of Dead Actors*

I. M.
Edward John Henley
(1861–1898)

WHERE are the passions they essayed,
    And where the tears they made to flow?
Where the wild humours they portrayed
For laughing worlds to see and know?
Othello's wrath and Juliet's woe?
Sir Peter's whims and Timon's gall?
And Millamant and Romeo?
Into the night go one and all.

Where are the braveries, fresh or frayed?
The plumes, the armours — friend and foe?
The cloth of gold, the rare brocade,
The mantles glittering to and fro?
The pomp, the pride, the royal show?
The cries of war and festival?
The youth, the grace, the charm, the glow?
Into the night go one and all.

24

WILLIAM ERNEST HENLEY

The curtain falls, the play is played:
The Beggar packs beside the Beau;
The Monarch troops, and troops the Maid;
The Thunder huddles with the Snow.
Where are the revellers high and low?
The clashing swords?   The lover's call?
The dancers gleaming row on row?
Into the night go one and all.

Envoy

Prince, in one common overthrow
The Hero tumbles with the Thrall:
As dust that drives, as straws that blow,
Into the night go one and all.

26

Invictus

OUT of the night that covers me,
  Black as the Pit from pole to pole,
I thank whatever gods may be
  For my unconquerable soul.

In the fell clutch of circumstance
  I have not winced nor cried aloud.
Under the bludgeonings of chance
  My head is bloody, but unbowed.

Beyond this place of wrath and tears
  Looms but the Horror of the shade,
And yet the menace of the years
  Finds, and shall find, me unafraid.

It matters not how strait the gate,
  How charged with punishments the scroll,
I am the master of my fate:
  I am the captain of my soul.

WILLIAM ERNEST HENLEY

All in a Garden Green

I TALKED one midnight with the jolly ghost
 Of a gray ancestor, Tom Heywood hight;
And, ' Here 's,' says he, his old heart liquor-lifted —
' Here 's how we did when Gloriana shone: '

  All in a garden green
   Thrushes were singing;
  Red rose and white between,
   Lilies were springing;
  It was the merry May;
   Yet sang my Lady: —
  ' Nay, Sweet, now nay, now nay!
   I am not ready.'

  Then to a pleasant shade
   I did invite her:
  All things a concert made,
   For to delight her;
  Under, the grass was gay;
   Yet sang my Lady: —
  ' Nay, Sweet, now nay, now nay!
   I am not ready.'

Since those we love and those we hate

S INCE those we love and those we hate,
 With all things mean and all things great,
Pass in a desperate disarray
Over the hills and far away:

WILLIAM ERNEST HENLEY

It must be, Dear, that, late or soon,
Out of the ken of the watching moon,
We shall abscond with Yesterday
Over the hills and far away.

What does it matter?   As I deem,
We shall but follow as brave a dream
As ever smiled a wanton May
Over the hills and far away.

We shall remember, and, in pride,
Fare forth, fulfilled and satisfied,
Into the land of Ever-and-Aye,
Over the hills and far away.

EDWIN JOHN ELLIS

1848–1918

29

From ' Himself '

AT Golgotha I stood alone,
   And trembled in the empty night:
The shadow of a cross was shown
   And Christ thereon who died upright.

The shadow murmured as I went,
   ' I cannot see thee, — who art thou?
Art thou my friend? or art thou sent
   In hate to rail upon me now?

' I cannot see thee.   Art thou one
   Of those I lived to save, — and saved?
I saved thee; but the sands that run
   Have filled the trace of words engraved.

EDWIN JOHN ELLIS

' I wrote with finger on the ground
    One pardon, then with blood on wood.
The priests and elders waited round,
    But none could read of all that stood.

' None read, and now I linger here,
    Only the ghost of one who died,
For God forsakes me, and the spear
    Runs ever cold into my side.

' I have believed in thee when then
    Thou wert not born, nor might I tell
Thy face among the souls of men
    Unborn, but yet I loved thee well.

' Pity me now for this my death;
    Love me a little for my love,
I loved and died, the story saith,
    And telleth over and above

' Of all my early days of want,
    And days of work, and then the end,
But telleth not how still I haunt
    My place of death and seek a friend.

' My God who lived in me to bless
    The earth He made has passed away;
And left me here companionless,
    A weary spectre night and day.

' I am the Ghost of Christ the Less,
    Jesus the man, whose ghost was bound
And banished in the wilderness
    And trodden deep beneath the ground.

28

EDWIN JOHN ELLIS

' I saw him go, and cried to him,
    " Eli, thou hast forsaken me! "
The nails were burning through each limb:
    He fled to find felicity.

' Ah! then I knew the foolish wrong
    That I upon myself had wrought,
Then floated off that Spirit strong
    That once had seemed my own heart's thought.

' Where is the life I might have known
    If God had never lit on me?
I might have loved one heart alone,
    A woman white as chastity.

' I might have hated devils and fled
    Whene'er they came. I might have turned
From sinners, and I might have led
    A life where no sin-knowledge burned.

' But between voice and voice I chose,
    Of these two selves and clave to this: —
Who left me here where no man knows,
    And fled to dwell with light in bliss.

' And left me here with wound of spears,
    A cast-off ghostly shade to rave,
And haunt the place for endless years,
    Crying, " Himself he cannot save! " '

So spoke the ghost of Joseph's son
    Haunting the place where Christ was slain.
I pray that e'er this world be done,
    Christ may relieve his piteous pain.

FREDERICK YORK POWELL

1850–1904

30 *The Sailor and the Shark*

THERE was a queen that fell in love with a jolly sailor
 bold,
But he shipped to the Indies, where he would seek for gold.
All in a good sea-boat, my boys, we fear no wind that blows!

There was a king that had a fleet of ships both tall and
     tarred;
He carried off this pretty queen, and she jumped overboard.
All in a good sea-boat, my boys, we fear no wind that blows!

The queen, the queen is overboard! a shark was cruising
     round,
He swallowed up this dainty bit alive and safe and sound.
All in a good sea-boat, my boys, we fear no wind that blows!

Within the belly of this shark it was both dark and cold,
But she was faithful still and true to her jolly sailor bold.
All in a good sea-boat, my boys, we fear no wind that blows!

The shark was sorry for her, and swam away so fast.
In the Indies, where the camels are, he threw her up at last.
All in a good sea-boat, my boys, we fear no wind that blows!

On one of these same goodly beasts, all in a palanquin,
She spied her own true love again — the Emperor of
     Tonquin.
All in a good sea-boat, my boys, we fear no wind that blows!

She called to him, ' O stay, my love, your queen is come,
    my dear.'
' Oh I've a thousand queens more fair within my kingdom
    here.'
All in a good sea-boat, my boys, we fear no wind that blows!

' You smell of the grave so strong, my dear.' ' I've sailed
    in a shark,' says she.
' It is not of the grave I smell; but I smell of the fish of the
    sea.'
All in a good sea-boat, my boys, we fear no wind that blows!

' My lady loves they smell so sweet; of rice-powder so fine.
The queen the King of Paris loves no sweeter smells than
    mine.'
All in a good sea-boat, my boys, we fear no wind that blows!

She got aboard the shark again, and weeping went her way;
The shark swam back again so fast to where the tall ships lay.
All in a good sea-boat, my boys, we fear no wind that blows!

The king he got the queen again, the shark away he swam.
The queen was merry as could be, and mild as any lamb.
All in a good sea-boat, my boys, we fear no wind that blows!

      *   *   *   *

Now all you pretty maidens what love a sailor bold,
You'd better ship along with him before his love grows cold.
                    (From the French of Paul Fort.)

31   *The Pretty Maid*

THE pretty maid she died, she died, in love-bed as she
    lay;
They took her to the churchyard: all at the break of day;
They laid her all alone there: all in her white array;

FREDERICK YORK POWELL

They laid her all alone there: a'coffin'd in the clay;
And they came back so merrily: all at the dawn of day;
A'singing all so merrily: ' *The dog must have his day!* '
The pretty maid is dead, is dead; in love-bed as she lay;
And they are off a-field to work: as they do every day.

(From the French of Paul Fort.)

ALICE MEYNELL

1847–1922

32   *I am the Way*

THOU art the Way.
  Hadst Thou been nothing but the goal,
    I cannot say
If Thou hadst ever met my soul.

    I cannot see —
I, child of process — if there lies
    An end for me,
Full of repose, full of replies.

    I'll not reproach
The road that winds, my feet that err.
    Access, approach
Art Thou, Time, Way, and Wayfarer.

33   *The Lady Poverty*

THE Lady Poverty was fair:
  But she has lost her looks of late,
With change of times and change of air.
Ah slattern! she neglects her hair,
Her gown, her shoes; she keeps no state
As once when her pure feet were bare.

Or — almost worse, if worse can be —
She scolds in parlours, dusts and trims,
Watches and counts.   Oh, is this she
Whom Francis met, whose step was free,
Who with Obedience carolled hymns,
In Umbria walked with Chastity?

Where is her ladyhood?   Not here,
Not among modern kinds of men;
But in the stony fields, where clear
Through the thin trees the skies appear,
In delicate spare soil and fen,
And slender landscape and austere.

34   *Renouncement*

I MUST not think of thee; and, tired yet strong,
I shun the thought that lurks in all delight —
The thought of thee — and in the blue Heaven's height,
And in the dearest passage of a song.
Oh, just beyond the fairest thoughts that throng
This breast, the thought of thee waits, hidden yet bright;
But it must never, never come in sight;
I must stop short of thee the whole day long.
But when sleep comes to close each difficult day,
When night gives pause to the long watch I keep,
And all my bonds I needs must loose apart,
Must doff my will as raiment laid away, —
With the first dream that comes with the first sleep
I run, I run, I am gathered to thy heart.

1852–1932

35   *Cold, Sharp Lamentation*

COLD, sharp lamentation
    In the cold bitter winds
Ever blowing across the sky;
Oh, there was loneliness with me!

The loud sounding of the waves
Beating against the shore,
Their vast, rough, heavy outcry,
Oh, there was loneliness with me!

The light sea-gulls in the air,
Crying sharply through the harbours,
The cries and screams of the birds
With my own heart!   Oh! that was loneliness.

The voice of the winds and the tide,
And the long battle of the mighty war;
The sea, the earth, the skies, the blowing of the winds,
Oh! there was loneliness in all of them together.

(*From the Irish of Douglas Hyde.*)

36   *He meditates on the Life of a Rich Man*

A   GOLDEN cradle under you, and you young;
    A right mother and a strong kiss.

A lively horse, and you a boy;
A school and learning and close companions.

A beautiful wife, and you a man;
A wide house and everything that is good.

34

A fine wife, children, substance;
Cattle, means, herds and flocks.

A place to sit, a place to lie down;
Plenty of food and plenty of drink.

After that, an old man among old men;
Respect on you and honour on you.

Head of the court, of the jury, of the meeting,
And the counsellors not the worse for having you.

At the end of your days death, and then
Hiding away; the boards and the church.

What are you better after tonight
Than Ned the beggar or Seaghan the fool?
(From the Irish of Douglas Hyde.)

37   *Will you be as hard?*

WILL you be as hard,
    Colleen, as you are quiet?
Will you be without pity
    On me for ever?

Listen to me, Noireen,
    Listen, aroon;
Put healing on me
    From your quiet mouth.

I am in the little road
    That is dark and narrow,
The little road that has led
    Thousands to sleep.
(From the Irish of Douglas Hyde.)

38   *I am Ireland*

I AM Ireland,
Older than the Hag of Beara.

Great my pride,
I gave birth to brave Cuchulain.

Great my shame,
My own children killed their mother.

I am Ireland,
Lonelier than the Hag of Beara.
              (*From the Irish of Padraig Pearse.*)

39   *A Poem written in Time of Trouble
by an Irish Priest who had taken
Orders in France*

MY thoughts, my grief! are without strength
My spirit is journeying towards death
My eyes are as a frozen sea
My tears my daily food;
There is nothing in life but only misery.
My poor heart is torn
And my thoughts are sharp wounds within me,
Mourning the miserable state of Ireland.

Misfortune has come upon us all together
The poor, the rich, the weak and the strong
The great lord by whom hundreds were maintained
The powerful strong man, and the man that holds the
        plough;
And the cross laid on the bare shoulder of every man.

    36

LADY GREGORY

Our feasts are without any voice of priests
And none at them but women lamenting
Tearing their hair with troubled minds
Keening miserably after the Fenians.

The pipes of our organs are broken
Our harps have lost their strings that were tuned
That might have made the great lamentations of Ireland.
Until the strong men come back across the sea
There is no help for us but bitter crying,
Screams, and beating of hands, and calling out.

I do not know of anything under the sky
That is friendly or favourable to the Gael
But only the sea that our need brings us to,
Or the wind that blows to the harbour
The ship that is bearing us away from Ireland;
And there is reason that these are reconciled with us,
For we increase the sea with our tears
And the wandering wind with our sighs.

(From the Irish.)

OSCAR WILDE

1856–1900

40   *From 'The Ballad of Reading
Gaol'*

HE did not wear his scarlet coat,
    For blood and wine are red,
And blood and wine were on his hands
    When they found him with the dead,
The poor dead woman whom he loved,
    And murdered in her bed.

He walked amongst the Trial Men
   In a suit of shabby grey;
A cricket cap was on his head,
   And his step seemed light and gay;
But I never saw a man who looked
   So wistfully at the day.

I never saw a man who looked
   With such a wistful eye
Upon that little tent of blue
   Which prisoners call the sky,
And at every drifting cloud that went
   With sails of silver by.

I walked, with other souls in pain,
   Within another ring,
And was wondering if the man had done
   A great or little thing,
When a voice behind me whispered low,
   ' That fellow's got to swing.'

     *   *   *   *

Six weeks our guardsman walked the yard,
   In the suit of shabby grey:
His cricket cap was on his head,
   And his step seemed light and gay,
But I never saw a man who looked
   So wistfully at the day.

I never saw a man who looked
   With such a wistful eye
Upon that little tent of blue
   Which prisoners call the sky,
And at every wandering cloud that trailed
   Its ravelled fleeces by.

OSCAR WILDE

He did not wring his hands, as do
    Those witless men who dare
To try to rear the changeling Hope
    In the cave of black Despair:
He only looked upon the sun,
    And drank the morning air.

He did not wring his hands nor weep,
    Nor did he peek or pine,
But he drank the air as though it held
    Some healthful anodyne;
With open mouth he drank the sun
    As though it had been wine!

And I and all the souls in pain,
    Who tramped the other ring,
Forgot if we ourselves had done
    A great or little thing,
And watched with gaze of dull amaze
    The man who had to swing.

And strange it was to see him pass
    With a step so light and gay,
And strange it was to see him look
    So wistfully at the day,
And strange it was to think that he
    Had such a debt to pay.

    *   *   *   *

For oak and elm have pleasant leaves
    That in the spring-time shoot:
But grim to see is the gallows-tree,
    With its adder-bitten root,
And, green or dry, a man must die
    Before it bears its fruit!

OSCAR WILDE

The loftiest place is that seat of grace
    For which all worldlings try:
But who would stand in hempen band
    Upon a scaffold high,
And through a murderer's collar take
    His last look at the sky?

It is sweet to dance to violins
    When Love and Life are fair:
To dance to flutes, to dance to lutes
    Is delicate and rare:
But it is not sweet with nimble feet
    To dance upon the air!

So with curious eyes and sick surmise
    We watched him day by day,
And wondered if each one of us
    Would end the self-same way,
For none can tell to what red Hell
    His sightless soul may stray.

At last the dead man walked no more
    Amongst the Trial Men,
And I knew that he was standing up
    In the black dock's dreadful pen,
And that never would I see his face
    In God's sweet world again.

Like two doomed ships that pass in storm
    We had crossed each other's way:
But we made no sign, we said no word,
    We had no word to say;
For we did not meet in the holy night,
    But in the shameful day.

A prison wall was round us both,
    Two outcast men we were:
The world had thrust us from its heart,
    And God from out His care:
And the iron gin that waits for Sin
    Had caught us in its snare.
       *   *   *   *

In Debtors' Yard the stones are hard,
    And the dripping wall is high,
So it was there he took the air
    Beneath the leaden sky,
And by each side a Warder walked,
    For fear the man might die.

Or else he sat with those who watched
    His anguish night and day;
Who watched him when he rose to weep,
    And when he crouched to pray;
Who watched him lest himself should rob
    Their scaffold of its prey.
       *   *   *   *

And twice a day he smoked his pipe,
    And drank his quart of beer:
His soul was resolute, and held
    No hiding-place for fear;
He often said that he was glad
    The hangman's hands were near.

But why he said so strange a thing
    No Warder dared to ask:
For he to whom a watcher's doom
    Is given as his task,
Must set a lock upon his lips,
    And make his face a mask.

Or else he might be moved, and try
   To comfort or console:
And what should Human Pity do
   Pent up in Murderers' Hole?
What word of grace in such a place
   Could help a brother's soul?

     *   *   *   *

We tore the tarry rope to shreds
   With blunt and bleeding nails;
We rubbed the doors, and scrubbed the floors,
   And cleaned the shining rails:
And, rank by rank, we soaped the plank,
   And clattered with the pails.

We sewed the sacks, we broke the stones,
   We turned the dusty drill:
We banged the tins, and bawled the hymns,
   And sweated on the mill:
But in the heart of every man
   Terror was lying still.

So still it lay that every day
   Crawled like a weed-clogged wave:
And we forgot the bitter lot
   That waits for fool and knave,
Till once, as we tramped in from work,
   We passed an open grave.

With yawning mouth the yellow hole
   Gaped for a living thing;
The very mud cried out for blood
   To the thirsty asphalte ring:
And we knew that ere one dawn grew fair
   Some prisoner had to swing.

Right in we went, with soul intent
　　On Death and Dread and Doom:
The hangman, with his little bag,
　　Went shuffling through the gloom:
And each man trembled as he crept
　　Into his numbered tomb.
　　　　*　　*　　*　　*
That night the empty corridors
　　Were full of forms of Fear,
And up and down the iron town
　　Stole feet we could not hear,
And through the bars that hide the stars
　　White faces seemed to peer.

He lay as one who lies and dreams
　　In a pleasant meadow-land,
The watchers watched him as he slept,
　　And could not understand
How one could sleep so sweet a sleep
　　With a hangman close at hand.

But there is no sleep when men must weep
　　Who never yet have wept:
So we — the fool, the fraud, the knave —
　　That endless vigil kept,
And through each brain on hands of pain
　　Another's terror crept.
　　　　*　　*　　*　　*
There is no chapel on the day
　　On which they hang a man:
The Chaplain's heart is far too sick,
　　Or his face is far too wan,
Or there is that written in his eyes
　　Which none should look upon.

43

So they kept us close till nigh on noon,
    And then they rang the bell,
And the Warders with their jingling keys
    Opened each listening cell,
And down the iron stair we tramped,
    Each from his separate Hell.

Out into God's sweet air we went,
    But not in wonted way,
For this man's face was white with fear,
    And that man's face was gray,
And I never saw sad men who looked
    So wistfully at the day.

I never saw sad men who looked
    With such a wistful eye
Upon that little tent of blue
    We prisoners called the sky,
And at every careless cloud that passed
    In happy freedom by.

The Warders strutted up and down,
    And kept their herd of brutes,
Their uniforms were spick and span,
    And they wore their Sunday suits,
But we knew the work they had been at,
    By the quicklime on their boots.

For where a grave had opened wide,
    There was no grave at all:
Only a stretch of mud and sand
    By the hideous prison-wall,
And a little heap of burning lime,
    That the man should have his pall.

44

For three long years they will not sow
  Or root or seedling there:
For three long years the unblessed spot
  Will sterile be and bare,
And look upon the wondering sky
  With unreproachful stare.

They think a murderer's heart would taint
  Each simple seed they sow.
It is not true! God's kindly earth
  Is kindlier than men know,
And the red rose would but blow more red,
  The white rose whiter blow.

THOMAS WILLIAM ROLLESTON

41   *Clonmacnoise*   1857–1920

IN a quiet water'd land, a land of roses,
    Stands Saint Kieran's city fair;
And the warriors of Erin in their famous generations
    Slumber there.

There beneath the dewy hillside sleep the noblest
    Of the clan of Conn,
Each below his stone with name in branching Ogham
    And the sacred knot thereon.

There they laid to rest the seven Kings of Tara,
    There the sons of Cairbrè sleep —
Battle-banners of the Gael that in Kieran's plain of crosses
    Now their final hosting keep.

And in Clonmacnoise they laid the men of Teffia,
    And right many a lord of Breagh;

45

Deep the sod above Clan Creidè and Clan Conaill,
  Kind in hall and fierce in fray.

Many and many a son of Conn the Hundred-fighter
  In the red earth lies at rest;
Many a blue eye of Clan Colman the turf covers,
  Many a swan-white breast.
     (*From the Irish of Angus O'Gillan.*)

ALFRED EDWARD HOUSMAN
         1859–1936

Grenadier

THE Queen she sent to look for me,
  The sergeant he did say,
' Young man, a soldier will you be
  For thirteen pence a day? '

For thirteen pence a day did I
  Take off the things I wore,
And I have marched to where I lie,
  And I shall march no more.

My mouth is dry, my shirt is wet,
  My blood runs all away,
So now I shall not die in debt
  For thirteen pence a day.

To-morrow after new young men
  The sergeant he must see,
For things will all be over then
  Between the Queen and me.

And I shall have to bate my price,
  For in the grave, they say,
Is neither knowledge nor device
  Nor thirteen pence a day.

46

43 *Soldier from the Wars returning*

SOLDIER from the wars returning,
    Spoiler of the taken town,
Here is ease that asks not earning;
    Turn you in and sit you down.

Peace is come and wars are over,
    Welcome you and welcome all,
While the charger crops the clover
    And his bridle hangs in stall.

Now no more of winters biting,
    Filth in trench from fall to spring,
Summers full of sweat and fighting
    For the Kesar or the King.

Rest you, charger, rust you, bridle;
    Kings and kesars, keep your pay;
Soldier, sit you down and idle
    At the inn of night for aye.

44 *The Chestnut casts his Flambeaux*

THE chestnut casts his flambeaux, and the flowers
    Stream from the hawthorn on the wind away,
The doors clap to, the pane is blind with showers.
    Pass me the can, lad; there's an end of May.

There's one spoilt spring to scant our mortal lot,
    One season ruined of our little store.
May will be fine next year as like as not:
    Oh ay, but then we shall be twenty-four.

47

We for a certainty are not the first
 Have sat in taverns while the tempest hurled
Their hopeful plans to emptiness, and cursed
 Whatever brute and blackguard made the world.

It is in truth iniquity on high
 To cheat our sentenced souls of aught they crave,
And mar the merriment as you and I
 Fare on our long fool's-errand to the grave.

Iniquity it is; but pass the can.
 My lad, no pair of kings our mothers bore;
Our only portion is the estate of man:
 We want the moon, but we shall get no more.

If here to-day the cloud of thunder lours
 To-morrow it will hie on far behests;
The flesh will grieve on other bones than ours
 Soon, and the soul will mourn in other breasts.

The troubles of our proud and angry dust
 Are from eternity, and shall not fail.
Bear them we can, and if we can we must.
 Shoulder the sky, my lad, and drink your ale.

45   *Could man be drunk for ever*

COULD man be drunk for ever
 With liquor, love, or fights,
Lief should I rouse at morning
 And lief lie down of nights.

But men at whiles are sober
 And think by fits and starts,
And if they think, they fasten
 Their hands upon their hearts.

46

The Deserter

WHAT sound awakened me, I wonder,
    For now 'tis dumb.'
' Wheels on the road most like, or thunder:
    Lie down; 'twas not the drum.'

Toil at sea and two in haven
    And trouble far:
Fly, crow, away, and follow, raven,
    And all that croaks for war.

' Hark, I heard the bugle crying,
    And where am I?
My friends are up and dressed and dying,
    And I will dress and die.'

' Oh love is rare and trouble plenty
    And carrion cheap,
And daylight dear at four-and-twenty:
    Lie down again and sleep.'

' Reach me my belt and leave your prattle:
    Your hour is gone;
But my day is the day of battle,
    And that comes dawning on.

' They mow the field of man in season:
    Farewell, my fair,
And, call it truth or call it treason,
    Farewell the vows that were.'

' Ay, false heart, forsake me lightly;
    'Tis like the brave.
They find no bed to joy in rightly
    Before they find the grave.

ALFRED EDWARD HOUSMAN

'Their love is for their own undoing,
    And east and west
They scour about the world a-wooing
    The bullet to their breast.

'Sail away the ocean over,
    Oh sail away,
And lie there with your leaden lover
    For ever and a day.'

ERNEST RHYS
1859—

47   *The Song of the Graves*

IN graves where drips the winter rain,
   Lie those that loved me most of men:
Cerwyd, Cywrid, Caw, lie slain.

In graves where the grass grows rank and tall,
Lie, well avenged ere they did fall:
Gwrien, Morien, Morial.

In graves where drips the rain, the dead
Lie, that not lightly bowed the head:
Gwrien, Gwen, and Gwried.

In Llan Beuno, where the sullen wave
Sounds night and day, is Dylan's grave,
In Bron Aren, Tydain the brave.

Where Corbre gives Tarw Torment space,
By a grave-yard wall, in a ruined place,
The stones hide Ceri Gledivor's face.

50

ERNEST RHYS

Where the ninth wave flows in Perython,
Is the grave of Gwalchmai, the peerless one:
In Llanbadarn lies Clydno's son.

Seithenin's lost mind sleeps by the shore,
Twixt Cinran and the grey sea's roar;
Where Caer Cenedir starts up before.

After many a death, in cold Camlan
Sleeps well the son of old Osvran:
Bedwyr the Brave lies in Tryvan.

In Abererch lies Rhyther' Hael,
Beneath the earth of Llan Morvael:
But Owain ab Urien in lonelier soil.

Clad in umber and red, the spear at his side,
With his shining horses he went in pride:
From his grave in Llan Heled he cannot ride.

After wounds, and bloody plains and red;
White horses to bear him, his helm on his head:
This, even this, is Cyndylan's bed.

Whose is the grave of the four square stones?
Who lies there, of the mighty ones?
Madawg the warrior, of Gwyneth's sons!

Mid the dreary moor, by the one oak-tree,
The grave of stately Siawn may be:
Stately, treacherous, and bitter was he!

Mid the salt sea-marsh, where the tides have been,
Lie the sweet maid, Sanaw: the warrior, Rhyn;
And Hennin's daughter, the pale Earwyn.

ERNEST RHYS

Where 's the grave of Beli, the bed of Braint?
One 's in the plain, and one in Llednaint;
By Clewaint water lies Dehewaint.

In Ardudwy, I bid my grief
Find the grave of Llia, the Gwythel chief,
Under the grass and the withered leaf.

And this may the grave of Gwythur be;
But who the world's great mystery, —
The grave of Arthur shall ever see?

Three graves on Celvi's ridge are made;
And there are Cynveli and Cynvael laid;
The third holds rough-browed Cynon's head.

The long graves in Gwanas — none has told
Their history — what men they hold,
What deeds, and death, beneath their mould.

Of Oeth's and Anoeth's fame we know:
Who seeks their kin, left naked now,
To dig in Gwanas' graves may go.
              (*From the Black Book of Carmarthen.*)

48   *The Lament for Urien*

(*i*)

A HEAD I bear; — the Eagle of Gál,
  Whose wing once brushed the mountain wall;
The Pillar of Prydain has come by a fall.

A head I bear by the side of my thigh:
He was the shield of his own country:
A wheel in battle; a sword borne high.

52

The Pillar of Prydain is fallen down:
Urien, Prince of our houses, is gone:
His heart was a castle, a walléd town.

A head I bear and hold in my hand,
That late was the Prince of Prydain's land,
That harried the host, as the sea the strand.

A head I bear, from the Riw to the wood:
His lips are closed on a foam of blood;
Woe to Reged! Let Urien be rued!

(*ii*)

The delicate white body will be buried to-day:
The delicate white body, be hidden away
Deep in the earth, and the stones, and the clay.

The delicate white body will be covered to-night,
Under earth and blue stones, from the eye of light:
The nettles shall cover it out of sight.

The delicate white body will be covered to-day,
The tumulus be reared, the green sod give way:
And there, oh Cynvarch, thy son they will lay.

The delicate white body will be covered to-night:
Oh Eurdyl, be sad: no more thy delight,
Thy brother shall rise from his sleep in might.
                    (*From the Red Book of Hergest.*)

49 *The Hound of Heaven*

I FLED Him, down the nights and down the **days**;
   I fled Him, down the arches of the years;
I fled Him, down the labyrinthine ways
   Of my own mind; and in the mist of tears
I hid from Him, and under running laughter.
            Up vistaed hopes I sped;
            And shot, precipitated,
Adown Titanic glooms of chasmèd fears,
   From those strong Feet that followed, **followed after.**
            But with unhurrying chase,
            And unperturbèd pace,
   Deliberate speed, majestic instancy,
            They beat — and a Voice beat
            More instant than the Feet —
   ' All things betray thee, who betrayest **Me.**'

            I pleaded, outlaw-wise,
By many a hearted casement, curtained red,
   Trellised with intertwining charities;
(For, though I knew His love Who followèd,
            Yet was I sore adread
Lest, having Him, I must have naught beside);
But, if one little casement parted wide,
   The gust of His approach would clash it to.
   Fear wist not to evade, as Love wist to pursue.
Across the margent of the world I fled,
   And troubled the gold gateways of the stars,
   Smiting for shelter on their clangèd bars;

54

FRANCIS THOMPSON.

          Fretted to dulcet jars
And silvern chatter the pale ports o' the moon.
I said to Dawn: Be sudden — to Eve: Be soon;
   With thy young skiey blossoms heap me over
        From this tremendous Lover —
Float thy vague veil about me, lest He see!
   I tempted all His servitors, but to find
My own betrayal in their constancy,
In faith to Him their fickleness to me,
   Their traitorous trueness, and their loyal deceit.
To all swift things for swiftness did I sue;
   Clung to the whistling mane of every wind.
       But whether they swept, smoothly fleet,
     The long savannahs of the blue;
        Or whether, Thunder-driven,
      They clanged his chariot 'thwart a heaven,
Plashy with flying lightnings round the spurn o' their feet: —
   Fear wist not to evade as Love wist to pursue.
        Still with unhurrying chase,
        And unperturbèd pace,
    Deliberate speed, majestic instancy,
       Came on the following Feet,
       And a Voice above their beat —
' Naught shelters thee, who wilt not shelter Me.'

I sought no more that after which I strayed
       In face of man or maid;
But still within the little children's eyes
       Seems something, something that replies,
They at least are for me, surely for me!
I turned me to them very wistfully;
But just as their young eyes grew sudden fair

With dawning answers there,
Their angel plucked them from me by the hair.
' Come then, ye other children, Nature's — share
With me ' (said I) ' your delicate fellowship;
   Let me greet you lip to lip,
   Let me twine with you caresses,
    Wantoning
   With our Lady-Mother's vagrant tresses,
    Banqueting
   With her in her wind-walled palace,
   Underneath her azured daïs,
   Quaffing, as your taintless way is,
    From a chalice
Lucent-weeping out of the dayspring.'
    So it was done:
I in their delicate fellowship was one —
Drew the bolt of Nature's secrecies.
   I knew all the swift importings
   On the willful face of skies;
   I knew how the clouds arise
   Spumèd of the wild sea-snortings;
    All that 's born or dies
   Rose and drooped with; made them shapers
Of mine own moods, or wailful or divine;
   With them joyed and was bereaven.
   I was heavy with the even,
   When she lit her glimmering tapers
   Round the day's dead sanctities.
   I laughed in the morning's eyes.
I triumphed and I saddened with all weather,
   Heaven and I wept together,
And its sweet tears were salt with mortal mine.

Against the red throb of its sunset-heart
      I laid my own to beat,
      And share commingling heat;
But not by that, by that, was eased my human smart.
In vain my tears were wet on Heaven's gray cheek.
For ah! we know not what each other says,
      These things and I; in sound *I* speak —
Their sound is but their stir, they speak by silences.
Nature, poor stepdame, cannot slake my drouth;
      Let her, if she would owe me,
Drop yon blue bosom-veil of sky, and show me
      The breasts o' her tenderness:
Never did any milk of hers once bless
      My thirsting mouth.
      Nigh and nigh draws the chase,
      With unperturbèd pace,
      Deliberate speed, majestic instancy;
      And past those noisèd Feet
      A Voice comes yet more fleet —
' Lo! naught contents thee, who content'st not Me.'

Naked I wait Thy love's uplifted stroke!
My harness piece by piece Thou hast hewn from me,
      And smitten me to my knee;
      I am defenceless utterly.
      I slept, methinks, and woke,
And, slowly gazing, find me stripped in sleep.
In the rash lustihead of my young powers,
      I shook the pillaring hours
And pulled my life upon me; grimed with smears,
I stand amid the dust o' the mounded years —
My mangled youth lies dead beneath the heap.

My days have crackled and gone up in smoke,
Have puffed and burst as sun-starts on a stream.
      Yea, faileth now even dream
The dreamer, and the lute the lutanist;
Even the linked fantasies, in whose blossomy twist
I swung the earth a trinket at my wrist,
Are yielding; cords of all too weak account
For earth with heavy griefs so overplussed.
      Ah! is Thy love indeed
A weed, albeit an amaranthine weed,
Suffering no flowers except its own to mount?
      Ah! must —
      Designer infinite! —
Ah! must Thou char the wood ere Thou canst limn
   with it?
My freshness spent its wavering shower i' the dust;
And now my heart is as a broken fount,
Wherein tear-drippings stagnate, spilt down ever
      From the dank thoughts that shiver
Upon the sighful branches of my mind.
      Such is; what is to be?
The pulp so bitter, how shall taste the rind?
I dimly guess what Time in mists confounds;
Yet ever and anon a trumpet sounds
From the hid battlements of Eternity;
Those shaken mists a space unsettle, then
Round the half-glimpsèd turrets slowly wash again.
      But not ere him who summoneth
      I first have seen, enwound
With glooming robes purpureal, cypress-crowned;
His name I know, and what his trumpet saith.
Whether man's heart or life it be which yields

Thee harvest, must Thy harvest-fields
Be dunged with rotten death?

Now of that long pursuit
Comes on at hand the bruit;
That Voice is round me like a bursting sea:
'And is thy earth so marred,
Shattered in shard on shard?
Lo, all things fly thee, for thou fliest Me!
Strange, piteous, futile thing!
Wherefore should any set thee love apart?
Seeing none but I make much of naught' (He said),
'And human love needs human meriting:
How hast thou merited —
Of all man's clotted clay the dingiest clot?
Alack, thou knowest not
How little worthy of any love thou art!
Whom wilt thou find to love ignoble thee
Save Me, save only Me?
All which I took from thee I did but take,
Not for thy harms,
But just that thou might'st seek it in My arms.
All which thy child's mistake
Fancies as lost, I have stored for thee at home:
Rise, clasp My hand, and come!'

Halts by me that footfall:
Is my gloom, after all,
Shade of His hand, outstretched caressingly?
'Ah, fondest, blindest, weakest,
I am He Whom thou seekest!
Thou dravest love from thee, who dravest Me.'

50 *From 'Sister Songs'*

BUT lo! at length the day is lingered out,
  At length my Ariel lays his viol by;
We sing no more to thee, child, he and I;
          The day is lingered out:
          In slow wreaths folden
      Around yon censer, sphered, golden,
          Vague Vesper's fumes aspire;
          And glimmering to eclipse,
          The long laburnum drips
Its honey of wild flame, its jocund spilth of fire.

          Now pass your ways, fair bird, and pass your ways
                  If you will;
          I have you through the days!
              And flit or hold you still,
              And perch you where you list
                  On what wrist, —
          You are mine through the times!
I have caught you fast for ever in a tangle of sweet rhymes.
          And in your young maiden morn
                  You may scorn,
                  But you must be
          Bound and sociate to me;
With this thread from out the tomb my dead hand shall
          tether thee!

The Heart (*i*)

51

THE heart you hold too small and local thing
　　Such spacious terms of edifice to bear.
And yet, since Poesy first shook out her wing,
　　The mighty Love has been impalaced there;
That has she given him as his wide demesne,
　　And for his sceptre ample empery;
Against its door to knock has Beauty been
　　Content; it has its purple canopy,
A dais for the sovreign lady spread
　　Of many a lover, who the heaven would think
Too low an awning for her sacred head.
　　The world, from star to sea, cast down its brink —
　　　　Yet shall that chasm, till He Who these did build
　　　　An awful Curtius make Him, yawn unfilled.

(*ii*)

O nothing, in this corporal earth of man,
　　That to the imminent heaven of his high soul
Responds with colour and with shadow, can
　　Lack correlated greatness. If the scroll
Where thoughts lie fast in spell of hieroglyph
　　Be mighty through its mighty habitants;
If God be in His Name; grave potence if
　　The sounds unbind of hieratic chants;
All's vast that vastness means. Nay, I affirm
　　Nature is whole in her least things exprest,
Nor know we with what scope God builds the worm.
　　Our towns are copies fragments from our breast;
　　　　And all man's Babylons strive but to impart
　　　　The grandeurs of his Babylonian heart.

MARY COLERIDGE

1861–1907

52 *Our Lady*

MOTHER of God! no lady thou:
　　Common woman of common earth
Our Lady ladies call thee now;
　　But Christ was never of gentle birth;
　　A common man of the common earth.

For God's ways are not as our ways.
　　The noblest lady in the land
Would have given up half her days,
　　Would have cut off her right hand,
　　To bear the child that was God of the land.

Never a lady did He choose,
　　Only a maid of low degree,
So humble she might not refuse
　　The carpenter of Galilee:
　　A daughter of the people, she.

Out she sang the song of her heart.
　　Never a lady so had sung.
She knew no letters, had no art;
　　To all mankind, in woman's tongue,
　　Hath Israelitish Mary sung.

And still for men to come she sings,
　　Nor shall her singing pass away.
' *He hath fillèd the hungry with good things* ' —
　　Oh, listen, lords and ladies gay! —
　　' *And the rich He hath sent empty away.*'

62

1861–1941

53 *Day after Day*

DAY after day, O lord of my life, shall I stand before thee face to face? With folded hands, O lord of all worlds, shall I stand before thee face to face?

Under thy great sky in solitude and silence, with humble heart shall I stand before thee face to face?

In this laborious world of thine, tumultuous with toil and with struggle, among hurrying crowds shall I stand before thee face to face?

And when my work shall be done in this world, O King of kings, alone and speechless shall I stand before thee face to face?

54 *If it is not my Portion*

IF it is not my portion to meet thee in this my life then let me ever feel that I have missed thy sight — let me not forget for a moment, let me carry the pangs of this sorrow in my dreams and in my wakeful hours.

As my days pass in the crowded market of this world and my hands grow full with the daily profits, let me ever feel that I have gained nothing — let me not forget for a moment, let me carry the pangs of this sorrow in my dreams and in my wakeful hours.

When I sit by the roadside, tired and panting, when I spread my bed low in the dust, let me ever feel that the long journey is still before me — let me not forget for a moment, let me carry the pangs of this sorrow in my dreams and in my wakeful hours.

When my rooms have been decked out and the flutes sound and the laughter there is loud, let me ever feel that I have not invited thee to my house — let me not forget for a moment, let me carry the pangs of this sorrow in my dreams and in my wakeful hours.

55 *I have got my Leave*

I HAVE got my leave. Bid me farewell, my brothers! I bow to you all and take my departure.

Here I give back the keys of my door — and I give up all claims to my house. I only ask for last kind words from you.

We were neighbours for long, but I received more than I could give. Now the day has dawned and the lamp that lit my dark corner is out. A summons has come and I am ready for my journey.

56 *On the Slope of the Desolate River*

ON the slope of the desolate river among tall grasses I asked her, 'Maiden, where do you go shading your lamp with your mantle? My house is all dark and lonesome — lend me your light!' She raised her dark eyes for a moment and looked at my face through the dusk. 'I have come to the river,' she said, 'to float my lamp on the stream when the daylight wanes in the west.' I stood alone among tall grasses and watched the timid flame of her lamp uselessly drifting in the tide.

In the silence of gathering night I asked her, 'Maiden, your lights are all lit — then where do you go with your lamp? My house is all dark and lonesome, — lend me your light.' She raised her dark eyes on my face and stood for a moment doubtful. ' I have come,' she said at last, ' to dedicate my lamp to the sky.' I stood and watched her light uselessly burning in the void.

In the moonless gloom of midnight I asked her, ' Maiden, what is your quest holding the lamp near your heart? My house is all dark and lonesome, — lend me your light.' She stopped for a minute and thought and gazed at my face in the dark. ' I have brought my light,' she said, ' to join the carnival of lamps.' I stood and watched her little lamp uselessly lost among lights.

57   *The Yellow Bird sings*

THE yellow bird sings in their tree and makes my heart dance with gladness.

We both live in the same village, and that is our one piece of joy.

Her pair of pet lambs come to graze in the shade of our garden trees.

If they stray into our barley field, I take them up in my arms.

The name of our village is Khanjanā, and Anjanā they call our river.

My name is known to all the village, and her name is Ranjanā.

Only one field lies between us.

Bees that have hived in our grove go to seek honey in theirs.

Flowers launched from their landing-stairs come floating by the stream where we bathe.

Baskets of dried *kusm* flowers come from their fields to our market.

The name of our village is Khanjanā, and Anjanā they call our river.

My name is known to all the village, and her name is Ranjanā.

The lane that winds to their house is fragrant in the spring with mango flowers.

When their linseed is ripe for harvest the hemp is in bloom in our field.

The stars that smile on their cottage send us the same twinkling look.

The rain that floods their tank makes glad our *kadam* forest.

The name of our village is Khanjanā, and Anjanā they call our river.

My name is known to all the village, and her name is Ranjanā.

58   *In the Dusky Path of a Dream*

IN the dusky path of a dream I went to seek the love who was mine in a former life.

Her house stood at the end of a desolate street.

In the evening breeze her pet peacock sat drowsing on its perch, and the pigeons were silent in their corner.

She set her lamp down by the portal and stood before me.

She raised her large eyes to my face and mutely asked, ' Are you well, my friend? '

I tried to answer, but our language had been lost and forgotten.

I thought and thought; our names would not come to my mind.

Tears shone in her eyes. She held up her right hand to me. I took it and stood silent.

One lamp had flickered in the evening breeze and died.

RABINDRANATH TAGORE

59   *Thou art the Sky*

THOU art the sky and Thou art also the nest.
    O Thou Beautiful! how in the nest thy love embraceth
    the soul with sweet sounds and colour and fragrant
    odours!
Morning cometh there, bearing in her golden basket the
    wreath of beauty, silently to crown the earth.
And there cometh Evening, o'er lonely meadows deserted
    of the herds, by trackless ways, carrying in her golden
    pitcher cool draughts of peace from the ocean-calms
    of the west.
But where thine infinite sky spreadeth for the soul to take
    her flight, a stainless white radiance reigneth; wherein
    is neither day nor night, nor form nor colour, nor ever
    any word.

                 (*All these poems are from his own Bengali.*)

SIR HENRY NEWBOLT

1862–1938

60   *Drake's Drum*

DRAKE he's in his hammock an' a thousand mile away,
    (Capten, art tha sleepin' there below?)
Slung atween the round shot in Nombre Dios Bay,
    An' dreamin' arl the time o' Plymouth Hoe.
Yarnder lumes the Island, yarnder lie the ships,
    Wi' sailor-lads a-dancin' heel-an'-toe,
An' the shore-lights flashin', an' the night-tide dashin',
    He sees et arl so plainly as he saw et long ago.

Drake he was a Devon man, an' rüled the Devon seas,
    (Capten, art tha sleepin' there below?)
Rovin' tho' his death fell, he went wi' heart at ease,
    An' dreamin' arl the time o' Plymouth Hoe.
' Take my drum to England, hang et by the shore,
    Strike et when your powder 's runnin' low;
If the Dons sight Devon, I'll quit the port o' Heaven,
    An' drum them up the Channel as we drumm'd them long
      ago.'

Drake he 's in his hammock till the great Armadas come,
    (Capten, art tha sleepin' there below?)
Slung atween the round shot, listenin' for the drum,
    An' dreamin' arl the time o' Plymouth Hoe.
Call him on the deep sea, call him up the Sound,
    Call him when ye sail to meet the foe;
Where the old trade 's plyin' an' the old flag flyin'
    They shall find him ware an' wakin', as they found him
      long ago!

MICHAEL FIELD

Katharine Bradley 1846–1914
Edith Cooper 1862–1913

61   *The Tragic Mary Queen of Scots. I*

AH me, if I grew sweet to man
   It was but as a rose that can
No longer keep the breath that heaves
And swells among its folded leaves.

The pressing fragrance would unclose
The flower, and I became a rose,
That unimpeachable and fair
Planted its sweetness in the air.

No art I used men's love to draw;
I lived but by my being's law,
As roses are by heaven designed
To bring the honey to the wind.

62 *The Tragic Mary Queen of Scots. II*

I COULD wish to be dead!
Too quick with life were the tears I shed,
Too sweet for tears is the life I led;
And ah, too lonesome my marriage-bed!
I could wish to be dead.

I could wish to be dead,
For just a word that rings in my head;
Too dear, too dear are the words he said,
They must never be rememberèd.
I could wish to be dead.

I could wish to be dead:
The wish to be loved is all mis-read,
And to love, one learns when one is wed,
Is to suffer bitter shame; instead
I could wish to be dead.

63 *Bury her at Even*

BURY her at even
That the stars may shine
Soon above her,
And the dews of twilight cover:
Bury her at even
Ye that love her.

Bury her at even
In the wind's decline;
Night receive her
Where no noise can ever grieve her!
Bury her at even,
And then leave her!

64   *And on my Eyes Dark Sleep by Night*

'Οφθαλμοῖς δὲ μέλαις νυκτὸς ἄωρος.

COME, dark-eyed Sleep, thou child of Night,
Give me thy dreams, thy lies;
Lead through the horny portal white
The pleasure day denies.

O bring the kiss I could not take
From lips that would not give
Bring me the heart I could not break
The bliss for which I live.

I care not if I slumber blest
By fond delusion; nay,
Put me on Phaon's lips to rest,
And cheat the cruel day!

65   *Gold is the Son of Zeus: neither Moth nor Worm may gnaw It*

Διὸς παῖς ὁ χρυσός·
κεῖνον οὐ σὴς οὐδὲ κὶς δάπτει.

Yea, gold is son of Zeus: no rust
Its timeless light can stain;
The worm that brings man's flesh to dust
Assaults its strength in vain:
More gold than gold the love I sing,
A hard, inviolable thing.

Men say the passions should grow old
With waning years; my heart
Is incorruptible as gold,
'Tis my immortal part:
Nor is there any god can lay
On love the finger of decay.

66 *Sweeter Far than the Harp,*
More Gold than Gold

Πολὺ **πάκτιδος** ἀδυμελεστέρα,
χρυσῶ χρυσοτέρα.

Thine elder that I am, thou must not cling
To me, nor mournful for my love entreat:
And yet, Alcaeus, as the sudden spring
Is love, yea, and to veiled Demeter sweet.

Sweeter than tone of harp, more gold than gold
Is thy young voice to me; yet, ah, the pain
To learn I am beloved now I am old,
Who, in my youth, loved, as thou must, in vain.

67 *If They Honoured Me, Giving*
Me Their Gifts

Αἴ με τιμίαν ἐπόησαν ἔργα
τὰ σφὰ δοῖσαι.

They bring me gifts, they honour me,
Now I am growing old;
And wondering youth crowds round my knee,
As if I had a mystery
And worship to unfold.

To me the tender, blushing bride
Doth come with lips that fail;
I feel her heart beat at my side
And cry: ' Like Ares in his pride,
Hail, noble bridegroom, hail! '

68   *To The Lord Love*

(*At the approach of old age*)

I AM thy fugitive, thy votary,
  Nor even thy mother tempts me from thy shrine:
Mirror, nor gold, nor ornament of mine
Appease her: thou art all my gods to me,
And I so breathless in my loyalty,
Youth hath slipped by and left no footprint sign:
Yet there are footsteps nigh.　My years decline.
Decline thy years?　Burns thy torch duskily?
Lord Love, to thy great altar I retire;
Time doth pursue me, age is on my brow,
And there are cries and shadows of the night.
Transform me, for I cannot quit thee now:
Love, thou hast weapons visionary, bright —
Keep me perpetual in grace and fire!

69   *Aridity*

O SOUL, canst thou not understand
  Thou art not left alone,
As a dog to howl and moan
His master's absence?　Thou art as a book
Left in a room that He forsook,

MICHAEL FIELD

But returns to by and by,
A book of His dear choice, —
That quiet waiteth for His Hand,
That quiet waiteth for His Eye,
That quiet waiteth for His Voice.

RUDYARD KIPLING

1865–1936

70 *A St. Helena Lullaby*

HOW far is St. Helena from a little child at play? '
What makes you want to wander there with all the
world between?
Oh, Mother, call your son again or else he'll run away.
(*No one thinks of winter when the grass is green!*)

' How far is St. Helena from a fight in Paris street? '
I haven't time to answer now — the men are falling fast.
The guns begin to thunder, and the drums begin to beat.
(*If you take the first step, you will take the last!*)

' How far is St. Helena from the field of Austerlitz? '
You couldn't hear me if I told — so loud the cannons roar.
But not so far for people who are living by their wits.
(' *Gay go up* ' means ' *Gay go down* ' *the wide world o'er!*)

' How far is St. Helena from an Emperor of France? '
I cannot see — I cannot tell — the crowns they dazzle so.
The Kings sit down to dinner, and the Queens stand up to
dance.
(*After open weather you may look for snow!*)

73

' How far is St. Helena from the Capes of Trafalgar? '
A longish way — a longish way — with ten year more to
  run.
It's South across the water underneath a falling star.
(*What you cannot finish you must leave undone!*)

' How far is St. Helena from the Beresina ice? '
An ill way — a chill way — the ice begins to crack.
But not so far for gentlemen who never took advice.
(*When you can't go forward you must e'en come back!*)

' How far is St. Helena from the field of Waterloo? '
A near way — a clear way — the ship will take you soon.
A pleasant place for gentlemen with little left to do.
(*Morning never tries you till the afternoon!*)

' How far from St. Helena to the Gate of Heaven's Grace? '
That no one knows — that no one knows — and no one
  ever will,
But fold your hands across your heart and cover up your
  face,
And after all your trapesings, child, lie still!

71   *The Looking-glass*
              (*A Country Dance*)

QUEEN *Bess was Harry's daughter. Stand forward
      partners all!*
In ruff and stomacher and gown
She danced King Philip down-a-down,
And left her shoe to show 'twas true —
    (*The very tune I'm playing you*)
In Norgem at Brickwall!

  74

The Queen was in her chamber, and she was middling old.
Her petticoat was satin, and her stomacher was gold.
Backwards and forwards and sideways did she pass,
Making up her mind to face the cruel looking-glass.
The cruel looking-glass that will never show a lass
As comely or as kindly as what she was!
Queen Bess was Harry's daughter. Now hand your partners all!

The Queen was in her chamber, a-combing of her hair.
There came Queen Mary's spirit and It stood behind her
    chair,
Singing ' Backwards and forwards and sideways may you pass,
But I will stand behind you till you face the looking-glass.
The cruel looking-glass that will never show a lass
As lovely or unlucky or as lonely as I was! '
Queen Bess was Harry's daughter. Now turn your partners all!

The Queen was in her chamber, a-weeping very sore,
There came Lord Leicester's spirit and It scratched upon the
    door,
Singing ' Backwards and forwards and sideways may you pass,
But I will walk beside you till you face the looking-glass.
The cruel looking-glass that will never show a lass,
As hard and unforgiving or as wicked as you was! '
Queen Bess was Harry's daughter. Now kiss your partners all!

The Queen was in her chamber, her sins were on her head.
She looked the spirits up and down and statelily she said: —
' Backwards and forwards and sideways though I've been,
Yet I am Harry's daughter and I am England's Queen! '

75

And she faced the looking-glass (and whatever else there was)
And she saw her day was over and she saw her beauty pass
In the cruel looking-glass, that can always hurt a lass
More hard than any ghost there is or any man there was!

ARTHUR SYMONS

1865–1945

72 *Mandoline*

THE singers of serenades
  Whisper their fated vows
Unto fair listening maids
Under the singing boughs.

Tircis, Aminte, are there,
Clitandre has waited long,
And Damis for many a fair
Tyrant makes many a song.

Their short vests, silken and bright,
Their long pale silken trains,
Their elegance of delight,
Twine soft blue silken chains.

And the mandolines and they,
Faintlier breathing, swoon
Into the rose and grey
Ecstasy of the moon.

(*From Paul Verlaine.*)

73 *Fantoches*

SCARAMOUCHE waves a threatening hand
  To Pulcinella, and they stand,
Two shadows, black against the moon.

76

The old doctor of Bologna pries
For simples with impassive eyes,
And mutters o'er a magic rune.

The while his daughter, scarce half-dressed,
Glides shyly 'neath the trees, in quest
Of her bold pirate lover's sail;

Her pirate from the Spanish main,
Whose passion thrills her in the pain
Of the loud languorous nightingale.

(*From Paul Verlaine.*)

74   *The Obscure Night of the Soul*

UPON an obscure night,
   Fevered with love in love's anxiety,
(O hapless-happy plight!)
I went, none seeing me,
Forth from my house where all things quiet be.

By night, secure from sight,
And by the secret stair, disguisedly,
(O hapless-happy plight!)
By night, and privily,
Forth from my house where all things quiet be.

Blest night of wandering,
In secret, where by none might I be spied,
Nor I see anything;
Without a light or guide,
Save that which in my heart burnt in my side.

ARTHUR SYMONS

That light did lead me on,
More surely than the shining of noontide,
Where well I knew that one
Did for my coming bide;
Where he abode might none but he abide.

O night that didst lead thus,
O night more lovely than the dawn of light,
O night that broughtest us,
Lover to lover's sight,
Lover with loved in marriage of delight!

Upon my flowery breast,
Wholly for him, and save himself for none,
There did I give sweet rest
To my beloved one;
The fanning of the cedars breathed thereon.

When the first moving air
Blew from the tower, and waved his locks aside,
His hand, with gentle care,
Did wound me in the side,
And in my body all my senses died.

All things I then forgot,
My cheek on him who for my coming came;
All ceased and I was not,
Leaving my cares and shame
Among the lilies, and forgetting them.

(From San Juan de la Cruz.)

1865–1923

75   *Jean Richepin's Song*

A POOR lad once and a lad so trim,
    Fol de rol de raly O!
        Fol de rol!
A poor lad once and a lad so trim
    Gave his love to her that loved not him.

And, says she, ' Fetch me to-night you rogue,'
    Fol de rol de raly O!
        Fol de rol!
And, says she, ' Fetch me to-night, you rogue,
    Your mother's heart to feed my dog! '

To his mother's house went that young man
    Fol de rol de raly O!
        Fol de rol!
To his mother's house went that young man
    Killed her, and took the heart, and ran.

And as he was running, look you, he fell
    Fol de rol de raly O!
        Fol de rol!
And as he was running, look you, he fell
    And the heart rolled on the ground as well.

And the lad, as the heart was a-rolling, heard
    (Fol de rol de raly O!
        Fol de rol!)
And the lad, as the heart was a-rolling, heard
    That the heart was speaking, and this was the word —

79

The heart was a-weeping, and crying so small
    (Fol de rol de raly O!
       Fol de rol!)
The heart was a-weeping, and crying so small
' Are you hurt my child, are you hurt at all? '

WILLIAM BUTLER YEATS

1865–1939

76   *After Long Silence*

SPEECH after long silence; it is right,
  All other lovers being estranged or dead,
Unfriendly lamplight hid under its shade,
The curtains drawn upon unfriendly night,
That we descant and yet again descant
Upon the supreme theme of Art and Song:
Bodily decrepitude is wisdom; young
We loved each other and were ignorant.

77   *Three Things*

O CRUEL Death, give three things back,'
   Sang a bone upon the shore;
' A child found all a child can lack,
Whether of pleasure or of rest,
Upon the abundance of my breast ':
A bone wave-whitened and dried in the wind.

' Three dear things that women know,'
Sang a bone upon the shore;
' A man if I but held him so
When my body was alive
Found all the pleasure that life gave ':
A bone wave-whitened and dried in the wind.

'The third thing that I think of yet,'
Sang a bone upon the shore;
'Is that morning when I met
Face to face my rightful man
And did after stretch and yawn ':
A bone wave-whitened and dried in the wind.

78 *Lullaby*

BELOVED, may your sleep be sound
That have found it where you fed.
What were all the world's alarms
To mighty Paris when he found
Sleep upon a golden bed
That first dawn in Helen's arms?

Sleep, beloved, such a sleep
As did that wild Tristram know
When, the potion's work being done,
Roe could run or doe could leap
Under oak and beechen bough,
Roe could leap or doe could run;

Such a sleep and sound as fell
Upon Eurotas' grassy bank
When the holy bird, that there
Accomplished his predestined will,
From the limbs of Leda sank
But not from her protecting care.

79 *Symbols*

A STORM—BEATEN old watch-tower,
A blind hermit rings the hour.

All-destroying sword-blade still
Carried by the wandering fool.

Gold-sewn silk on the sword-blade,
Beauty and fool together laid.

80 *From ' Vacillation '*

MUST we part, Von Hügel, though much alike, for we
Accept the miracles of the saints and honour sanctity?
The body of Saint Teresa lies undecayed in tomb,
Bathed in miraculous oil, sweet odours from it come,
Healing from its lettered slab. Those self-same hands perchance
Eternalized the body of a modern saint that once
Had scooped out Pharaoh's mummy. I — though heart might find relief
Did I become a Christian man and choose for my belief
What seems most welcome in the tomb — play a predestined part.
Homer is my example and his unchristened heart.
The lion and the honeycomb, what has Scripture said?
So get you gone, Von Hügel, though with blessings on your head.

81 *Sailing to Byzantium*

THAT is no country for old men. The young
In one another's arms; birds in the trees,
— Those dying generations — at their song;
The salmon-falls, the mackerel-crowded seas,

82

Fish, flesh, or fowl, commend all summer long
Whatever is begotten, born, and dies.
Caught in that sensual music all neglect
Monuments of unageing intellect.

An aged man is but a paltry thing,
A tattered coat upon a stick, unless
Soul clap its hands and sing, and louder sing
For every tatter in its mortal dress,
Nor is there singing school but studying
Monuments of its own magnificence;
And therefore I have sailed the seas and come
To the holy city of Byzantium.

O sages standing in God's holy fire
As in the gold mosaic of a wall,
Come from the holy fire, perne in a gyre,
And be the singing-masters of my soul.
Consume my heart away; sick with desire
And fastened to a dying animal
It knows not what it is; and gather me
Into the artifice of eternity.

Once out of nature I shall never take
My bodily form from any natural thing,
But such a form as Grecian goldsmiths make
Of hammered gold and gold enamelling
To keep a drowsy Emperor awake;
Or set upon a golden bough to sing
To lords and ladies of Byzantium
Of what is past, or passing, or to come.

82   *The Rose Tree*

'O WORDS are lightly spoken,'
Said Pearse to Connolly,
' Maybe a breath of politic words
Has withered our Rose Tree;
Or maybe but a wind that blows
Across the bitter sea.'

' It needs to be but watered,'
James Connolly replied,
' To make the green come out again
And spread on every side,
And shake the blossom from the bud
To be the garden's pride.'

' But where can we draw water,'
Said Pearse to Connolly,
' When all the wells are parched away?
O plain as plain can be
There's nothing but our own red blood
Can make a right Rose Tree.'

83   *On a Political Prisoner*

SHE that but little patience knew,
From childhood on, had now so much
A grey gull lost its fear and flew
Down to her cell and there alit,
And there endured her fingers' touch
And from her fingers ate its bit.

84

Did she in touching that lone wing
Recall the years before her mind
Became a bitter, an abstract thing,
Her thought some popular enmity:
Blind and leader of the blind
Drinking the foul ditch where they lie?

When long ago I saw her ride
Under Ben Bulben to the meet,
The beauty of her country-side
With all youth's lonely wildness stirred,
She seemed to have grown clean and sweet
Like any rock-bred, sea-borne bird:

Sea-borne, or balanced on the air
When first it sprang out of the nest
Upon some lofty rock to stare
Upon the cloudy canopy,
While under its storm-beaten breast
Cried out the hollows of the sea.

84   *In Memory of Eva Gore-Booth
and Con Markiewicz*

THE light of evening, Lissadell,
  Great windows open to the south,
Two girls in silk kimonos, both
Beautiful, one a gazelle.
But a raving autumn shears
Blossom from the summer's wreath;
The older is condemned to death,
Pardoned, drags out lonely years
Conspiring among the ignorant.

I know not what the younger dreams —
Some vague Utopia — and she seems,
When withered old and skeleton-gaunt,
An image of such politics.
Many a time I think to seek
One or the other out and speak
Of that old Georgian mansion, mix
Pictures of the mind, recall
That table and the talk of youth,
Two girls in silk kimonos, both
Beautiful, one a gazelle.
Dear shadows, now you know it all,
All the folly of a fight
With a common wrong or right.
The innocent and the beautiful
Have no enemy but time;
Arise and bid me strike a match
And strike another till time catch;
Should the conflagration climb,
Run till all the sages know.
We the great gazebo built,
They convicted us of guilt;
Bid me strike a match and blow.

85   *To a Friend whose Work has
come to Nothing*

NOW all the truth is out,
  Be secret and take defeat
From any brazen throat,
For how can you compete,

86

Being honour bred, with one
Who, were it proved he lies,
Were neither shamed in his own
Nor in his neighbours' eyes?
Bred to a harder thing
Than Triumph, turn away
And like a laughing string
Whereon mad fingers play
Amid a place of stone,
Be secret and exult,
Because of all things known
That is most difficult.

86   *An Irish Airman foresees his
Death*

I KNOW that I shall meet my fate
Somewhere among the clouds above;
Those that I fight I do not hate,
Those that I guard I do not love;
My country is Kiltartan Cross,
My countrymen Kiltartan's poor,
No likely end could bring them loss
Or leave them happier than before.
Nor law, nor duty bade me fight,
Nor public men, nor cheering crowds,
A lonely impulse of delight
Drove to this tumult in the clouds;
I balanced all, brought all to mind,
The years to come seemed waste of breath,
A waste of breath the years behind
In balance with this life, this death.

Coole Park, 1929

I MEDITATE upon a swallow's flight,
Upon an aged woman and her house,
A sycamore and lime tree lost in night
Although that western cloud is luminous,
Great works constructed there in nature's spite
For scholars and for poets after us,
Thoughts long knitted into a single thought,
A dance-like glory that those walls begot.

There Hyde before he had beaten into prose
That noble blade the Muses buckled on,
There one that ruffled in a manly pose
For all his timid heart, there that slow man,
That meditative man, John Synge, and those
Impetuous men, Shaw Taylor and Hugh Lane,
Found pride established in humility,
A scene well set and excellent company.

They came like swallows and like swallows went,
And yet a woman's powerful character
Could keep a swallow to its first intent;
And half a dozen in formation there,
That seemed to whirl upon a compass-point,
Found certainty upon the dreaming air,
The intellectual sweetness of those lines
That cut through time or cross it withershins.

Here, traveller, scholar, poet, take your stand
When all those rooms and passages are gone,
When nettles wave upon a shapeless mound
And saplings root among the broken stone,

And dedicate — eyes bent upon the ground,
Back turned upon the brightness of the sun
And all the sensuality of the shade —
A moment's memory to that laurelled head.

88   *Coole and Ballylee, 1931*

UNDER my window-ledge the waters race,
   Otters below and moor-hens on the top,
Run for a mile undimmed in Heaven's face
Then darkening through ' dark ' Raftery's ' cellar ' drop,
Run underground, rise in a rocky place
In Coole demesne, and there to finish up
Spread to a lake and drop into a hole.
What's water but the generated soul?

Upon the border of that lake 's a wood
Now all dry sticks under a wintry sun,
And in·a copse of beeches there I stood,
For Nature 'd pulled her tragic buskin on
And all the rant a mirror of my mood:
At sudden thunder of the mounting swan
I turned about and looked where branches broke
The glittering reaches of the flooded lake.

Another emblem there!   That stormy white
But seems a concentration of the sky;
And, like the soul, it sails into the sight
And in the morning 's gone, no man knows why;
And is so lovely that it sets to right
What knowledge or its lack has set awry,
So arrogantly pure, a child might think
It can be murdered with a spot of ink.

Sound of a stick upon the floor, a sound
From somebody that toils from chair to chair;
Beloved books that famous hands have bound,
Old marble heads, old pictures everywhere;
Great rooms where travelled men and children found
Content or joy; a last inheritor
Where none has reigned that lacked a name and fame
Or out of folly into folly came.

A spot whereon the founders lived and died
Seemed once more dear than life; ancestral trees,
Or gardens rich in memory glorified
Marriages, alliances and families,
And every bride's ambition satisfied.
Where fashion or mere fantasy decrees
Man shifts about — all that great glory spent —
Like some poor Arab tribesman and his tent.

We were the last romantics — chose for theme
Traditional sanctity and loveliness;
Whatever's written in what poets name
The book of the people; whatever most can bless
The mind of man or elevate a rhyme;
But all is changed, that high horse riderless,
Though mounted in that saddle Homer rode
Where the swan drifts upon a darkening flood.

89   *From 'Oedipus at Colonus'*

ENDURE what life God gives and ask no longer span;
  Cease to remember the delights of youth, travel-
      wearied aged man;
Delight becomes death-longing if all longing else be vain.

  90

Even from that delight memory treasures so,
Death, despair, division of families, all entanglements of
    mankind grow,
As that old wandering beggar and these God-hated children
    know.

In the long echoing street the laughing dancers throng,
The bride is carried to the bridegroom's chamber through
    torchlight and tumultuous song;
I celebrate the silent kiss that ends short life or long.

Never to have lived is best, ancient writers say;
Never to have drawn the breath of life, never to have
    looked into the eye of day;
The second best 's a gay goodnight and quickly turn away.

ERNEST DOWSON

1867–1900

90   *Villanelle of the Poet's Road*

WINE and woman and song,
   Three things garnish our way:
Yet is day over long.

Lest we do our youth wrong,
   Gather them while we may:
Wine and woman and song.

Three things render us strong,
   Vine leaves, kisses and bay;
Yet is day over long.

Unto us they belong,
   Us the bitter and gay,
Wine and woman and song.

We, as we pass along,
  Are sad that they will not stay;
Yet is day over long.

Fruits and flowers among,
  What is better than they:
Wine and woman and song?
  Yet is day over long.

91 *Non sum qualis eram bonae sub regno Cynarae*

LAST night, ah, yesternight, betwixt her lips and mine
  There fell thy shadow, Cynara! thy breath was shed
Upon my soul between the kisses and the wine;
And I was desolate and sick of an old passion,
  Yea, I was desolate and bowed my head:
I have been faithful to thee, Cynara! in my fashion.

All night upon mine heart I felt her warm heart beat,
Night-long within mine arms in love and sleep she lay;
Surely the kisses of her bought red mouth were sweet;
But I was desolate and sick of an old passion,
  When I awoke and found the dawn was gray:
I have been faithful to thee, Cynara! in my fashion.

I have forgot much, Cynara! gone with the wind,
Flung roses, roses riotously with the throng,
Dancing, to put thy pale, lost lilies out of mind;
But I was desolate and sick of an old passion,
  Yea, all the time, because the dance was long:
I have been faithful to thee, Cynara! in my fashion.

I cried for madder music and for stronger wine,
But when the feast is finished and the lamps expire,
Then falls thy shadow, Cynara! the night is thine;
And I am desolate and sick of an old passion,
    Yea hungry for the lips of my desire:
I have been faithful to thee, Cynara! in my fashion.

Flos Lunae

I WOULD not alter thy cold eyes,
  Nor trouble the calm fount of speech
With aught of passion or surprise.
The heart of thee I cannot reach:
I would not alter thy cold eyes!

I would not alter thy cold eyes;
Nor have thee smile, nor make thee weep:
Though all my life droops down and dies,
Desiring thee, desiring sleep,
I would not alter thy cold eyes.

I would not alter thy cold eyes;
I would not change thee if I might,
To whom my prayers for incense rise,
Daughter of dreams! my moon of night!
I would not alter thy cold eyes.

I would not alter thy cold eyes,
With trouble of the human heart:
Within their glance my spirit lies,
A frozen thing, alone, apart;
I would not alter thy cold eyes.

93

Exchanges

ALL that I had I brought,
   Little enough I know;
A poor rhyme roughly wrought,
   A rose to match thy snow:
All that I had I brought.

Little enough I sought:
   But a word compassionate,
A passing glance, or thought,
   For me outside the gate:
Little enough I sought.

Little enough I found:
   All that you had, perchance!
With the dead leaves on the ground,
   I dance the devil's dance.
All that you had I found.

94 *O mors! quam amara est memoria tua
homini pacem habenti in substantiis suis*

EXCEEDING sorrow
   Consumeth my sad heart!
Because to-morrow
   We must depart,
Now is exceeding sorrow
   All my part!

Give over playing,
  Cast thy viol away:
Merely laying
  Thine head my way:
Prithee, give over playing,
  Grave or gay.

Be no word spoken;
  Weep nothing: let a pale
Silence, unbroken
  Silence prevail!
Prithee, be no word spoken,
  Lest I fail!

Forget to-morrow!
  Weep nothing: only lay
In silent sorrow
  Thine head my way:
Let us forget to-morrow,
  This one day!

95   *Vesperal*

STRANGE grows the river on the sunless evenings!
  The river comforts me, grown spectral, vague and
    dumb:
Long was the day; at last the consoling shadows come:
Sufficient for the day are the day's evil things!

Labour and longing and despair the long day brings;
Patient till evening men watch the sun go west;
Deferred, expected night at last brings sleep and rest:
Sufficient for the day are the day's evil things!

95

At last the tranquil Angelus of evening rings
Night's curtain down for comfort and oblivion
Of all the vanities observed by the sun:
Sufficient for the day are the day's evil things!

So, some time, when the last of all our evenings
Crowneth memorially the last of all our days,
Not loth to take his poppies man goes down and says,
' Sufficient for the day were the day's evil things! '

96   *Dregs*

THE fire is out, and spent the warmth thereof,
    (This is the end of every song man sings!)
The golden wine is drunk, the dregs remain,
Bitter as wormwood and as salt as pain;
And health and hope have gone the way of love
Into the drear oblivion of lost things.
Ghosts go along with us until the end;
This was a mistress, this, perhaps, a friend.
With pale, indifferent eyes, we sit and wait
For the dropt curtain and the closing gate:
This is the end of all the songs man sings.

97   *To One in Bedlam*

WITH delicate, mad hands, behind his sordid bars,
    Surely he hath his posies, which they tear and twine;
Those scantless wisps of straw, that miserably line
His strait, caged universe, whereat the dull world stares,

Pedant and pitiful. O, how his rapt gaze wars
With their stupidity! Know they what dreams divine
Lift his long, laughing reveries like enchaunted wine,
And make his melancholy germane to the stars'?

O lamentable brother! if those pity thee,
Am I not fain of all thy lone eyes promise me;
Half a fool's kingdom, far from men who sow and reap,
All their days, vanity? Better than mortal flowers,
Thy moon-kissed roses seem: better than love or sleep,
The star-crowned solitude of thine oblivious hours!

98   *Extreme Unction*

U PON the eyes, the lips, the feet,
   On all the passages of sense,
The atoning oil is spread with sweet
   Renewal of lost innocence.

The feet, that lately ran so fast
   To meet desire, are soothly sealed;
The eyes, that were so often cast
   On vanity, are touched and healed.

From troublous sights and sounds set free;
   In such a twilight hour of breath,
Shall one retrace his life, or see,
   Through shadows, the true face of death?

Vials of mercy! Sacring oils!
   I know not where nor when I come,
Nor through what wanderings and toils,
   To crave of you Viaticum.

Yet, when the walls of flesh grow weak,
   In such an hour, it well may be,
Through mist and darkness, light will break,
   And each anointed sense will see.

THOMAS BOYD

1867–

99 *The King's Son*

WHO rideth through the driving rain
At such a headlong speed?
Naked and pale he rides amain
　Upon a naked steed.

Nor hollow nor height his going bars,
　His wet steed shines like silk,
His head is golden to the stars
　And his limbs are white as milk.

But, lo, he dwindles as a light
　That lifts from a black mere,
And, as the fair youth wanes from sight,
　The steed grows mightier.

What wizard by yon holy tree
　Mutters unto the sky
Where Macha's flame-tongued horses flee
　On hooves of thunder by?

Ah, 'tis not holy so to ban
　The youth of kingly seed:
Ah! woe, the wasting of a man
　Who changes to a steed.

Nightly upon the Plain of Kings
　When Macha's day is nigh
He gallops; and the dark wind brings
　His lonely human cry.

100   *Reconciliation*

I BEGIN through the grass once again to be bound to the
    Lord;
  I can see, through a face that has faded, the face full of
    rest
Of the earth, of the mother, my heart with her heart in
    accord,
  As I lie 'mid the cool green tresses that mantle her breast
I begin with the grass once again to be bound to the Lord.

By the hand of a child I am led to the throne of the King
  For a touch that now fevers me not is forgotten and far,
And His infinite sceptred hands that sway us can bring
  Me in dreams from the laugh of a child to the song of
    a star.
On the laugh of a child I am borne to the joy of the King.

101   *Immortality*

WE must pass like smoke or live within the spirit's fire;
  For we can no more than smoke unto the flame
    return
If our thought has changed to dream, our will unto desire,
    As smoke we vanish though the fire may burn.

Lights of infinite pity star the grey dusk of our days:
Surely here is soul: with it we have eternal breath:
In the fire of love we live, or pass by many ways,
    By unnumbered ways of dream to death.

99

GEORGE WILLIAM RUSSELL (Æ)

Desire

WITH Thee a moment! Then what dreams have play!
  Traditions of eternal toil arise,
Search for the high, austere and lonely way
The Spirit moves in through eternities.
Ah, in the soul what memories arise!

And with what yearning inexpressible,
Rising from long forgetfulness I turn
To Thee, invisible, unrumoured, still:
White for Thy whiteness all desires burn.
Ah, with what longing once again I turn!

The Great Breath

ITS edges foamed with amethyst and rose,
  Withers once more the old blue flower of day:
There where the ether like a diamond glows
    Its petals fade away.

A shadowy tumult stirs the dusky air;
Sparkle the delicate dews, the distant snows;
The great deep thrills, for through it everywhere
    The breath of Beauty blows.

I saw how all the trembling ages past,
Moulded to her by deep and deeper breath,
Neared to the hour when Beauty breathes her last
    And knows herself in death.

The Gay

THOSE moon-gilded dancers
  Prankt like butterflies,
Theirs was such lovely folly
It stayed my rapt eyes:
But my heart that was pondering
Was sadly wise.

To be so lighthearted
What pain was left behind;
What fetters fallen gave them
Unto this airy mind:
What dark sins were pardoned;
What God was kind!

I with long anguish bought
Joy that was soon in flight;
And wondered what these paid
For years of young delight;
Ere they were born what tears
Through what long night.

All these gay cheeks, light feet,
Were telling over again,
But in a heavenly accent,
A tale of ancient pain
That, the joy spent, must pass
To sorrow again.

I went into the wilderness
Of night to be alone,

Holding sorrow and joy
Hugged to my heart as one,
Lest they fly on those wild ways
And life be undone.

105 *The Cities*

THEY shall sink under water,
They shall rise up again:
They shall be peopled
By millions of men.

Cleansed of their scarlet,
Absolved of their sin,
They shall be like crystal
All stainless within.

Paris and Babel,
London and Tyre,
Reborn from the darkness,
Shall sparkle like fire.

From the folk who throng in
Their gardens and towers
Shall be blown fragrance
Sweeter than flowers.

Faery shall dance in
The streets of the town,
And from sky headlands
The gods looking down.

106   *New York*

WITH these heaven-assailing spires
       All that was in clay or stone
Fabled of rich Babylon
By these children is outdone.

Earth has split her fire in these
To make them of her mightier kind;
Has she that precious fire to give,
The starry-pointing Magian mind,

That soared from the Chaldean plains
Through zones of mystic air, and found
The Master of the Zodiac,
The Will that makes the Wheel go round?

107   *Germinal*

CALL not thy wanderer home as yet
      Though it be late.
Now is his first assailing of
    The invisible gate.
Be still through that light knocking. The hour
    Is thronged with fate.

To that first tapping at the invisible door
    Fate answereth.
What shining image or voice, what sigh
    Or honied breath,
Comes forth, shall be the master of life
    Even to death.

Satyrs may follow after.   Seraphs
   On crystal wing
May blaze.   But the delicate first comer
   It shall be King.
They shall obey, even the mightiest,
   That gentle thing.

All the strong powers of Dante were bowed
   To a child's mild eyes,
That wrought within him that travail
   From depths up to skies,
Inferno, Purgatorio
   And Paradise.

Amid the soul's grave councillors
   A petulant boy
Laughs under the laurels and purples, the elf
   Who snatched at his joy,
Ordering Caesar's legions to bring him
   The world for his toy.

In ancient shadows and twilights
   Where childhood had strayed,
The world's great sorrows were born
   And its heroes were made.
In the lost boyhood of Judas
   Christ was betrayed.

Let thy young wanderer dream on:
   Call him not home.
A door opens, a breath, a voice
   From the ancient room,
Speaks to him now.   Be it dark or bright
   He is knit with his doom.

1867–1902

108   *The Dark Angel*

DARK Angel, with thine aching lust
      To rid the world of penitence:
Malicious Angel, who still dost
My soul such subtile violence!

Because of thee, no thought, no thing
Abides for me undesecrate:
Dark Angel, ever on the wing,
Who never reachest me too late!

When music sounds, then changest thou
Its silvery to a sultry fire:
Nor will thine envious heart allow
Delight untortured by desire.

Through thee, the gracious Muses turn
To Furies, O mine Enemy!
And all the things of beauty burn
With flames of evil ecstasy.

Because of thee, the land of dreams
Becomes a gathering-place of fears:
Until tormented slumber seems
One vehemence of useless tears.

When sunlight glows upon the flowers,
Or ripples down the dancing sea:
Thou, with thy troop of passionate powers,
Beleaguerest, bewilderest me.

Within the breath of autumn woods,
Within the winter silences:
Thy venomous spirit stirs and broods,
O Master of impieties!

LIONEL JOHNSON

The ardour of red flame is thine,
And thine the steely soul of ice:
Thou poisonest the fair design
Of nature, with unfair device.

Apples of ashes, golden bright;
Waters of bitterness, how sweet!
O banquet of a foul delight,
Prepared by thee, dark Paraclete.

Thou art the whisper in the gloom,
The hinting tone, the haunting laugh:
Thou art the adorner of my tomb,
The minstrel of mine epitaph.

I fight thee, in the Holy Name!
Yet, what thou dost, is what God saith:
Tempter! should I escape thy flame,
Thou wilt have helped my soul from Death:

The second Death, that never dies,
That cannot die, when time is dead:
Live Death, wherein the lost soul cries,
Eternally uncomforted.

Dark Angel, with thine aching lust!
Of two defeats, of two despairs:
Less dread, a change to drifting dust,
Than thine eternity of cares.

Do what thou wilt, thou shalt not so,
Dark Angel! triumph over me:
Lonely, unto the Lone I go;
Divine, to the Divinity.

109   *The Age of a Dream*

IMAGERIES of dreams reveal a gracious age:
Black armour, falling lace, and altar lights at morn.
The courtesy of Saints, their gentleness and scorn,
Lights on an earth more fair, than shone from Plato's page:
The courtesy of knights, fair calm and sacred rage:
The courtesy of love, sorrow for love's sake borne.
Vanished, those high conceits! Desolate and forlorn,
We hunger against hope for the lost heritage.

Gone now, the carven work! Ruined, the golden shrine!
No more the glorious organs pour their voice divine;
No more rich frankincense drifts through the Holy Place:
Now from the broken tower, what solemn bell still tolls,
Mourning what piteous death? Answer, O saddened souls!
Who mourn the death of beauty and the death of grace.

110   *The Church of a Dream*

SADLY the dead leaves rustle in the whistling wind,
Around the weather-worn, grey church, low down the
    vale:
The Saints in golden vesture shake before the gale;
The glorious windows shake, where still they dwell en-
    shrined;
Old Saints by long-dead, shrivelled hands, long since de-
    signed:
There still, although the world autumnal be, and pale,
Still in their golden vesture the old Saints prevail;
Alone with Christ, desolate else, left by mankind.

Only one ancient Priest offers the Sacrifice,
Murmuring holy Latin immemorial:
Swaying with tremulous hands the old censer full of spice,
In grey, sweet incense clouds; blue, sweet clouds mystical:
To him, in place of men, for he is old, suffice
Melancholy remembrances and vesperal.

111   *Te Martyrum Candidatus*

AH, see the fair chivalry come, the companions of Christ!
    White Horsemen, who ride on white horses, the
        Knights of God!
They, for their Lord and their Lover who sacrificed
All, save the sweetness of treading, where He first trod!

These, through the darkness of death, the dominion of
        night,
Swept, and they woke in white places at morning tide:
They saw with their eyes, and sang for joy of the sight,
They saw with their eyes the Eyes of the Crucified.

Now, whithersoever He goeth, with Him they go:
White Horsemen, who ride on white horses, oh, fair to see!
They ride, where the Rivers of Paradise flash and flow,
White Horsemen, with Christ their Captain: for ever He!

112   *To Morfydd*

A VOICE on the winds,
    A voice by the waters,
        Wanders and cries:
    Oh! what are the winds?
    And what are the waters?
        Mine are your eyes!

108

LIONEL JOHNSON

Western the winds are,
And western the waters,
  Where the light lies:
Oh! what are the winds?
And what are the waters?
  Mine are your eyes!

Cold, cold, grow the winds,
And wild grow the waters,
  Where the sun dies:
Oh! what are the winds?
And what are the waters?
  Mine are your eyes!

And down the night winds,
And down the night waters,
  The music flies:
Oh! what are the winds?
And what are the waters?
Cold be the winds,
And wild be the waters,
  So mine be your eyes!

113   *By the Statue of King Charles*
           at Charing Cross

SOMBRE and rich, the skies;
Great glooms, and starry plains.
Gently the night wind sighs;
Else a vast silence reigns.

LIONEL JOHNSON

The splendid silence clings
Around me: and around
The saddest of all kings
Crowned, and again discrowned.

Comely and calm, he rides
Hard by his own Whitehall:
Only the night wind glides:
No crowds, nor rebels, brawl.

Gone, too, his Court: and yet,
The stars his courtiers are:
Stars in their stations set;
And every wandering star.

Alone he rides, alone,
The fair and fatal king:
Dark night is all his own,
That strange and solemn thing.

Which are more full of fate:
The stars; or those sad eyes?
Which are more still and great:
Those brows; or the dark skies?

Although his whole heart yearn
In passionate tragedy:
Never was face so stern
With sweet austerity.

Vanquished in life, his death
By beauty made amends:
The passing of his breath
Won his defeated ends.

LIONEL JOHNSON

Brief life, and hapless?   Nay:
Through death, life grew sublime.
Speak after sentence?   Yea:
And to the end of time.

Armoured he rides, his head
Bare to the stars of doom:
He triumphs now, the dead,
Beholding London's gloom.

Our wearier spirit faints,
Vexed in the world's employ:
His soul was of the saints;
And art to him was joy.

King, tried in fires of woe!
Men hunger for thy grace:
And through the night I go,
Loving thy mournful face.

Yet, when the city sleeps;
When all the cries are still:
The stars and heavenly deeps
Work out a perfect will.

LAURENCE BINYON

1869–1943

114   *Tristram's End*

(i)

TRISTRAM lies sick to death;
   Dulled is his kingly eye,
Listless his famed right arm: earth-weary breath
Hath force alone to sigh
The one name that re-kindles life's low flame,

111

Isoult! — And thou, fair moon of Tristram's eve,
Who with that many-memoried name didst take
A glory for the sake
Of her who shone the sole light of his days and deeds,
Thou canst no more relieve
This heart that inly bleeds
With all thy love, with all thy tender lore,
No, nor thy white hands soothe him any more.
Still, the day long, she hears
Kind words that are more sharp to her than spears.
Ah, loved he more, he had not been so kind!
And still with pricking tears
She watches him, and still must seem resigned;
Though well she knows what face his eyes require,
And jealous pangs, like coiled snakes in her mind,
Cling tighter, as that voice more earnestly
Asks heavy with desire
From out that passionate past which is not hers,
' Sweet wife, is there no sail upon the sea? '

Tenderest hearts by pain grow oft the bitterest,
And haste to wound the thing they love the best.
At evening, at sun-set, to Tristram's bed
News on her lips she brings!
She comes with eyes bright in divining dread,
Hardening her anguished heart she bends above his head.
' O Tristram! ' — How her low voice strangely rings! —
' There comes a ship, ah, rise not, turn not pale.
I know not what this means, it is a sail
Black, black as night! ' She shot her word, and fled.
But Tristram cried
With a great cry, and rose upon his side.

LAURENCE BINYON

' It cannot be, it cannot, shall not be!
I will not die until mine own eyes see.'
Despair, more strong than hope, lifts his weak limbs;
He stands and draws deep effort from his breath,
He trembles, his gaze swims,
He gropes his steps in pain,
Nigh fainting, till he gain
Salt air and brightness from the outer door
That opens on the cliff-built bastion floor
And the wide ocean gleaming far beneath.
He gazes, his lips part,
And all the blood pours back upon his heart.

Close thine eyes, Tristram, lest joy blind thee quite!
So swift a splendour burns away thy doubt.
Nay, Tristram, gaze, gaze, lest bright Truth go out
Ere she hath briefly shone.
White, dazzling white,
A sail swells onward, filling all his sight
With snowy light!
As on a gull's sure wing the ship comes on;
She towers upon the wave, she speeds for home.
Tristram on either doorpost must sustain
His arms for strength to gaze his fill again.
She shivers off the wind; the shining foam
Bursts from her pitching prow,
The sail drops as she nears,
Poised on the joyous swell; and Tristram sees
The mariners upon the deck; he hears
Their eager cries: the breeze
Blows a blue cloak; and now
Like magic brought to his divining ears,

A voice, that empties all the earth and sky,
Comes clear across the water, ' It is I! '

Isoult is come!   Victorious saints above,
Who suffered anguish ere to bliss you died,
Have pity on him whom Love so sore hath tried,
Who sinned yet greatly suffered for his love.
That dear renouncèd love when now he sees,
Heavy with joy, he sinks upon his knees.
O had she wings to lift her to his side!
But she is far below
Where the spray breaks upon the rusted rail
And rock-hewn steps, and there
Stands gazing up, and lo!
Tristram, how faint and pale!
A pity overcomes her like despair.
How shall her strength avail
To conquer that steep stair,
Dark, terrible, and ignorant as Time,
Up which her feet must climb
To Tristram?   His outstretching arms are fain
To help her, yet are helpless; and his pain
Is hers, and her pain Tristram's; with long sighs
She mounts, then halts again,
Till she have drawn strength from his loved-dimmed eyes:
But when that wasted face anew she sees,
Despair anew subdues her knees:
She fails, yet still she mounts by sad degrees,
With all her soul into her gaze upcast,
Until at last, at last . . .
What tears are like the wondering tears
Of that entranced embrace,

When out of desolate and divided years
Face meets belovèd face?
What cry most exquisite of grief or bliss
The too full heart shall tell,
When the new-recovered kiss
Is the kiss of last farewell?

(*ii*)

Isoult

O Tristram, is this true?
Is it thou I see
With my own eyes, clasp in my arms? I knew,
I knew that this must be.
Thou couldst not suffer so,
And I not feel the smart,
Far, far away. But oh,
How pale, my love, thou art!

Tristram

'Tis I, Isoult, 'tis I
That thee enfold.
I have seen thee, my own life, and yet I die.
O for my strength of old!
O that thy love could heal
This wound that conquers me!
But the night is come, I feel,
And the last sun set for me.

Isoult

Tristram, 'twas I that healed thy hurt,
That old, fierce wound of Morolt's poisoned sword.
Stricken to death, pale, pale as now thou wert:
Yet was thy strength restored.

Have I forgot my skill?
This wound shall yet be healed.
Love shall be master still,
And Death again shall yield!

Tristram

Isoult, if Time could bring me back
That eve, that first eve, and that Irish shore,
Then should I fear not, no nor nothing lack,
And life were mine once more.
But now too late thou art come;
Too long we have dwelt apart;
I have pined in an alien home:
This new joy bursts my heart.

Isoult

Hark, Tristram, to the breaking sea!
So sounded the dim waves, at such an hour
On such an eve, when thy voice came to me
First in my father's tower.
I heard thy sad harp from the shore beneath,
It stirred my soul from sleep.
Then it was bliss to breathe;
But now, but now, I weep.

Tristram

Shipwrecked, without hope, without friend, alone
On a strange shore, stricken with pang on pang,
I stood sad-hearted by that tower unknown,
Yet soon for joy I sang.

For could I see thee and on death believe?
Ah, glad would I die to attain
The beat of my heart, that eve,
And the song in my mouth again!

Isoult

Young was I then and fair,
Thou too wast fair and young;
How comely the brown hair
Down on thy shoulder hung!
O Tristram, all grows dark as then it grew,
But still I see thee on that surge-beat shore;
Thou camest, and all was new
And changed for evermore.

Tristram

Isoult, dost thou regret?
Behold my wasted cheek.
With salt tears it is wet,
My arms how faint, how weak!
And thou, since that far day, what hast thou seen
Save strife, and tears, and failure, and dismay?
Had that hour never been,
Peace had been thine, this day.

Isoult

Look, Tristram, in my eyes!
My own love, I could feed
Life well with miseries
So thou wert mine indeed.

Proud were the tears I wept;
That day, that hour I bless,
Nor would for peace accept
One single pain the less.

Tristram

Isoult, my heart is rent.
What pangs our bliss hath bought!
Only joy we meant,
Yet woe and wrong we have wrought.
I vowed a vow in the dark,
And thee, who wert mine, I gave
For a word's sake, to King Mark!
Words, words have digged our grave.

Isoult

Tristram, despite thy love,
King Mark had yet thine oath.
Ah, surely thy heart strove
How to be true to both.
Blame not thyself! for woe
'Twixt us was doomed to be.
One only thing I know;
Thou hast been true to me.

Tristram

Accurst be still that day,
When lightly I vowed the king
Whatever he might pray
Home to his hands I'd bring!

Thee, thee he asked! And I
Who never feared man's sword,
Yielded my life to a lie,
To save the truth of a word.

Isoult

Think not of that day, think
Of the day when our lips desired,
Unknowing, that cup to drink!
The cup with a charm was fired
From thee to beguile my love:
But now in my soul it shall burn
For ever, nor turn, nor remove,
Till the sun in his course shall turn.

Tristram

Or ever that draught we drank,
Thy heart, Isoult, was mine,
My heart was thine. I thank
God's grace, no wizard wine,
No stealth of a drop distilled
By a spell in the night, no art,
No charm, could have ever filled
With aught but thee my heart.

Isoult

When last we said farewell,
Remember how we dreamed
Wild love to have learned to quell;
Our hearts grown wise we deemed.

Tender, parted friends
We vowed to be; but the will
Of Love meant other ends.
Words fool us, Tristram, still.

Tristram

Not now, Isoult, not now!
I am thine while I have breath.
Words part us not, nor vow —
No, nor King Mark, but death.
I hold thee to my breast.
Our sins, our woes are past;
Thy lips were the first I prest,
Thou art mine, thou art mine at the last!

Isoult

O Tristram, all grows old,
Enfold me closer yet!
The night grows vast and cold,
And the dew on thy hair falls wet.
And never shall Time rebuild
The places of our delight;
Those towers and gardens are filled
With emptiness now, and night!

Tristram

Isoult, let it all be a dream,
The days and the deeds, let them be
As the bough that I cast on the stream
And that lived but to bring thee to me;

LAURENCE BINYON

As the leaves that I broke from the bough
To float by thy window, and say
That I waited thy coming — O now
Thou art come, let the world be as they!

Isoult

How dark is the strong waves' sound!
Tristram, they fill me with fear!
We two are but spent waves, drowned
In the coming of year upon year.
Long dead are our friends and our foes,
Old Rual, Brangian, all
That helped us, or wrought us woes;
And we, the last, we fall.

Tristram

God and his great saints guard
True friends that loved us well,
And all false foes be barred
In the fiery gates of hell.
But broken be all those towers,
And sunken be all those ships!
Shut out those old, dead hours;
Life, life, is on thy lips!

Isoult

Tristram, my soul is afraid!

Tristram

Isoult, Isoult, thy kiss!
To sorrow though I was made,
I die in bliss, in bliss.

LAURENCE BINYON

Isoult

Tristram, my heart must break.
O leave me not in the grave
Of the dark world!   Me too take!
Save me, O Tristram, save!

(*iii*)

Calm, calm the moving waters all the night
On to that shore roll slow,
Fade into foam against the cliff's dim height,
And fall in a soft thunder, and upsurge
For ever out of unexhausted might,
Lifting their voice below
Tuned to no human dirge;
Nor from their majesty of music bend
To wail for beauty's end
Or towering spirit's most fiery overthrow;
Nor tarrieth the dawn, though she unveil
To weeping eyes their woe,
The dawn that doth not know
What the dark night hath wrought,
And over the far wave comes pacing pale,
Of all that she reveals regarding nought. —
But ere the dawn there comes a faltering **tread**;
Isoult, the young wife, stealing from her bed,
Sleepless with dread,
Creeps by still wall and blinded corridor,
Till from afar the salt scent of the air
Blows on her brow; and now

In that pale space beyond the open door
What mute, clasped shadow dulls her to despair
By keen degrees aware
That with the dawn her widowhood is there?

Is it wild envy or remorseful fear
Transfixes her young heart, unused to woe,
Crying to meet wrath, hatred, any foe,
Not silence drear!
Not to be vanquished so
By silence on the lips that were so dear!
Ah, sharpest stab! it is another face
That leans to Tristram's piteous embrace,
Another face she knows not, yet knows well,
Whose hands are clasped about his helpless head,
Propping it where it fell
In a vain tenderness,
But dead, — her great dream-hated rival dead,
Invulnerably dead,
Dead as her love, and cold,
And on her heart a grief heavy as stone is rolled.
She bows down, stricken in accusing pain,
And love, long-baffled, surges back again
Over her heart; she wails a shuddering cry,
While the tears blindly rain,
' I, I have killed him, I that loved him, I
That for his dear sake had been glad to die.
I loved him not enough, I could not keep
His heart, and yet I loved him, O how deep!
I cannot touch him. Will none set him free
From those, those other arms and give him me?
Alas, I may not vex him from that sleep.

He is thine in the end, thou proud one, he is thine,
Not mine, not mine!
I loved him not enough, I could not hold
My tongue from stabbing, and forsook him there.
I had not any care
To keep him from the darkness and the cold.
O all my wretched servants, where were ye?
Hath none in my house tended him but she?
Where are ye now?   Can ye not hear my call?
Come hither, laggards all!
Nay, hush not so affrighted, nor so stare
Upon your lord; 'tis he!
Put out your torches, for the dawn grows clear.
And set me out within the hall a bier,
And wedding robes, the costliest that are
In all my house, prepare,
And lay upon the silks these princely dead,
And bid the sailors take that funeral bed
And set it in the ship, and put to sea,
And north to Cornwall steer.
Farewell, my lord, thy home is far from here.
Farewell, my great love, dead and doubly dear!
Carry him hence, proud queen, for he is thine,
Not mine, not mine, not mine! '

Within Tintagel walls King Mark awaits his queen.
The south wind blows, surely she comes to-day!
No light hath his eye seen
Since she is gone, no pleasure; he grows gray;
His knights apart make merry and wassail,
With dice and chessboard, hound at knee, they play;
But he sits solitary all the day,

Thinking of what hath been.
And now through all the castle rings a wail;
The king arises; all his knights are dumb;
The queen, the queen is come.
Not as she came of old,
Sweeping with gesture proud
To meet her wronged lord, royally arrayed,
And music ushered her, and tongues were stayed,
And all hearts beat, her beauty to behold;
But mute she comes and cold,
Borne on a bier, apparelled in a shroud,
Daisies about her sprinkled; and now bowed
Is her lord's head; and hushing upon all
Thoughts of sorrow fall,
As the snow softly, without any word;
And every breast is stirred
With wonder in its weeping;
For by her sleeping side,
In that long sleep no morning shall divide,
Is Tristram sleeping;
Tristram who wept farewell, and fled, and swore
That he would clasp his dear love never more,
And sailed far over sea
Far from his bliss and shame,
And dreamed to die at peace in Brittany
And to uncloud at last the glory of his name.
Yet lo, with fingers clasping both are come,
Come again home
In all men's sight, as when of old they came,
And Tristram led Isoult, another's bride,
True to his vow, but to his heart untrue,
And silver trumpets blew

To greet them stepping o'er the flower-strewn floor,
And King Mark smiled upon them, and men cried
On Tristram's name anew,
Tristram, the king's strong champion and great pride.

Silently gazing long
On them that wrought him wrong,
Still stands the stricken king, and to his eyes
Such tears as old men weep, yet shed not, rise:
Lifting his head at last, as from a trance, he sighs.
' Beautiful ever, O Isoult, wast thou,
And beautiful art thou now,
Though never again shall I, reproaching thee,
Make thy proud head more beautiful to me;
But this is the last reproach, and this the last
Forgiveness that thou hast.
Lost is the lost, Isoult, and past the past!
O Tristram, no more shalt thou need to hide
Thy thought from my thought, sitting at my side,
Nor need to wrestle sore
With thy great love and with thy fixèd oath,
For now Death leaves thee loyal unto both,
Even as thou wouldst have been, for evermore.
Now, after all thy pain, thy brow looks glad;
But I lack all things that I ever had,
My wife, my friend, yea, even my jealous rage;
And empty is the house of my old age.
Behold, I have laboured all my days to part
These two, that were the dearest to my heart.
Isoult, I would have fenced thee from men's sight,
My treasure, that I found so very fair,
The treasure I had taken with a snare:

To keep thee mine, this was my life's delight.
And now the end is come, alone I stand,
And the hand that lies in thine is not my hand.'

HILAIRE BELLOC

1870–

115   *Tarantella*

DO you remember an Inn,
    Miranda?
Do you remember an Inn?
And the tedding and the spreading
Of the straw for a bedding,
And the fleas that tease in the High Pyrenees,
And the wine that tasted of the tar?
And the cheers and the jeers of the young muleteers
(Under the dark of the vine verandah)?
Do you remember an Inn, Miranda,
Do you remember an Inn?
And the cheers and the jeers of the young muleteers
Who hadn't got a penny,
And who weren't paying any,
And the hammer at the doors and the Din?
And the Hip! Hop! Hap!
Of the clap
Of the hands to the twirl and the swirl
Of the girl gone chancing,
Glancing,
Dancing,
Backing and advancing,
Snapping of the clapper to the spin
Out and in —

And the Ting, Tong, Tang of the guitar!
Do you remember an Inn,
Miranda?
Do you remember an Inn!

Never more;
Miranda,
Never more.
Only the high peaks hoar:
And Aragon a torrent at the door.
No sound
In the walls of the Halls where falls
The tread
Of the feet of the dead to the ground.
No sound:
Only the boom
Of the far Waterfall like Doom.

WILLIAM HENRY DAVIES

1871–1940

116   *Joy and Pleasure*

NOW, Joy is born of parents poor,
    And Pleasure of our richer kind;
Though Pleasure 's free, she cannot sing
    As sweet a song as Joy confined.

Pleasure 's a Moth, that sleeps by day
    And dances by false glare at night;
But Joy 's a Butterfly, that loves
    To spread its wings in Nature's light.

128

Joy 's like a Bee that gently sucks
   Away on blossoms its sweet hour;
But Pleasure 's like a greedy Wasp,
   That plums and cherries would devour.

Joy 's like a Lark that lives alone,
   Whose ties are very strong, though few;
But Pleasure like a Cuckoo roams,
   Makes much acquaintance, no friends true.

Joy from her heart doth sing at home,
   With little care if others hear;
But Pleasure then is cold and dumb,
   And sings and laughs with strangers near.

117   *Truly Great*

MY walls outside must have some flowers,
   My walls within must have some books;
A house that 's small; a garden large,
   And in it leafy nooks.

A little gold that 's sure each week;
   That comes not from my living kind,
But from a dead man in his grave,
   Who cannot change his mind.

A lovely wife, and gentle too;
   Contented that no eyes but mine
Can see her many charms, nor voice
   To call her beauty fine.

Where she would in that stone cage live,
    A self-made prisoner, with me;
While many a wild bird sang around,
    On gate, on bush, on tree.

And she sometimes to answer them,
    In her far sweeter voice than all;
Till birds, that loved to look on leaves,
    Will doat on a stone wall.

With this small house, this garden large,
    This little gold, this lovely mate,
With health in body, peace at heart —
    Show me a man more great.

118   *Money*

WHEN I had money, money, O!
    I knew no joy till I went poor;
For many a false man as a friend
    Came knocking all day at my door.

Then felt I like a child that holds
    A trumpet that he must not blow
Because a man is dead; I dared
    Not speak to let this false world know.

Much have I thought of life, and seen
    How poor men's hearts are ever light;
And how their wives do hum like bees
    About their work from morn till night.

So, when I hear these poor ones laugh,
  And see the rich ones coldly frown —
Poor men, think I, need not go up
  So much as rich men should come down.

When I had money, money, O!
  My many friends proved all untrue;
But now I have nó money, O!
  My friends are real, though very few.

119   *Leisure*

WHAT is this life if, full of care,
    We have no time to stand and stare.

No time to stand beneath the boughs
And stare as long as sheep or cows.

No time to see, when woods we pass,
Where squirrels hide their nuts in grass.

No time to see, in broad daylight,
Streams full of stars, like skies at night.

No time to turn at Beauty's glance,
And watch her feet, how they can dance.

No time to wait till her mouth can
Enrich that smile her eyes began.

A poor life this if, full of care,
We have no time to stand and stare.

120 ### *The Sluggard*

A JAR of cider and my pipe,
  In summer, under shady tree;
A book of one that made his mind
  Live by its sweet simplicity:
Then must I laugh at kings who sit
  In richest chambers, signing scrolls;
And princes cheered in public ways,
  And stared at by a thousand fools.

Let me be free to wear my dreams,
  Like weeds in some mad maiden's hair,
When she believes the earth has not
  Another maid so rich and fair;
And proudly smiles on rich and poor,
  The queen of all fair women then:
So I, dressed in my idle dreams,
  Will think myself the king of men.

121 ### *The Best Friend*

N OW shall I walk,
  Or shall I ride?
'Ride,' Pleasure said;
  'Walk,' Joy replied.

Now what shall I —
  Stay home or roam?
'Roam,' Pleasure said;
  And Joy — 'Stay home.'

Now shall I dance,
    Or sit for dreams?
' Sit,' answers Joy;
    ' Dance,' Pleasure screams.

Which of ye two
    Will kindest be?
Pleasure laughed sweet,
    But Joy kissed me.

School 's out

GIRLS scream,
    Boys shout;
Dogs bark,
    School 's out.

Cats run,
    Horses shy;
Into trees
    Birds fly.

Babes wake
    Open-eyed;
If they can,
    Tramps hide.

Old man,
    Hobble home;
Merry mites,
    Welcome.

MANMOHAN GHOSE

1870–1924

123 *Who is it talks of Ebony?*

WHO is it talks of ebony,
  Who of the raven's plume?
The glory of your tresses black
  Will yield to neither room.

So thick the ambrosial dusk of you
  Glooms in your locks, soul, sight,
The world itself is swallowed up
  In darkness and delight.

Tell me no more that black must be
  Light's baffle, colour's loss.
Your tresses shoot into the sun
  A richly purple gloss.

It was the sunshine white of you
  Which cast that wealth of shade.
There from the burning light of you
  The world and I am laid.

THOMAS STURGE MOORE

1870–1944

124 *The Dying Swan*

O SILVER-THROATED Swan
  Struck, struck! a golden dart
Clean through thy breast has gone
  Home to thy heart.

134

Thrill, thrill, O silver throat!
O silver trumpet, pour
Love for defiance back
On him who smote!
And brim, brim o'er
With love; and ruby-dye thy track
Down thy last living reach
Of river, sail the golden light . . .
Enter the sun's heart . . . even teach,
O wondrous-gifted Pain, teach thou
The god to love, let him learn how.

125   *Kindness*

OF the beauty of kindness I speak,
   Of a smile, of a charm
On the face it is pleasure to meet,
   That gives no alarm!

Of the soul that absorbeth itself
   In discovering good,
Of that power which outlasts health,
   As the spell of a wood

Outlasts the sad fall of the leaves,
   And in winter is fine,
And from snow and from frost receives
   A garment divine.

Oh! well may the lark sing of this,
   As through rents of huge cloud,
He broacheth blue gulfs that are bliss,
   For they make his heart proud

With the power of wings deployed
In delightfullest air.
Yea, thus among things enjoyed
Is kindness rare.

For even the weak with surprise
Spread wings, utter song,
They can launch . . . in this blue they can rise,
In this kindness are strong, . . .

They can launch like a ship into calm.
Which was penned up by storm,
Which sails for the islands of balm
Luxuriant and warm.

126 *Response to Rimbaud's Later Manner*

THE cow eats green grass;
　　Alas, alas!
Nothing to eat
Surrounds my feet!

Diamond clad
In the stream the naïad
Never sips, dips
All save her lips.

They, they, and not I,
Never ask why
The Cathedral tower
Dreams like a flower.

They, they, are healed
From thought congealed
That ploughs up the heart
Which takes its own part.

They, they, have refound
Eternity;
Which is the sun bound
In the arms of the sea.

127   *Variation on Ronsard*

TIME flits away, time flits away, lady;
    Alas, not time, but we
Whose childish limbs once skipped so fairily,
And still to dance are free.

Things are forgot, things are forgot, lady;
Alas, not things alone,
But dames whose sweet, sweet names chimed airily
Are no more loved or known.

How bright those stars! and think, each bright star stays,
Though all else fair be brief;
Leisure have they and peace and length of days
And love, 'tis my belief.

For Love gives light, Love vows his light will last,
And Love instilleth peace . ∴ .
As lake returns the star-rays downward cast,
Be thou the Love, Love sees.

128   *The Event*

SHAPED and vacated
　See rhythms lie scattered like shells!
Heed one and through it
What stimulus swells!

Let meaning now mate it;
As pallor may quit a hushed face
And health re-endue it
With courage and grace,

Lilt, pulsed to a tune when
Some storm has been lulled on the deep,
Resurgent can capture
Words from their sleep.

T'ward him who shall croon them
Lo! Psyche herself rides the wave
With ear all rapture
At a thought in its cave.

— Knees bend you before
Vision woven of sound,
That floats like a shell to the shore,
Both given and found.

129   *The Gazelles*

WHEN the sheen on tall summer grass is pale,
　Across blue skies white clouds float on
In shoals, or disperse and singly sail,
Till, the sun being set, they all are gone:

138

THOMAS STURGE MOORE

Yet, as long as they may shine bright in the sun,
They flock or stray through the daylight bland,
While their stealthy shadows like foxes run
Beneath where the grass is dry and tanned:

And the waste, in hills that swell and fall,
Goes heaving into yet dreamier haze;
And a wonder of silence is over all
Where the eye feeds long like a lover's gaze:

Then, cleaving the grass, gazelles appear
(The gentler dolphins of kindlier waves)
With sensitive heads alert of ear;
Frail crowds that a delicate hearing saves,

That rely on the nostrils' keenest power,
And are governed from trance-like distances
By hopes and fears, and, hour by hour,
Sagacious of safety, snuff the breeze.

They keep together, the timid hearts;
And each one's fear with a panic thrill
Is passed to an hundred; and if one starts
In three seconds all are over the hill.

A Nimrod might watch, in his hall's wan space,
After the feast, on the moonlit floor,
The timorous mice that troop and race,
As tranced o'er those herds the sun doth pour;

Like a wearied tyrant sated with food
Who envies each tiniest thief that steals
A crumb from his abstracted mood,
For the zest and daring it reveals.

He alone, save the quite dispassionate moon,
Sees them; she stares at the prowling pard
Who surprises their sleep and, ah! how soon
Is riding the weakest or sleepiest hard!

Let an agony's nightmare course begin,
Four feet with five spurs a-piece control,
Like a horse thief reduced to save his skin
Or a devil that rides a human soul!

The race is as long as recorded time,
Yet brief as the flash of assassin's knife;
For 'tis crammed as history is with crime
'Twixt the throbs at taking and losing life;

Then the warm wet clutch on the nape of the neck,
Through which the keen incisors drive;
Then the fleet knees give, down drops the wreck
Of yesterday's pet that was so alive.

Yet the moon is naught concerned, ah no!
She shines as on a drifting plank
Far in some northern sea-stream's flow
From which two numbed hands loosened and sank.

Such thinning their number must suffer; and wors
When hither at times the Shah's children roam,
Their infant listlessness to immerse
In energy's ancient upland home:

For here the shepherd in years of old
Was taught by the stars, and bred a race
That welling forth from these highlands rolled
In tides of conquest o'er earth's face:

THOMAS STURGE MOORE

On piebald ponies or else milk-white,
Here, with green bridles in silver bound,
A crescent moon on the violet night
Of their saddle cloths, or a sun rayed round,

With tiny bells on their harness ringing,
And voices that laugh and are shrill by starts,
Prancing, curvetting, and with them bringing
Swift chetahs cooped up in light-wheeled carts,

They come, and their dainty pavilions pitch
In some valley, beside a sinuous pool,
Where a grove of cedars towers in which
Herons have built, where the shade is cool;

Where they tether their ponies to low-hung boughs,
Where long through the night their red fires gleam,
Where the morning's stir doth them arouse
To their bath in the lake, as from dreams to a dream.

And thence in an hour their hunt rides forth,
And the chetahs course the shy gazelle
To the east or west or south or north;
And every eve in a distant vale

A hecatomb of the slaughtered beasts
Is piled; tongues loll from breathless throats;
Round large jet eyes the horsefly feasts . . .
Jet eyes, which now a blue film coats:

Dead there they bleed, and each prince there
Is met by his sister, wife, or bride . . .
Delicious ladies with long dark hair,
And soft dark eyes, and brows arched wide,

THOMAS STURGE MOORE

In quilted jacket, embroidered sash,
And tent-like skirts of pleated lawn;
While their silk-lined jewelled slippers flash
Round bare feet bedded like pools at dawn:

So choicefully prepared to please,
Young, female, royal of race and mood,
In indolent compassion these
O'er those dead beauteous creatures brood:

They lean some minutes against their friend,
A lad not slow to praise himself,
Who tells how this one met his end
Out-raced, or trapped by leopard stealth,

And boasts his chetahs fleetest are;
Through his advice the chance occurred,
That leeward vale by which the car
Was well brought round to head the herd.

Seeing him bronzed by sun and wind,
She feels his power and owns him lord,
Then, that his courage may please her mind,
With a soft coy hand half draws his sword,

Just shudders to see the cold steel gleam,
And drops it back in the long curved sheath;
She will merge his evening meal in a dream
And embalm his slumber like the wreath

Of heavy-lidded flowers bewitched
To murmur words of ecstasy
For king who, though with all else enriched,
Pays warlock for tones the young hear free.

THOMAS STURGE MOORE

But, while they sleep, the orphaned herd
And wounded stragglers, through the night
Wander in pain, and wail unheard
To the moon and the stars so cruelly bright.

Why are they born? ah! why beget
They in the long November gloom
Heirs of their beauty, their fleetness . . . yet
Heirs of their panics, their pangs, their doom?

That to princely spouses children are born
To be daintily bred and taught to please,
Has a fitness like the return of morn:
But why perpetuate lives like these?

Why, with horns that jar and with fiery eyes,
Should the male stags fight for the shuddering does
Through the drear dark nights, with frequent cries
From tyrant lust or outlawed woes?

Doth the meaningless beauty of their lives
Rave in the spring, when they course afar
Like the shadows of birds, and the young fawn strives
Till its parents no longer the fleetest are?

Like the shadows of flames which the sun's rays throw
On a kiln's blank wall, where glaziers dwell,
Pale shadows as those from glasses they blow,
Yet that lap at the blank wall and rebel . . .

Even so to my curious trance-like thought
Those herds move over those pallid hills,
With fever as of a frail life caught
In circumstance o'er-charged with ills;

143

More like the shadow of lives than life,
Or most like the life that is never born
From baffled purpose and foredoomed strife,
That in each man's heart must be hidden from scorn,

Yet with something of beauty very rare
Unseizable, fugitive, half discerned;
The trace of intentions that might have been fair
In action, left on a face that yearned

But long has ceased to yearn, alas!
So faint a trace do they leave on the slopes
Of hills as sleek as their coats with grass;
So faint may the trace be of noblest hopes.

Yet why are they born to roam and die?
Can their beauty answer thy query, O soul?
Nay, nor that of hopes which were born to fly,
But whose pinions the common and coarse day stole.

Like that region of grassy hills outspread,
A realm of our thought knows days and nights
And summers and winters, and has fed
Ineffectual herds of vanished delights.

JOHN MILLINGTON SYNGE

1871–1909

130   *Queens*

SEVEN dog-days we let pass
    Naming Queens in Glenmacnass,
All the rare and royal names
Wormy sheepskin yet retains:
Etain, Helen, Maeve and Fand,
Golden Deirdre's tender hand;

144

JOHN MILLINGTON SYNGE

Bert, the big-foot, sung by Villon,
Cassandra, Ronsard found in Lyon.
Queens of Sheba, Meath and Connaught,
Coifed with crown, or gaudy bonnet;
Queens whose finger once did stir men,
Queens were eaten of fleas and vermin,
Queens men drew like Monna Lisa,
Or slew with drugs in Rome and Pisa.
We named Lucrezia Crivelli,
And Titian's lady with amber belly,
Queens acquainted in learned sin,
Jane of Jewry's slender shin:
Queens who cut the bogs of Glanna,
Judith of Scripture, and Gloriana,
Queens who wasted the East by proxy,
Or drove the ass-cart, a tinker's doxy.
Yet these are rotten — I ask their pardon —
And we've the sun on rock and garden;
These are rotten, so you're the Queen
Of all are living, or have been.

131   *On an Anniversary*

After reading the dates in a book of Lyrics

WITH Fifteen-ninety or Sixteen-sixteen
We end Cervantes, Marot, Nashe or Green:
Then Sixteen-thirteen till two score and nine,
Is Crashaw's niche, that honey-lipped divine.
They'll say I came in Eighteen-seventy-one,
And died in Dublin . . . What year will they write
For my poor passage to the stall of night?

132 *On a Birthday*

FRIEND of Ronsard, Nashe and Beaumont,
Lark of Ulster, Meath, and Thomond,
Heard from Smyrna and Sahara
To the surf of Connemara,
Lark of April, June, and May,
Sing loudly this my Lady-day.

133 *A Question*

I ASKED if I got sick and died, would you
With my black funeral go walking too,
If you'd stand close to hear them talk or pray
While I'm let down in that steep bank of clay.

And, No, you said, for if you saw a crew
Of living idiots pressing round that new
Oak coffin — they alive, I dead beneath
That board — you'd rave and rend them with your teeth.

134 *In Glencullen*

THRUSH, linnet, stare and wren,
Brown lark beside the sun,
Take thought of kestrel, sparrow-hawk,
Birdlime and roving gun.

You great-great-grand-children
Of birds I've listened to,
I think I robbed your ancestors
When I was young as you.

146

JOHN MILLINGTON SYNGE

135   *I've Thirty Months*

I'VE thirty months, and that 's my pride,
   Before my age 's a double score,
Though many lively men have died
At twenty-nine or little more.

I've left a long and famous set
Behind some seven years or three,
But there are millions I'd forget
Will have their laugh at passing me.

136   *Prelude*

STILL south I went and west and south again,
   Through Wicklow from the morning till the night,
And far from cities, and the sights of men,
Lived with the sunshine, and the moon's delight.

I knew the stars, the flowers, and the birds,
The grey and wintry sides of many glens,
And did but half remember human words,
In converse with the mountains, moors, and fens.

137   *Winter*

(With little money in a great city)

THERE 'S snow in every street
   Where I go up and down,
And there 's no woman, man, or dog
That knows me in the town.

147

I know each shop, and all
These Jews, and Russian Poles,
For I go walking night and noon
To spare my sack of coals.

138   He wishes he might die and follow Laura

IN the years of her age the most beautiful and the most flowery — the time Love has his mastery — Laura, who was my life, has gone away leaving the earth stripped and desolate. She has gone up into the Heavens, living and beautiful and naked, and from that place she is keeping her Lordship and her rein upon me, and I crying out: Ohone, when will I see that day breaking that will be my first day with herself in Paradise?

My thoughts are going after her, and it is that way my soul would follow her, lightly, and airily, and happily, and I would be rid of all my great troubles. But what is delaying me is the proper thing to lose me utterly, to make me a greater weight on my own self.

Oh, what a sweet death I might have died this day three years to-day!

(From Petrarch.)

139   He understands the Great Cruelty of Death

MY flowery and green age was passing away, and I feeling a chill in the fires had been wasting my heart, for I was drawing near the hillside that is above the grave.

148

Then my sweet enemy was making a start, little by little, to give over her great wariness, the way she was wringing a sweet thing out of my sharp sorrow. The time was coming when Love and Decency can keep company, and lovers may sit together and say out all the things are in their hearts. But Death had his grudge against me, and he got up in the way, like an armed robber, with a pike in his hand.

(From Petrarch.)

140   *Laura waits for him in Heaven*

THE first day she passed up and down through the Heavens, gentle and simple were left standing, and they in great wonder, saying one to the other:

'What new light is that? What new beauty at all? The like of her hasn't risen up these long years from the common world.'

And herself, well pleased with the Heavens, was going forward, matching herself with the most perfect that were before her, yet one time, and another, waiting a little, and turning her head back to see if myself was coming after her. It's for that I'm lifting up all my thoughts and will into the Heavens, because I do hear her praying that I should be making haste for ever.

(From Petrarch.)

141   *An Old Woman's Lamentations*

THE man I had a love for — a great rascal would kick me in the gutter — is dead thirty years and over it, and it is I am left behind, grey and aged.

JOHN MILLINGTON SYNGE

When I do be minding the good days I had, minding what I was one time, and what it is I'm come to, and when I do look on my own self, poor and dry, and pinched together, it wouldn't be much would set me raging in the streets.

Where is the round forehead I had, and the fine hair, and the two eyebrows, and the eyes with a big gay look out of them would bring folly from a great scholar? Where is my straight, shapely nose, and two ears, and my chin with a valley in it, and my lips were red and open?

Where are the pointed shoulders were on me, and the long arms and nice hands to them? Where is my bosom was as white as any, or my straight rounded sides?

It's the way I am this day — my forehead is gone away into furrows, the hair of my head is grey and whitish, my eyebrows are tumbled from me, and my two eyes have died out within my head — those eyes that would be laughing to the men — my nose has a hook on it, my ears are hanging down, and my lips are sharp and skinny.

That's what's left over from the beauty of a right woman — a bag of bones, and legs the like of two shrivelled sausages going beneath it.

It's of the like of that we old hags do be thinking, of the good times are gone away from us, and we crouching on our hunkers by a little fire of twigs, soon kindled and soon spent, we that were the pick of many.

(From Villon.)

RALPH HODGSON

1872–

142 *The Bull*

SEE an old unhappy bull,
  Sick in soul and body both,
Slouching in the undergrowth
Of the forest beautiful,
Banished from the herd he led,
Bulls and cows a thousand head.

Cranes and gaudy parrots go
Up and down the burning sky;
Tree-top cats purr drowsily
In the dim-day green below;
And troops of monkeys, nutting, some,
All disputing, go and come;

And things abominable sit
Picking offal buck or swine,
On the mess and over it
Burnished flies and beetles shine,
And spiders big as bladders lie
Under hemlocks ten foot high;

And a dotted serpent curled
Round and round and round a tree,
Yellowing its greenery,
Keeps a watch on all the world,
All the world and this old bull
In the forest beautiful.

Bravely by his fall he came:
One he led, a bull of blood
Newly come to lustihood,
Fought and put his prince to shame,
Snuffed and pawed the prostrate head
Tameless even while it bled.

There they left him, every one,
Left him there without a lick,
Left him for the birds to pick,
Left him there for carrion,
Vilely from their bosom cast
Wisdom, worth and love at last.

When the lion left his lair
And roared his beauty through the hills,
And the vultures pecked their quills
And flew into the middle air,
Then this prince no more to reign
Came to life and lived again.

He snuffed the herd in far retreat,
He saw the blood upon the ground,
And snuffed the burning airs around
Still with beevish odours sweet,
While the blood ran down his head
And his mouth ran slaver red.

Pity him, this fallen chief,
All his splendour, all his strength,
All his body's breadth and length
Dwindled down with shame and grief,
Half the bull he was before,
Bones and leather, nothing more.

RALPH HODGSON

See him standing dewlap-deep
In the rushes at the lake,
Surly, stupid, half asleep,
Waiting for his heart to break
And the birds to join the flies
Feasting at his bloodshot eyes;

Standing with his head hung down
In a stupor, dreaming things:
Green savannas, jungles brown,
Battlefields and bellowings,
Bulls undone and lions dead
And vultures flapping overhead.

Dreaming things: of days he spent
With his mother gaunt and lean
In the valley warm and green,
Full of baby wonderment,
Blinking out of silly eyes
At a hundred mysteries;

Dreaming over once again
How he wandered with a throng
Of bulls and cows a thousand strong,
Wandered on from plain to plain,
Up the hill and down the dale,
Always at his mother's tail;

How he lagged behind the herd,
Lagged and tottered, weak of limb,
And she turned and ran to him
Blaring at the loathly bird
Stationed always in the skies,
Waiting for the flesh that dies.

Dreaming maybe of a day
When her drained and drying paps
Turned him to the sweets and saps,
Richer fountains by the way,
And she left the bull she bore
And he looked to her no more;

And his little frame grew stout,
And his little legs grew strong,
And the way was not so long;
And his little horns came out,
And he played at butting trees
And boulder-stones and tortoises,

Joined a game of knobby skulls
With the youngsters of his year,
All the other little bulls,
Learning both to bruise and bear,
Learning how to stand a shock
Like a little bull of rock.

Dreaming of a day less dim,
Dreaming of a time less far,
When the faint but certain star
Of destiny burned clear for him,
And a fierce and wild unrest
Broke the quiet of his breast,

And the gristles of his youth
Hardened in his comely pow,
And he came to fighting growth,
Beat his bull and won his cow,
And flew his tail and trampled off
Past the tallest, vain enough,

And curved about in splendour full
And curved again and snuffed the airs
As who should say Come out who dares!
And all beheld a bull, a Bull,
And knew that here was surely one
That backed for no bull, fearing none.

And the leader of the herd
Looked and saw, and beat the ground,
And shook the forest with his sound,
Bellowed at the loathly bird
Stationed always in the skies,
Waiting for the flesh that dies.

Dreaming, this old bull forlorn,
Surely dreaming of the hour
When he came to sultan power,
And they owned him master-horn,
Chiefest bull of all among
Bulls and cows a thousand strong;

And in all the tramping herd
Not a bull that barred his way,
Not a cow that said him nay,
Not a bull or cow that erred
In the furnace of his look
Dared a second, worse rebuke;

Not in all the forest wide,
Jungle, thicket, pasture, fen,
Not another dared him then,
Dared him and again defied;
Not a sovereign buck or boar
Came a second time for more;

RALPH HODGSON

Not a serpent that survived
Once the terrors of his hoof
Risked a second time reproof,
Came a second time and lived,
Not a serpent in its skin
Came again for discipline;

Not a leopard bright as flame,
Flashing fingerhooks of steel
That a wooden tree might feel,
Met his fury once and came
For a second reprimand,
Not a leopard in the land;

Not a lion of them all,
Not a lion of the hills,
Hero of a thousand kills,
Dared a second fight and fall,
Dared that ram terrific twice,
Paid a second time the price.

Pity him, this dupe of dream,
Leader of the herd again
Only in his daft old brain,
Once again the bull supreme
And bull enough to bear the part
Only in his tameless heart.

Pity him that he must wake;
Even now the swarm of flies
Blackening his bloodshot eyes
Bursts and blusters round the lake,
Scattered from the feast half-fed,
By great shadows overhead;

RALPH HODGSON

And the dreamer turns away
From his visionary herds
And his splendid yesterday,
Turns to meet the loathly birds
Flocking round him from the skies,
Waiting for the flesh that dies.

WALTER DE LA MARE

1873–

143   *The Listeners*

IS there anybody there?' said the Traveller,
   Knocking on the moonlit door;
And his horse in the silence champed the grasses
   Of the forest's ferny floor:
And a bird flew up out of the turret,
   Above the Traveller's head:
And he smote upon the door again a second time;
   ' Is there anybody there? ' he said.
But no one descended to the Traveller;
   No head from the leaf-fringed sill
Leaned over and looked into his grey eyes,
   Where he stood perplexed and still.
But only a host of phantom listeners
   That dwelt in the lone house then
Stood listening in the quiet of the moonlight
   To that voice from the world of men:
Stood thronging the faint moonbeams on the dark stair,
   That goes down to the empty hall,
Hearkening in an air stirred and shaken
   By the lonely Traveller's call.
And he felt in his heart their strangeness,
   Their stillness answering his cry,

157

While his horse moved, cropping the dark turf,
   'Neath the starred and leafy sky;
For he suddenly smote on the door, even
   Louder, and lifted his head: —
' Tell them I came, and no one answered,
   That I kept my word,' he said.
Never the least stir made the listeners,
   Though every word he spake
Fell echoing through the shadowiness of the still house
   From the one man left awake:
Ay, they heard his foot upon the stirrup,
   And the sound of iron on stone,
And how the silence surged softly backward,
   When the plunging hoofs were gone.

144   *Winter*

CLOUDED with snow
   The cold winds blow,
And shrill on leafless bough
The robin with its burning breast
   Alone sings now.

   The rayless sun,
   Day's journey done,
Sheds its last ebbing light
On fields in leagues of beauty spread
   Unearthly white.

   Thick draws the dark,
   And spark by spark,
The frost-fires kindle, and soon
Over that sea of frozen foam
   Floats the white moon.

145 *The Scribe*

WHAT lovely things
        Thy hand hath made:
The smooth-plumed bird
        In its emerald shade,
The seed of the grass,
        The speck of stone
Which the wayfaring ant
        Stirs — and hastes on!

Though I should sit
        By some tarn in thy hills,
Using its ink
        As the spirit wills
To write of Earth's wonders,
        Its live, willed things,
Flit would the ages
        On soundless wings
Ere unto Z
        My pen drew nigh;
Leviathan told,
        And the honey-fly:

And still would remain
        My wit to try —
My worn reeds broken,
        The dark tarn dry,
All words forgotten —
        Thou, Lord, and I.

146 *All that's Past*

VERY old are the woods;
  And the buds that break
Out of the brier's boughs,
  When March winds wake,
So old with their beauty are —
  Oh, no man knows
Through what wild centuries
  Roves back the rose.

Very old are the brooks;
  And the rills that rise
Where snow sleeps cold beneath
  The azure skies
Sing such a history
  Of come and gone,
Their every drop is as wise
  As Solomon.

Very old are we men;
  Our dreams are tales
Told in dim Eden
  By Eve's nightingales;
We wake and whisper awhile,
  But, the day gone by,
Silence and sleep like fields
  Of amaranth lie.

147 *Echo*

WHO called? ' I said, and the words
  Through the whispering glades,
Hither, thither, baffled the birds —
  ' Who called?   Who called? '

160

The leafy boughs on high
   Hissed in the sun;
The dark air carried my cry
   Faintingly on:

Eyes in the green, in the shade,
   In the motionless brake,
Voices that said what I said,
   For mockery's sake:

' Who cares? ' I bawled through my tears:
   The wind fell low:
In the silence, ' Who cares? who cares? '
   Wailed to and fro.

148   *The Silver Penny*

S AILORMAN, I'll give to you
   My bright silver penny,
If out to sea you'll sail me
   And my dear sister Jenny.'

' Get in, young sir, I'll sail ye
   And your dear sister Jenny,
But pay she shall her golden locks
   Instead of your penny.'

They sail away, they sail away,
   O fierce the winds blew!
The foam flew in clouds,
   And dark the night grew!

And all the wild sea-water
   Climbed steep into the boat;
Back to the shore again
   Sail they will not.

WALTER DE LA MARE

Drowned is the sailorman,
    Drowned is sweet Jenny,
And drowned in the deep sea
    A bright silver penny.

GORDON BOTTOMLEY
1874–

149   *To Iron-Founders and Others*

WHEN you destroy a blade of grass
    You poison England at her roots:
Remember no man's foot can pass
    Where evermore no green life shoots.

You force the birds to wing too high
    Where your unnatural vapours creep:
Surely the living rocks shall die
    When birds no rightful distance keep.

You have brought down the firmament
    And yet no heaven is more near;
You shape huge deeds without event,
    And half made men believe and fear.

Your worship is your furnaces,
    Which, like old idols, lost obscenes,
Have molten bowels; your vision is
    Machines for making more machines.

O, you are busied in the night,
    Preparing destinies of rust;
Iron misused must turn to blight
    And dwindle to a tettered crust.

GORDON BOTTOMLEY

The grass, forerunner of life, has gone,
    But plants that spring in ruins and shards
Attend until your dream is done:
    I have seen hemlock in your yards.

The generations of the worm
    Know not your loads piled on their soil;
Their knotted ganglions shall wax firm
    Till your strong flagstones heave and toil.

When the old hollowed earth is cracked,
    And when, to grasp more power and feasts,
Its ores are emptied, wasted, lacked,
    The middens of your burning beasts

Shall be raked over till they yield
    Last priceless slags for fashionings high,
Ploughs to make grass in every field,
    Chisels men's hands to magnify.

GILBERT KEITH CHESTERTON
1872–1936
150   *The Rolling English Road*

BEFORE the Roman came to Rye or out to Severn strode,
    The rolling English drunkard made the rolling English
        road.
A reeling road, a rolling road, that rambles round the shire,
And after him the parson ran, the sexton and the squire;
A merry road, a mazy road, and such as we did tread
The night we went to Birmingham by way of Beachy Head.

I knew no harm of Bonaparte and plenty of the Squire,
And for to fight the Frenchman I did not much desire;
But I did bash their baggonets because they came arrayed

163

To straighten out the crooked road an English drunkard
    made,
Where you and I went down the lane with ale-mugs in our
    hands,
The night we went to Glastonbury by way of Goodwin
    Sands.

His sins they were forgiven him; or why do flowers run
Behind him; and the hedges all strengthening in the sun?
The wild thing went from left to right and knew not which
    was which,
But the wild rose was above him when they found him in
    the ditch.
God pardon us, nor harden us; we did not see so clear
The night we went to Bannockburn by way of Brighton
    Pier.

My friends, we will not go again or ape an ancient rage,
Or stretch the folly of our youth to be the shame of age,
But walk with clearer eyes and ears this path that wandereth,
And see undrugged in evening light the decent inn of
    death;
For there is good news yet to hear and fine things to be seen,
Before we go to Paradise by way of Kensal Green.

151   *Lepanto*

WHITE founts falling in the courts of the sun,
    And the Soldan of Byzantium is smiling as they run;
There is laughter like the fountains in that face of all men
    feared,

GILBERT KEITH CHESTERTON

It stirs the forest darkness, the darkness of his beard,
It curls the blood-red crescent, the crescent of his lips,
For the inmost sea of all the earth is shaken with his ships.
They have dared the white republics up the capes of Italy,
They have dashed the Adriatic round the Lion of the Sea,
And the Pope has cast his arms abroad for agony and loss,
And called the kings of Christendom for swords about the
      Cross,
The cold queen of England is looking in the glass;
The shadow of the Valois is yawning at the Mass;
From evening isles fantastical rings faint the Spanish gun,
And the Lord upon the Golden Horn is laughing in the sun.
Dim drums throbbing, in the hills half heard,
Where only on a nameless throne a crownless prince has
      stirred,
Where, risen from a doubtful seat and half-attainted stall,
The last knight of Europe takes weapons from the wall,
The last and lingering troubadour to whom the bird has
      sung,
That once went singing southward when all the world was
      young,
In that enormous silence, tiny and unafraid,
Comes up along a winding road the noise of the Crusade.
Strong gongs groaning as the guns boom far,
Don John of Austria is going to the war,
Stiff flags straining in the night-blasts cold
In the gloom black-purple, in the glint old-gold,
Torchlight crimson on the copper kettle-drums,
Then the tuckets, then the trumpets, then the cannon, and
      he comes.
Don John laughing in the brave beard curled,
Spurning of his stirrups like the thrones of all the world,

GILBERT KEITH CHESTERTON

Holding his head up for a flag of all the free.
Love-light of Spain — hurrah!
Death-light of Africa!
Don John of Austria
Is riding to the sea.

Mahound is in his paradise above the evening star,
(*Don John of Austria is going to the war.*)
He moves a mighty turban on the timeless houri's knees,
His turban that is woven of the sunset and the seas.
He shakes the peacock gardens as he rises from his ease,
And he strides among the tree-tops and is taller than the
 trees,
And his voice through all the garden is a thunder sent to
 bring
Black Azrael and Ariel and Ammon on the wing.
Giants and the Genii,
Multiplex of wing and eye,
Whose strong obedience broke the sky
When Solomon was king.

They rush in red and purple from the red clouds of the
 morn,
From temples where the yellow gods shut up their eyes in
 scorn;
They rise in green robes roaring from the green hells of the
 sea
Where fallen skies and evil hues and eyeless creatures be;
On them the sea-valves cluster and the grey sea-forests curl,
Splashed with a splendid sickness, the sickness of the pearl;
They swell in sapphire smoke out of the blue cracks of the
 ground, —

They gather and they wonder and give worship to Ma-
    hound.
And he saith, ' Break up the mountains where the hermit-
    folk can hide,
And sift the red and silver sands lest bone of saint abide,
And chase the Giaours flying night and day, not giving rest,
For that which was our trouble comes again out of the west.
We have set the seal of Solomon on all things under sun,
Of knowledge and of sorrow and endurance of things done,
But a noise is in the mountains, in the mountains, and I
    know
The voice that shook our palaces — four hundred years ago:
It is he that saith not ' Kismet '; it is he that knows not Fate;
It is Richard, it is Raymond, it is Godfrey in the gate!
It is he whose loss is laughter when he counts the wager
    worth,
Put down your feet upon him, that our peace be on the
    earth.'
For he heard drums groaning and he heard guns jar,
(*Don John of Austria is going to the war.*)
Sudden and still — hurrah!
Bolt from Iberia!
Don John of Austria
Is gone by Alcalar.

St. Michael 's on his Mountain in the sea-roads of the north
(*Don John of Austria is girt and going forth.*)
Where the grey seas glitter and the sharp tides shift
And the sea folk labour and the red sails lift.
He shakes his lance of iron and he claps his wings of stone;
The noise is gone through Normandy; the noise is gone
    alone;

The North is full of tangled things and texts and aching
    eyes
And dead is all the innocence of anger and surprise,
And Christian killeth Christian in a narrow dusty room,
And Christian dreadeth Christ that hath a newer face of
    doom,
And Christian hateth Mary that God kissed in Galilee,
But Don John of Austria is riding to the sea.
Don John calling through the blast and the eclipse
Crying with the trumpet, with the trumpet of his lips,
Trumpet that sayeth ha!
   Domino Gloria!
Don John of Austria
Is shouting to the ships.

King Philip's in his closet with the Fleece about his neck
(*Don John of Austria is armed upon the deck.*)
The walls are hung with velvet that is black and soft as sin,
And little dwarfs creep out of it and little dwarfs creep in.
He holds a crystal phial that has colours like the moon,
He touches, and it tingles, and he trembles very soon,
And his face is as a fungus of a leprous white and grey
Like plants in the high houses that are shuttered from the
    day,
And death is in the phial, and the end of noble work,
But Don John of Austria has fired upon the Turk.
Don John's hunting, and his hounds have bayed —
Booms away past Italy the rumour of his raid.
Gun upon gun, ha! ha!
Gun upon gun, hurrah!
Don John of Austria
Has loosed the cannonade.

The Pope was in his chapel before day or battle broke,
(*Don John of Austria is hidden in the smoke.*)
The hidden room in man's house where God sits all the
    year,
The secret window whence the world looks small and very
    dear.
He sees as in a mirror on the monstrous twilight sea
The crescent of his cruel ships whose name is mystery;
They fling great shadows foe-wards, making Cross and
    Castle dark,
They veil the plumèd lions on the galleys of St. Mark;
And above the ships are palaces of brown, black-bearded
    chiefs,
And below the ships are prisons, where with multitudinous
    griefs,
Christian captives sick and sunless, all a labouring race re-
    pines
Like a race in sunken cities, like a nation in the mines.
They are lost like slaves that swat, and in the skies of morn-
    ing hung
The stairways of the tallest gods when tyranny was young.
They are countless, voiceless, hopeless as those fallen or flee-
    ing on
Before the high Kings' horses in the granite of Babylon.
And many a one grows witless in his quiet room in hell
Where a yellow face looks inward through the lattice of his
    cell,
And he finds his God forgotten, and he seeks no more a
    sign —
(*But Don John of Austria has burst the battle-line!*)
Don John pounding from the slaughter-painted poop,
Purpling all the ocean like a bloody pirate's sloop,

Scarlet running over on the silvers and the golds,
Breaking of the hatches up and bursting of the holds,
Thronging of the thousands up that labour under sea
White for bliss and blind for sun and stunned for liberty.
Vivat Hispania!
Domino Gloria!
Don John of Austria
Has set his people free!

Cervantes on his galley sets the sword back in the sheath
(*Don John of Austria rides homeward with a wreath.*)
And he sees across a weary land a straggling road in Spain,
Up which a lean and foolish knight forever rides in vain,
And he smiles, but not as Sultans smile, and settles back the
    blade. . . .
(*But Don John of Austria rides home from the Crusade.*)

ALFRED EDGAR COPPARD

1878–

152   *Mendacity*

TRUTH is love and love is truth,
    Either neither in good sooth:
Truth is truth and love is love,
Give us grace to taste thereof;
But if truth offend my sweet,
Then I will have none of it,
And if love offend the other,
Farewell truth, I will not bother.

Happy truth when truth accords
With the love in lovers' words!
Harm not truth in any part,
But keep its shadow from love's heart.

170

Men must love, though lovers' lies
Outpoll the stars in florid skies,
And none may keep, and few can merit,
The fond joy that they inherit.

Who with love at his command
Dares give truth a welcome hand?
Believe it, or believe it not,
'Tis a lore most vainly got.
Truth requites no penny-fee,
Niggard's honey feeds no bee;
Ere this trick of truth undo me,
Little love, my love, come to me.

153   *The Apostate*

I'LL go, said I, to the woods and hills,
   In a park of doves I'll make my fires,
And I'll fare like the badger and fox, I said,
   And be done with mean desires.

Never a lift of the hand I'll give
   Again in the world to bidders and buyers;
I'll live with the snakes in the hedge, I said,
   And be done with mean desires.

I'll leave — and I left — my own true love.
   O faithful heart that never tires!
I will return, tho' I'll not return
   To perish of mean desires.

Farewell, farewell to my kinsmen all,
   The worst were thieves and the best were liars,
But the devil must take what he gave, I said,
   For I'm done with mean desires.

171

ALFRED EDGAR COPPARD

But the snake, the fox, the badger and I
    Are one in blood, like sons and sires,
And as far from home as kingdom come
    I follow my mean desires.

154   *Epitaph*

L IKE silver dew are the tears of love,
    Like gold the smile of joy,
But I had neither, silver, gold,
    Nor wit for their employ.

I had no gifts or fancies fair
    This poverty to mend:
I was the son of my father,
    And had no other friend.

Though he that brings no grist to mill
    May con the reckoning o'er,
Who comes into the world with naught
    Can scarce go out with more.

WILFRID GIBSON

1878–

155   *Breakfast*

W E ate our breakfast lying on our backs
    Because the shells were screeching overhead.
I bet a rasher to a loaf of bread
That Hull United would beat Halifax
When Jimmy Stainthorpe played full-back instead
Of Billy Bradford. Ginger raised his head
And cursed, and took the bet, and dropt back dead.
We ate our breakfast lying on our backs
Because the shells were screeching overhead.

172

156   *Old Skinflint*

'TWIXT Carrowbrough Edge and Settlingstones
    See old daddy Skinflint dance in his bones,
Old Skinflint on the gallows-tree,
Old daddy Skinflint, the father of me.

Why do you dance, do you dance so high?
Why do you dance in the windy sky?
Why do you dance in your naked bones
'Twixt Carrowbrough Edge and Settlingstones?

Old daddy Skinflint, the father of me,
Why do you dance on the gallows-tree,
Who never tripped on a dancing-floor
Or flung your heels in a reel before?

You taught me many a cunning thing,
But never taught me to dance and sing;
Yet I must do whatever you do,
So when you dance I must dance too.

'Twixt Carrowbrough Edge and Settlingstones
See old daddy Skinflint dance in his bones,
Old Skinflint on the gallows-tree,
Old daddy Skinflint, the father of me.

157   *Luck*

WHAT bring you, sailor, home from the sea —
    Coffers of gold and of ivory?

When first I went to sea as a lad
A new jack-knife was all I had:

And I've sailed for fifty years and three
To the coasts of gold and of ivory:

And now at the end of a lucky life,
Well, still I've got my old jack-knife.

158 *The Parrot*

LONG since I'd ceased to care
        Though he should curse and swear
The little while he spent at home with me:
And yet I couldn't bear
To hear his parrot swear
The day I learned my man was drowned at sea.

He'd taught the silly bird
To jabber word for word
Outlandish oaths that he'd picked up at sea;
And now it seemed I heard
In every wicked word
The dead man from the deep still cursing me.

A flood of easing tears,
Though I'd not wept for years,
Brought back old long-forgotten dreams to me,
The foolish hopes and fears
Of the first half-happy years
Before his soul was stolen by the sea.

OLIVER ST. JOHN GOGARTY

1878–

159   *Portrait with Background*

DERVORGILLA'S supremely lovely daughter,
   Recalling him, of all the Leinstermen Ri,
Him whose love and hate brought o'er the water,
      Strongbow and Henry;

Brought rigid law, the long spear and the horsemen
Riding in steel; and the rhymed, romantic, high line;
Built those square keeps on the forts of the Norsemen,
      Still on our sky-line.

I would have brought, if I saw a chance of losing
You, many more — we are living in War-rife time —
Knights of the air and submarine men cruising,
      Trained through a life-time;

Brought the implacable hand with law-breakers,
Drilled the Too-many and broken their effrontery;
Broken the dream of the men of a few acres
      Ruling a country;

Brought the long day with its leisure and its duty,
Built once again the limestone lordly houses —
Founded on steel is the edifice of Beauty,
      All it avows is.

Here your long limbs and your golden hair affright men,
Slaves are their souls, and instinctively they hate them,
Knowing full well that such charms can but invite men,
      Heroes to mate them.

175

160 *Ringsend*

(*After reading Tolstoi*)

I WILL live in Ringsend
 With a red-headed whore,
And the fan-light gone in
Where it lights the hall-door;
And listen each night
For her querulous shout,
As at last she streels in
And the pubs empty out.
To soothe that wild breast
With my old-fangled songs,
Till she feels it redressed
From inordinate wrongs,
Imagined, outrageous,
Preposterous wrongs,
Till peace at last comes,
Shall be all I will do,
Where the little lamp blooms
Like a rose in the stew;
And up the back-garden
The sound comes to me
Of the lapsing, unsoilable,
Whispering sea.

161 *Marcus Curtius*

In response to an oracle which declared that a gulf recently
opened in the Forum could only be closed by casting into it
that which Rome held dearest, Marcus Curtius, fully armed,

176

mounted his war-horse and plunged, for that which Rome
held dearest was her chivalry.

'TIS not by brooding on delight
　　That men take heart of pride, and force
To pull the saddle-girthings tight
And close the gulf on staring horse.

From softness only softness comes;
Urged by a bitterer shout within,
Men of the trumpets and the drums
Seek, with appropriate discipline,

That Glory past the pit or wall
Which contradicts and stops the breath,
And with immortalizing gall
Builds the most stubborn things on death.

162　　　　*The Conquest*

SINCE the Conquest none of us
　　Has died young except in battle.'
I knew that hers was no mean house,
And that beneath her innocent prattle
There was likely hid in words
What could never anger Fame;
The glory of continuous swords,
The obligations of a name.
Had I grown incredulous,
Thinking for a little space:
Though she has the daring brows,
She has not the falcon face;
In the storm from days of old

It is hard to keep at poise,
And it is the over-bold,
Gallant-hearted Fate destroys:
Could I doubt that her forbears
Kept their foot-hold on the sands,
Triumphed through eight hundred years,
From the hucksters kept their lands,
And still kept the conquering knack —
I who had myself gone down
Without waiting the attack
Of their youngest daughter's frown?

163   *Per Iter Tenebricosum*

ENOUGH! Why should a man bemoan
A Fate that leads the natural way?
Or think himself a worthier one
Than those who braved it in their day?
If only gladiators died,
Or heroes, Death would be his pride;
But have not little maidens gone,
And Lesbia's sparrow — all alone?

164   *Verse*

WHAT should we know,
For better or worse,
Of the Long Ago,
Were it not for Verse:
What ships went down;
What walls were razed;
Who won the crown;

What lads were praised?
A fallen stone,
Or a waste of sands;
And all is known
Of Art-less lands.
But you need not delve
By the sea-side hills
Where the Muse herself
All Time fulfills,
Who cuts with his scythe
All things but hers;
All but the blithe
Hexameters.

165   *After Galen*

ONLY the Lion and the Cock,
  As Galen says, withstand Love's shock.
So, Dearest, do not think me rude
If I yield now to lassitude,
But sympathize with me. I know
You would not have me roar, or crow.

166   *With a Coin from Syracuse*

WHERE is the hand to trace
   The contour of her face:
The nose so straight and fine
Down from the forehead's line;

The curved and curtal lip
Full in companionship
With that lip's overplus,
Proud and most sumptuous,

179

Which draws its curve within,
Swelling the faultless chin?
What artist knows the tech-
nique of the Doric neck:

The line that keeps with all
The features vertical,
Crowned with the thickly rolled
And corrugated gold?

The curious hands are lost
On the sweet Asian coast,
That made the coins enwrought
(Fairer than all they bought)

With emblems round the proud
Untroubled face of god
And goddess. Or they lie
At Syracuse hard by

The Fountain Arethuse.
Therefore from Syracuse
I send this face to her
Whose face is lovelier,

Alas, and as remote
As hers around whose throat
The curving fishes swim,
As round a fountain's brim.

It shows on the reverse
Pherenikos the horse;
And that 's as it should be:
Horses she loves, for she

Is come of the old stock,
Lords of the limestone rock
And acres fit to breed
Many a likely steed,

Straight in the back and bone,
With head high, like her own,
And blood that, tamed and mild,
Can suddenly go wild.

167 *Non Dolet*

OUR friends go with us as we go
   Down the long path where Beauty wends,
Where all we love forgathers, so
   Why should we fear to join our friends?

Who would survive them to outlast
   His children; to outwear his fame —
Left when the Triumph has gone past —
   To win from Age, not Time, a name?

Then do not shudder at the knife
   That Death's indifferent hand drives home,
But with the Strivers leave the Strife,
   Nor, after Caesar, skulk in Rome.

168 *O Boys! O Boys!*

O BOYS, the times I've seen!
   The things I've done and known!
If you knew where I have been?
Or half the joys I've had,
You never would leave me alone;

181

But pester me to tell,
Swearing to keep it dark,
What . . . but I know quite well:
Every solicitor's clerk
Would break out and go mad;
And all the dogs would bark!

There was a young fellow of old
Who spoke of a wonderful town,
Built on a lake of gold,
With many a barge and raft
Afloat in the cooling sun,
And lutes upon the lake
Played by such courtesans . . .
The sight was enough to take
The reason out of a man's
Brain; and to leave him daft,
Babbling of lutes and fans.

The tale was right enough:
Willows and orioles,
And ladies skilled in love.
But they listened only to smirk,
For he spoke to incredulous fools,
And, maybe, was sorry he spoke;
For no one believes in joys,
And Peace on Earth is a joke,
Which, anyhow, telling destroys;
So better go on with your work:
But Boys! O Boys! O Boys!

169   *To Petronius Arbiter*

PROCONSUL of Bithynia,
   Who loved to turn the night to day,
Yet for your ease had more to show
Than others for their push and go,
Teach us to save the Spirit's expense,
And win to Fame through indolence.

170   *The Image-Maker*

HARD is the stone, but harder still
   The delicate preforming will
That, guided by a dream alone,
Subdues and moulds the hardest stone,
Making the stubborn jade release
The emblem of eternal peace.

If but the will be firmly bent,
No stuff resists the mind's intent;
The adamant abets his skill
And sternly aids the artist's will,
To clothe in perdurable pride
Beauty his transient eyes descried.

171   *Palinode*

TWENTY years are gone
   Down the winding road,
Years in which it shone
   More often than it snowed;
And now old Time brings on,
   Brings on the palinode.

OLIVER ST. JOHN GOGARTY

I have been full of mirth;
   I have been full of wine;
And I have trod the earth
   As if it all were mine;
And laughed to bring to birth
   The lighter lyric line.

Before it was too late,
   One thing I learnt and saw:
Prophets anticipate
   What Time brings round by law;
Call age before its date
   To darken Youth with awe.

Why should you drink the rue?
   Or leave in righteous rage
A world that will leave you
   Howe'er you walk the stage?
Time needs no help to do
   His miracle of age.

A few years more to flow
   From miracle-working Time,
And surely I shall grow
   Incapable of rhyme,
Sans Love and Song, and so
   An echo of a mime.

Yet if my stone set forth
   The merry Attic blade's
Remark, I shall have worth
   Achieved before Life fades:
' A gentle man on Earth
   And gentle 'mid the Shades.'

OLIVER ST. JOHN GOGARTY

172   *To Death*

B UT for your Terror
    Where would be Valour?
What is Love for
    But to stand in your way?
Taker and Giver,
For all your endeavour
You leave us with more
    Than you touch with decay!

173   *To a Boon Companion*

I F medals were ordained for drinks,
    Or soft communings with a minx,
Or being at your ease belated,
By Heavens, you'd be decorated.
And not Alcmena's chesty son
Have room to put your ribands on!

174   *Dedication*

T ALL unpopular men,
    Slim proud women who move
As women walked in the islands when
Temples were built to Love,
I sing to you. With you
Beauty at best can live,
Beauty that dwells with the rare and **few,**
Cold and imperative.
He who had Caesar's ear
Sang to the lonely and strong.
Virgil made an austere
Venus Muse of his song.

175 *Colophon*

WHILE the Tragedy's afoot,
    Let us play in the high boot;
Once the trumpets' notes are gone,
Off, before the Fool comes on!

JOHN MASEFIELD

1878–

176 *Sea-Change*

GONEYS an' gullies an' all o' the birds o' the sea
    They ain't no birds, not really,' said Billy the Dane.
' Not mollies, nor gullies, nor goneys at all,' said he,
    ' But simply the sperrits of mariners livin' again.

' Them birds goin' fishin' is nothin' but souls o' the drowned,
    Souls o' the drowned an' the kicked as are never no more;
An' that there haughty old albatross cruisin' around,
    Belike he's Admiral Nelson or Admiral Noah.

' An' merry 's the life they are living. They settle and dip,
    They fishes, they never stands watches, they waggle their
        wings;
When a ship comes by, they fly to look at the ship
    To see how the nowaday mariners manages things.

' When freezing aloft in a snorter, I tell you I wish —
    (Though maybe it ain't like a Christian) — I wish I
        could be
A haughty old copper-bound albatross dipping for fish
    And coming the proud over all o' the birds o' the sea.'

186

177   *' Port of Many Ships '*

IT 'S a sunny pleasant anchorage, is Kingdom Come,
  Where crews is always layin' aft for double-tots o' rum,
'N' there 's dancin' 'n' fiddlin' of ev'ry kind o' sort,
It 's a fine place for sailor-men is that there port.
          'N' I wish —
          I wish as I was there.

' The winds is never nothin' more than jest light airs,
'N' no-one gets belayin'-pinned, 'n' no-one never swears,
Yer free to loaf an' laze around, yer pipe atween yer lips,
Lollin' on the fo'c's'le, sonny, lookin' at the ships.
          'N' I wish —
          I wish as I was there.

' For ridin' in the anchorage the ships of all the world
Have got one anchor down 'n' all sails furled.
All the sunken hookers 'n' the crews as took 'n' died
They lays there merry, sonny, swingin' to the tide.
          'N' I wish —
          I wish as I was there.

' Drowned old wooden hookers green wi' drippin' wrack,
Ships as never fetched to port, as never came back,
Swingin' to the blushin' tide, dippin' to the swell,
'N' the crews all singin', sonny, beatin' on the bell.
          'N' I wish —
          I wish as I was there.'

178 A Valediction (Liverpool Docks)

A CRIMP.   A DRUNKEN SAILOR.

*I*S *there anything as I can do ashore for you*
   When you've dropped down the tide? —

You can take 'n' tell Nan I'm goin' about the world agen,
        'N' that the world's wide.
'N' tell her that there ain't no postal service
        Not down on the blue sea.
'N' tell her that she'd best not keep her fires alight
        Nor set up late for me.
'N' tell her I'll have forgotten all about her
        Afore we cross the Line.
'N' tell her that the dollars of any other sailorman
        Is as good red gold as mine.

Is there anything as I can do aboard for you
Afore the tow-rope's taut?

I'm new to this packet and all the ways of her,
        'N' I don't know of aught;
But I knows as I'm goin' down to the seas agen
        'N' the seas are salt 'n' drear;
But I knows as all the doin' as you're man enough for
        Won't make them lager-beer.

'N' ain't there nothin' *as I can do ashore for you*
When you've got fair afloat? —

You can buy a farm with the dollars as you've done me of
'N' cash my advance-note.

Is there anythin' you'd fancy for your breakfastin'
When you're home across Mersey Bar? —

I wants a red herrin' 'n' a prairie oyster
'N' a bucket of Three Star,
'N' a girl with redder lips than Polly has got,
'N' prettier ways than Nan —

Well, so-long, Billy, 'n' a spankin' heavy pay-day to you!

So-long, my fancy man!

179   *Trade Winds*

IN the harbour, in the island, in the Spanish Seas,
Are the tiny white houses and the orange-trees,
And day-long, night-long, the cool and pleasant breeze
    Of the steady Trade Winds blowing.

There is the red wine, the nutty Spanish ale,
The shuffle of the dancers, the old salt's tale,
The squeaking fiddle, and the soughing in the sail
    Of the steady Trade Winds blowing.

And o' nights there 's fire-flies and the yellow moon,
And in the ghostly palm-trees the sleepy tune
Of the quiet voice calling me, the long low croon
    Of the steady Trade Winds blowing.

180   *Cargoes*

QUINQUIREME of Nineveh from distant Ophir
Rowing home to haven in sunny Palestine,
With a cargo of ivory,
And apes and peacocks,
Sandalwood, cedarwood, and sweet white wine.

Stately Spanish galleon coming from the Isthmus,
Dipping through the Tropics by the palm-green shores,
With a cargo of diamonds,
Emeralds, amethysts,
Topazes, and cinnamon, and gold moidores.

Dirty British coaster with a salt-caked smoke stack
Butting through the Channel in the mad March days,
With a cargo of Tyne coal,
Road-rail, pig-lead,
Firewood, iron-ware, and cheap tin trays.

Tettenhall.

181   *Port of Holy Peter*

THE blue laguna rocks and quivers,
   Dull gurgling eddies twist and spin,
The climate does for people's livers,
   It's a nasty place to anchor in
      Is Spanish port,
      Fever port,
      Port of Holy Peter.

The town begins on the sea-beaches,
   And the town's mad with the stinging flies,
The drinking water's mostly leeches,
   It's a far remove from Paradise
      Is Spanish port,
      Fever port,
      Port of Holy Peter.

JOHN MASEFIELD

There 's sand-bagging and throat-slitting,
   And quiet graves in the sea slime,
Stabbing, of course, and rum-hitting,
   Dirt, and drink, and stink, and crime,
      In Spanish port,
      Fever port,
      Port of Holy Peter.

All the day the wind 's blowing
   From the sick swamp below the hills,
All the night the plague 's growing,
   And the dawn brings the fever chills,
      In Spanish port,
      Fever port,
      Port of Holy Peter.

You get a thirst there 's no slaking,
   You get the chills and fever-shakes,
Tongue yellow and head aching,
   And then the sleep that never wakes.
And all the year the heat 's baking,
   The sea rots and the earth quakes,
      In Spanish port,
      Fever port,
      Port of Holy Peter.

Tettenhall.

EDWARD THOMAS

1878–1917

182   *If I should ever by Chance*

IF I should ever by chance grow rich
I 'll buy Codham, Cockridden, and Childerditch,
Roses, Pyrgo, and Lapwater,
And let them all to my elder daughter.
The rent I shall ask of her will be only
Each year's first violets, white and lonely,
The first primroses and orchises —
She must find them before I do, that is.
But if she finds a blossom on furze
Without rent they shall all for ever be hers,
Codham, Cockridden, and Childerditch,
Roses, Pyrgo, and Lapwater, —
I shall give them all to my elder daughter.

JOSEPH CAMPBELL

1879–

183   *The Dancer*

THE tall dancer dances
With slowly taken breath:
In his feet music,
And on his face death.

His face is a mask,
It is so still and white:
His withered eyes shut,
Unmindful of light.

JOSEPH CAMPBELL

The old fiddler fiddles
The merry ' *Silver Tip* '
With softly beating foot
And laughing eye and lip.

And round the dark walls
The people sit and stand,
Praising the art
Of the dancer of the land.

But he dances there
As if his kin were dead:
Clay in his thoughts,
And lightning in his tread!

HAROLD MONRO

1879–1932

184   *Milk for the Cat*

WHEN the tea is brought at five o'clock,
    And all the neat curtains are drawn with care,
The little black cat with bright green eyes
Is suddenly purring there.

At first she pretends, having nothing to do,
She has come in merely to blink by the grate,
But, though tea may be late or the milk may be sour,
She is never late.

And presently her agate eyes
Take a soft large milky haze,
And her independent casual glance
Becomes a stiff, hard gaze.

HAROLD MONRO

Then she stamps her claws or lifts her ears,
Or twists her tail and begins to stir,
Till suddenly all her lithe body becomes
One breathing, trembling purr.

The children eat and wriggle and laugh;
The two old ladies stroke their silk:
But the cat is grown small and thin with desire,
Transformed to a creeping lust for milk.

The white saucer like some full moon descends
At last from the clouds of the table above;
She sighs and dreams and thrills and glows,
Transfigured with love.

She nestles over the shining rim,
Buries her chin in the creamy sea;
Her tail hangs loose; each drowsy paw
Is doubled under each bending knee.

A long, dim ecstasy holds her life;
Her world is an infinite shapeless white,
Till her tongue has curled the last holy drop,
Then she sinks back into the night,

Draws and dips her body to heap
Her sleepy nerves in the great arm-chair,
Lies defeated and buried deep
Three or four hours unconscious there.

185 *Cat's Meat*

HO, all you cats in all the street;
Look out, it is the hour of meat:
The little barrow is crawling along,
And the meat-boy growling his fleshy song.

194

Hurry, Ginger! Hurry, White!
Don't delay to court or fight.

Wandering Tabby, vagrant Black,
Yamble from adventure back!

Slip across the shining street,
Meat! Meat! Meat! Meat!

Lift your tail and dip your feet;
Find your penny — Meat! Meat!

Where 's your mistress?   Learn to purr:
Pennies emanate from her.

Be to her, for she is Fate,
Perfectly affectionate.

(You, domestic Pinkie-Nose,
Keep inside and warm your toes.)

Flurry, flurry in the street —
Meat! Meat! Meat! Meat!

186   *Hearthstone*

I WANT nothing but your fire-side now.
Friend, you are sitting there alone I know,
And the quiet flames are licking up the soot,
Or crackling out of some enormous root:
All the logs on your hearth are four feet long.
Everything in your room is wide and strong
According to the breed of your hard thought.
Now you are leaning forward; you have caught
That great dog by his paw and are holding it,
And he looks sidelong at you, stretching a bit,

Drowsing with open eyes, huge, warm and wide,
The full hearth-length on his slow-breathing side.
Your book has dropped unnoticed: you have read
So long you cannot send your brain to bed.
The low quiet room and all its things are caught
And linger in the meshes of your thought.
(Some people think they know time cannot pause).
Your eyes are closing now though not because
Of sleep. You are searching something with your brain;
You have let the old dog's paw drop down again. . . .
Now suddenly you hum a little catch,
And pick up the book. The wind rattles the latch;
There's a patter of light cool rain and the curtain shakes;
The silly dog growls, moves, and almost wakes.
The kettle near the fire one moment hums.
Then a long peace upon the whole room comes.
So the sweet evening will draw to its bedtime end.
I want nothing now but your fire-side, friend.

187 *Bitter Sanctuary*

(i)

SHE lives in the porter's room; the plush is nicotined.
Clients have left their photos there to perish.
She watches through green shutters those who press
To reach unconsciousness.

She licks her varnished thin magenta lips,
She picks her foretooth with a finger nail,
She pokes her head out to greet new clients, or
To leave them (to what torture) waiting at the door.

196

(*ii*)

Heat has locked the heavy earth,
Given strength to every sound,
He, where his life still holds him to the ground,
In anaesthesia, groaning for re-birth,
Leans at the door.
From out the house there comes the dullest flutter;
A lackey; and thin giggling from behind that shutter.

(*iii*)

His lost eyes lean to find and read the number.
Follows his knuckled rap, and hesitating curse.
He cannot wake himself; he may not slumber;
While on the long white wall across the road
Drives the thin outline of a dwindling hearse.

(*iv*)

Now the door opens wide.

He: 'Is there room inside? '
She: 'Are you past the bounds of pain? '
He: 'May my body lie in vain
    Among the dreams I cannot keep! '
She: 'Let him drink the cup of sleep.'

(*v*)

Thin arms and ghostly hands; faint sky-blue eyes;
Long drooping lashes, lids like full-blown moons,
Clinging to any brink of floating skies:
What hope is there?   What fear? — Unless to wake
    and see
Lingering flesh, or cold eternity.

HAROLD MONRO

O yet some face, half living, brings
Far gaze to him and croons:
She: ' You 're white.   You are alone.
    Can you not approach my sphere? '
He: ' I 'm changing into stone.'
She: ' Would *I* were!   Would *I* were! '
Then the white attendants fill the cup.

(*vi*)

In the morning through the world,
Watch the flunkeys bring the coffee;
Watch the shepherds on the downs,
Lords and ladies at their toilet,
Farmers, merchants, frothing towns.

But look how he, unfortunate, now fumbles
Through unknown chambers, unheedful stumbles.
Can he evade the overshadowing night?
Are there not somewhere chinks of braided light?

(*vii*)

How do they leave who once are in those rooms?
Some may be found, they say, deeply asleep
In ruined tombs.
Some in white beds, with faces round them.   Some
Wander the world, and never find a home.

188   *From ' Midnight Lamentation '*

WHEN you and I go down
    Breathless and cold,
Our faces both worn back
To earthly mould,

198

HAROLD MONRO

How lonely we shall be!
What shall we do,
You without me,
I without you?

I cannot bear the thought
You, first, may die,
Nor of how you will weep,
Should I.
We are too much alone;
What can we do
To make our bodies one:
You, me; I, you?

We are most nearly born
Of one same kind;
We have the same delight,
The same true mind.
Must we then part, we part;
Is there no way
To keep a beating heart,
And light of day?

I cannot find a way
Through love and through;
I cannot reach beyond
Body, to you.
When you or I must go
Down evermore,
There 'll be no more to say
— But a locked door.

HAROLD MONRO

From 'Natural History'

THE vixen woman,
  Long gone away,
Came to haunt me
Yesterday.

I sit and faint
Through year on year.
Was it yesterday
I thought her dear?

Is hate then love?
Can love be hate?
Can they both rule
In equal state?

Young, young she was,
And young was I.
We cried: Love! Come!
Love heard our cry.

Her whom I loved
I loathe to-day:
The vixen woman
Who came my way.

JOHN FREEMAN

1880—1929

Asylum

A HOUSE ringed round with trees and in the trees
  One lancet where the crafty light slides through;
Comely, forsaken, unhusbanded,
Blind-eyed and mute, unlamped and smokeless, yet
Safe from the humiliation of death.

JOHN FREEMAN

The porch is mossy, the roof-shingles are mossy,
Green furs the window-sills and beards the drip-stones,
A staring board, *To Let*, leans thigh-deep in
Grave-clothes of grass; and no one sees or cares.

One day, may be, a school will open here,
Or hospital, or home for fallen girls —
A fallen house for fallen girls, may be.
Laughter will shrill these silences away,
Break every pane of peace with foolishness,
And all the waiting, anxious memories
Abashed will slink through the trees away, away.

So calm a house should not be given to noise,
Nor scornful feet.   But old men here should come,
When apprehension first shall haunt their eyes.
Fire should warm all the rooms and smoke the chimneys,
Creeper renew its blood on the cold stones,
A porch light shine on the rain-sodden path
And watery ruts; and wise men here should find
Asylum from the thought and fear of Death.

191   *To end her Fear*

B E kind to her
  O Time.
She is too much afraid of you
    Because yours is a land unknown,
    Wintry, dark and lone.

'Tis not for her
To pass
Boldly upon your roadless waste.
    Roads she loves, and the bright ringing
    Of quick heels, and clear singing.

She is afraid
Of Time,
Forty to seventy sadly fearing . . .
   O, all those unknown years,
   And these sly, stoat-like fears!

Shake not on her
Your snows,
But on the rich, the proud, the wise
   Who have that to make them glow
   With warmth beneath the snow.

If she grow old
At last,
Be it yet unknown to her; that she
   Not until her last prayer is prayed
   May whisper, ' I am afraid! '

192 *The Hounds*

FAR off a lonely hound
  Telling his loneliness all round
To the dark woods, dark hills, and darker sea;

And, answering, the sound
Of that yet lonelier sea-hound
Telling his loneliness to the solitary stars.

Hearing, the kennelled hound
Some neighbourhood and comfort found,
And slept beneath the comfortless high stars.

But that wild sea-hound
Unkennelled, called all night all round —
The unneighboured and uncomforted cold sea.

1881–1938

193 *Hope and Despair*

SAID God, ' You sisters, ere ye go
Down among men, my work to do,
I will on each a badge bestow:
Hope I love best, and gold for her,
Yet a silver glory for Despair,
For she is my angel too.'

Then like a queen, Despair
Put on the stars to wear.
But Hope took ears of corn, and round
Her temples in a wreath them bound. —
Which think ye lookt the more fair?

194 *The Fear*

AS over muddy shores a dragon flock
Went, in an early age from ours discrete,
Before the grim race found oblivion meet;
And as Time harden'd into iron rock
That unclean mud, and into cliffs did lock
The story of those terrifying feet
With hooked claws and wrinkled scale complete,
Till quarrying startles us with amaz'd shock:

So there was something wont to pass along
The plashy marge of early consciousness.
Now the quagmires are turned to pavement strong;
Those outer twilight regions bold I may
Explore, — yet still I shudder with distress
To find detested tracks of his old way.

195   *The Stream's Song*

MAKE way, make way,
 You thwarting stones;
Room for my play,
Serious ones.

Do you not fear,
O rocks and boulders,
To feel my laughter
On your grave shoulders?

Do you not know
My joy at length
Will all wear out
Your solemn strength?

You will not for ever
Cumber my play;
With joy and a song
I clear my way.

Your faith of rock
Shall yield to me,
And be carried away
By the song of my glee.

Crumble, crumble,
Voiceless things;
No faith can last
That never sings.

For the last hour
To joy belongs;
The steadfast perish,
But not the songs.

Yet for a while
Thwart me, O boulders;
I need for laughter
Your serious shoulders.

And when my singing
Has razed you quite,
I shall have lost
Half my delight.

196   *Mary and the Bramble*

THE great blue ceremony of the air
        Did a new morrow for the earth prepare;
The silver troops of mist were almost crept
Back to the streams where through the day they slept;
And, high up on his tower of song, the glad
Galloping wings of a lark already had
A message from the sun, to give bright warning
That he would shortly make a golden morning.
It was a dawn when the year is earliest.
Mary, in her rapt girlhood, from her rest
Came for the hour to wash her soul. Now she
Beheld, with eyes like the rain-shadowed sea,
Of late an urgency disturb the world;
Her thought that, like a curtain wide unfurl'd
With stir of a hurrying throng against it prest,
Seen things flutter'd with spiritual haste
Behind them, as a rush of winged zeal
Made with its gusty passage shiver and reel,
Like a loose weaving, all the work of sense.
Surely not always could such vehemence

Of Spirit stay all shrouded in the green
Appearance of earth's knowledgeable mien:
Ay, see this morning trembling like a sail!
Can it still hold the strain? must it not fail
Even now? for lo how it doth thrill and bend!
Will not, as a torn cloth, earth's season rend
Before this shaking wind of Heaven's speed,
And show her God's obediences indeed
Burning along behind it?   Never yet
Was such a fever in the frail earth set
By those hid throngs posting behind its veil!

Unfearing were her eyes; yet would they quail
A little when the curtain seemed nigh torn,
The shining weft of kind clear-weather'd morn,
In pressure of near Spirit forcing it.
And as she walkt, the marvel would permit
Scarce any love for the earth's delighted dress.
Through meadows flowering with happiness
Went Mary, feeling not the air that laid
Honours of gentle dew upon her head;
Nor that the sun now loved with golden stare
The marvellous behaviour of her hair,
Bending with finer swerve from off her brow
Than water which relents before a prow:
Till in the shining darkness many a gleam
Of secret bronze-red lustres answered him.

The Spirit of Life vaunted itself: 'Ho ye
Who wear the Heavens, now look down to me!
I too can praise.   My dark encumberment
Of earth, whereinto I was hardly sent,

206

I have up-wielded as the fire wields flame,
And turned it into glory of God's name:
Till now a praise as good as yours I can,
For now my speech, the long-stammer'd being of **Man**,
Rises into its mightiest, sweetest word.'
Not vain his boast: for seemly to the Lord,
Blue-robed and yellow-kerchieft, Mary went.
There never was to God such worship sent
By any angel in the Heavenly ways,
As this that Life had utter'd for God's praise,
This girlhood — as the service that Life said
In the beauty and the manners of this maid.
Never the harps of Heaven played such song
As her grave walking through the grasses long.
Yea, out of Jewry came the proof in her
That the angel Life was God's best worshipper.

Now in her vision'd walk beside a brake
Is Mary passing, wherein brambles make
A tangled malice, grown to such a riddle
That any grimness crouching in the middle
Were not espied. Bewildered was the place,
Like a brain full of folly and disgrace;
And with its thorny toils it seemed to be
A naughty heart devising cruelty.
Ready it was with all its small keen spite
To catch at anything that walkt upright,
Although a miching weasel safely went
Therethrough. And close to this entanglement,
This little world out of unkindness made,
With eyes beyond her path young Mary strayed.

As an unheeded bramble's reach she crost,
Her breast a spiny sinew did accost
With eager thorns, tearing her dress to seize
And harm her hidden white virginities.
To it she spake, with such a gentle air
That the thing might not choose but answer her.

'What meanest thou, O Bramble,
    So to hurt my breast?
Why is thy sharp cruelty
    Against my heart prest?'

'How can I help, O Mary,
    Dealing wound to thee?
Thou hast Heaven's favour:
    I am mortality.'

'If I, who am thy sister,
    Am in Heaven's love,
If it be so, then should it not
    Thee to gladness move?'

'Nay, nay, it moves me only
    Quietly to wait,
Till I can surely seize thy heart
    In my twisting hate.'

'Ah, thou hast pierced my paps, bramble,
    Thy thorns are in my blood;
Tell me for why, thou cruel growth,
    Thy malice is so rude.'

' Thou art looking, Mary,
   Beyond the world to be:
If I cannot grapple thee down to the world,
   I can injure thee.'

' Ah, thy wicked daggers now
   Into my nipple cling:
It is like guilt, so to be held
   In thy harsh fingering.'

   The little leaves were language still,
And gave their voice to Mary's will;
But till the bramble's word was said,
Thorns clutcht hard upon the maid.
' Yes, like guilt, for guilt am I,
Sin and wrong and misery.
For thy heart guilt is feeling;
Hurt for which there is no healing
Must the bramble do to thee,
If thou wilt not guilty be.
Know'st thou me? These nails of hate
Are the fastenings of the weight
Of substance which thy God did bind
Upon thy upward-meaning mind.
Life has greatly sworn to be
High as the brows of God in thee;
But I am heaviness, and I
Would hold thee down from being high.
Thou thyself by thy straining
Hast made my weight a wicked thing;
Here in the bramble now I sit
And tear thy flesh with the spines of it.

Yet into my desires come,
And like a worshipping bridegroom
I will turn thy life to dream,
All delicious love to seem.
But if in Heaven God shall wear
Before any worship there
Thy Spirit, and Life boasteth this,
Thou must break through the injuries
And shames I will about thee wind,
The hooks and thickets of my kind;
The whole earth's nature will come to be
Full of my purpose against thee:
Yea, worse than a bramble's handling, men
Shall use thy bosom, Mary, then.
And yet I know that by these scars
I make thee better than the stars
For God to wear; and thou wilt ride
On the lusts that have thee tried,
The murders that fell short of thee,
Like charioting in a victory;
Like shafted horses thou wilt drive
The crimes that I on earth made thrive
Against thee, into Heaven to draw
Thy soul out of my heinous law.
But now in midst of my growth thou art,
And I have thee by the heart;
And closer shall I seize on thee
Even than this; a gallows-tree
Shall bear a bramble-coil on high;
Then twisted about thy soul am I,
Then a withe of my will is bound
Strangling thy very ghost around.'

LASCELLES ABERCROMBIE

Homeward went Mary, nursing fearfully
The bleeding badges of that cruelty.
Now closer spiritual turbulence whirled
Against her filmy vision of the world,
Which ras like shaken silk, so gravely leant
The moving of that throng'd astonishment
On the far side: the time was near at hand
When Gabriel with the fiery-flower'd wand
Would part the tissue of her bodily ken,
And to the opening all God's shining men
Would crowd to watch the message that he took
To earthly life: ' Hail, Mary, that dost look
Delightful to the Lord; I bid thee know
That answering God's own love thy womb shall throe.'

FRANK PEARCE STURM

197   *Still-heart*

D READ are the death-pale Kings
     Who bend to the oar,
Dread is the voice that sings
On the starless shore,
Lamentations and woes:
Cold on the wave
Beautiful Still-heart goes
To the rock-hewn grave.
The limbs are bound, and the breasts
That I kissed are cold;
Beautiful Still-heart rests
With the queens of old.

1881–

198　　　　*Old Soldier*

WE wander now who marched before,
　Hawking our bran from door to door,
While other men from the mill take their flour:
　　So it is to be an Old Soldier.

Old, bare and sore, we look on the hound
Turning upon the stiff frozen ground,
Nosing the mould, with the night around:
　　So it is to be an Old Soldier.

And we who once rang out like a bell,
Have nothing now to show or to sell;
Old bones to carry, old stories to tell:
　　So it is to be an Old Soldier.

199　　　　*A Drover*

TO Meath of the pastures,
　From wet hills by the sea,
Through Leitrim and Longford,
Go my cattle and me.

I hear in the darkness
Their slipping and breathing —
I name them the by-ways
They're to pass without heeding;

PADRAIC COLUM

Then the wet, winding roads,
Brown bogs with black water,
And my thoughts on white ships
And the King o' Spain's daughter.

O farmer, strong farmer!
You can spend at the fair,
But your face you must turn
To your crops and your care;

And soldiers, red soldiers!
You've seen many lands,
But you walk two by two,
And by captain's commands!

O the smell of the beasts,
The wet wind in the morn,
And the proud and hard earth
Never broken for corn!

And the crowds at the fair,
The herds loosened and blind,
Loud words and dark faces,
And the wild blood behind!

(O strong men with your best
I would strive breast to breast,
I could quiet your herds
With my words, with my words!)

I will bring you, my kine,
Where there 's grass to the knee,
But you'll think of scant croppings
Harsh with salt of the sea.

PADRAIC COLUM

The Poor Girl's Meditation

I AM sitting here
  Since the moon rose in the night,
Kindling a fire,
And striving to keep it alight;
The folk of the house are lying
In slumber deep;
The geese will be gabbling soon:
The whole of the land is asleep.

May I never leave this world
Until my ill-luck is gone;
Till I have cows and sheep,
And the lad that I love for my own;
I would not think it long,
The night I would lie at his breast,
And the daughters of spite, after that,
Might say the thing they liked best.

Love takes the place of hate,
If a girl have beauty at all:
On a bed that was narrow and high,
A three-month I lay by the wall:
When I bethought on the lad
That I left on the brow of the hill,
I wept from dark until dark,
And my cheeks have the tear-tracks still.

And, O young lad that I love,
I am no mark for your scorn;
All you can say of me is
Undowered I was born:

And if I've no fortune in hand,
Nor cattle and sheep of my own,
This I can say, O lad,
I am fitted to lie my lone!

201 *No Child*

I HEARD in the night the pigeons
Stirring within their nest:
The wild pigeons' stir was tender,
Like a child's hand at the breast.

I cried, ' O stir no more!
(My breast was touched with tears)
O pigeons, make no stir —
A childless woman hears.'

JOHN DRINKWATER

1882–1937

202 *Moonlit Apples*

AT the top of the house the apples are laid in rows,
And the skylight lets the moonlight in, and those
Apples are deep-sea apples of green.   There goes
    A cloud on the moon in the autumn night.

A mouse in the wainscot scratches, and scratches, and then
There is no sound at the top of the house of men
Or mice; and the cloud is blown, and the moon again
    Dapples the apples with deep-sea light.

They are lying in rows there, under the gloomy beams;
On the sagging floor; they gather the silver streams
Out of the moon, those moonlit apples of dreams,
    And quiet is the steep stair under.

In the corridors under there is nothing but sleep,
And stiller than ever on orchard boughs they keep
Tryst with the moon, and deep is the silence, deep
   On moon-washed apples of wonder.

203   *Who were before me*

LONG time in some forgotten churchyard earth of War-
    wickshire,
My fathers in their generations lie beyond desire,
And nothing breaks the rest, I know, of John Drinkwater
   now,
Who left in sixteen-seventy his roan team at plough.

And James, son of John, is there, a mighty ploughman too,
Skilled he was at thatching and the barleycorn brew,
And he had a heart-load of sorrow in his day,
But ten score of years ago he put it away.

Then Thomas came, and played a fiddle cut of mellow
   wood,
And broke his heart, they say, for love that never came to
   good.
A hundred winter peals and more have rung above his
   bed —
O, poor eternal grief, so long, so lightly, comforted.

And in the gentle yesterday these were but glimmering
   tombs,
Or tales to tell on fireside eves of legendary dooms;
I being life while they were none, what had their dust to
   bring
But cold intelligence of death upon my tides of Spring?

JOHN DRINKWATER

Now grief is in my shadow, and it seems well enough
To be there with my fathers, where neither fear nor love
Can touch me more, nor spite of men, nor my own teasing
    blame,
While the slow mosses weave an end of my forgotten name.

JAMES JOYCE

1882–1941

204 *A Flower given to my Daughter*

    FRAIL the white rose and frail are
      Her hands that gave
    Whose soul is sere and paler
    Than time's wan wave.

    Rosefrail and fair — yet frailest
    A wonder wild
    In gentle eyes thou veilest,
    My blueveined child.

Trieste 1913.

205   *Tutto è Sciolto*

    A BIRDLESS heaven, seadusk, one lone star
      Piercing the west,
As thou, fond heart, love's time, so faint, so far,
Rememberest.

The clear young eyes' soft look, the candid brow,
    The fragrant hair,
Falling as through the silence falleth now
    Dusk of the air.

217

Why then, remembering those shy
Sweet lures, repine
When the dear love she yielded with a sigh
Was all but thine?

Trieste 1914.

206   *On the Beach at Fontana*

WIND whines and whines the shingle,
    The crazy pierstakes groan;
A senile sea numbers each single
Slimesilvered stone.

From whining wind and colder
Grey sea I wrap him warm
And touch his trembling fineboned shoulder
And boyish arm.

Around us fear, descending
Darkness of fear above
And in my heart how deep unending
Ache of love!

Trieste 1914.

JAMES STEPHENS

1882–

207   *Deirdre*

DO not let any woman read this verse!
    It is for men, and after them their sons,
And their sons' sons!

The time comes when our hearts sink utterly;
When we remember Deirdre, and her tale,
And that her lips are dust.

218

Once she did tread the earth: men took her hand;
They looked into her eyes and said their say,
And she replied to them.

More than two thousand years it is since she
Was beautiful: she trod the waving grass;
She saw the clouds.

Two thousand years!   The grass is still the same;
The clouds as lovely as they were that time
When Deirdre was alive.

But there has been again no woman born
Who was so beautiful; not one so beautiful
Of all the women born.

Let all men go apart and mourn together!
No man can ever love her!   Not a man
Can dream to be her lover!

No man can bend before her!   No man say —
What could one say to her?   There are no words
That one could say to her!

Now she is but a story that is told
Beside the fire!   No man can ever be
The friend of that poor queen!

208   *Blue Blood*

WE thought at first, this man is a king for sure,
    Or the branch of a mighty and ancient and famous
        lineage
— That silly, sulky, illiterate, black-avisèd boor
Who was hatched by foreign vulgarity under a hedge!

219

The good men of Clare were drinking his health in a flood,
And gazing, with me, in awe at the princely lad;
And asking each other from what bluest blueness of blood
His daddy was squeezed, and the pa of the da of his dad?

We waited there, gaping and wondering, anxiously,
Until he'd stop eating, and let the glad tidings out;
And the slack-jawed booby proved to the hilt that he
Was lout, son of lout, by old lout, and was da to a lout!

(From the Irish.)

209   *A Glass of Beer*

THE lanky hank of a she in the inn over there
      Nearly killed me for asking the loan of a glass of beer;
May the devil grip the whey-faced slut by the hair,
And beat bad manners out of her skin for a year.

That parboiled ape, with the toughest jaw you will see
On virtue's path, and a voice that would rasp the dead,
Came roaring and raging the minute she looked at me,
And threw me out of the house on the back of my head!

If I asked her master he'd give me a cask a day;
But she, with the beer at hand, not a gill would arrange!
May she marry a ghost and bear him a kitten, and may
The High King of Glory permit her to get the mange.

(From the Irish.)

210   *Egan O Rahilly*

HERE in a distant place I hold my tongue;
      I am O Rahilly!

When I was young,
Who now am young no more,

I did not eat things picked up from the shore:
The periwinkle, and the tough dog-fish
At even-tide have got into my dish!

The great, where are they now! the great had said —
This is not seemly! Bring to him instead
That which serves his and serves our dignity —
And that was done.

I am O Rahilly!
Here in a distant place he holds his tongue,
Who once said all his say, when he was young!
(From the Irish.)

211   *Inis Fál*

NOW may we turn aside and dry our tears!
And comfort us! And lay aside our fears,
For all is gone!

All comely quality!
All gentleness and hospitality!
All courtesy and merriment

Is gone!
Our virtues, all, are withered every one!
Our music vanished, and our skill to sing!

Now may we quiet us and quit our moan!
Nothing is whole that could be broke! No thing
Remains to us of all that was our own.
(From the Irish.)

212 *The Rivals*

I HEARD a bird at dawn
   Singing sweetly on a tree,
That the dew was on the lawn,
And the wind was on the lea;
But I didn't listen to him,
For he didn't sing to me!

I didn't listen to him,
For he didn't sing to me
That the dew was on the lawn,
And the wind was on the lea!
I was singing at the time,
Just as prettily as he!

I was singing all the time,
Just as prettily as he,
About the dew upon the lawn,
And the wind upon the lea!
So I didn't listen to him,
As he sang upon a tree!

213 *In the Night*

THERE always is a noise when it is dark!
   It is the noise of silence, and the noise
Of blindness!

The noise of silence, and the noise of blindness
Do frighten me!
They hold me stark and rigid as a tree!

These frighten me!
These hold me stark and rigid as a tree!
Because at last their tumult is more loud
Than thunder!

Because
Their tumult is more loud than thunder,
They terrify my soul!   They tear
My heart asunder!

214   *The Main-deep*

THE long-rólling,
         Steady-póuring,
Deep-trenchéd
Green billów:

The wide-topped,
Unbróken,
Green-glacid,
Slow-sliding,

Cold-flushing,
— On — on — on —
Chill-rushing,
Hush — hushing,

. . . Hush — hushing . . .

SHRI PUROHIT SWAMI
                                       1882–
215   *I Know that I am a Great Sinner*

I KNOW that I am a great sinner,
   That there is no remedy,
But let Thy will be done.
If my Lord wishes He need not speak to me.
All I ask is that of His bounty

He walk by my side through my life.
I will behave well
Though He never embrace me —
O Lord, Thou art my Master
And I Thy slave.

(From his own Hindi.)

216
Shall I do this

SHALL I do this?
Shall I do that?
My hands are empty,
All that talk amounts to nothing.
Never will I do anything,
Never, never will I do anything;
Having been commanded to woo Thee
I should keep myself wide awake
Or else sleep away my life.
I am unfit to do the first,
But I can sleep with open eyes,
And I can always pretend to laugh,
And I can weep for the state I am in;
But my laugh has gone for good,
And gone the charm of tears.

(From his own Urdu.)

217
A Miracle indeed

A MIRACLE indeed!
Thou art Lord of All Power.
I asked a little power,
Thou gavest me a begging-bowl.

(From his own Urdu.)

224

JAMES ELROY FLECKER

1884–1915

Santorin

(*A Legend of the Ægean*)

WHO are you, Sea Lady,
    And where in the seas are we?
I have too long been steering
By the flashes in your eyes.
Why drops the moonlight through my heart,
And why so quietly
Go the great engines of my boat
As if their souls were free? '
' Oh ask me not, bold sailor;
Is not your ship a magic ship
That sails without a sail:
Are not these isles the Isles of Greece
And dust upon the sea?
But answer me three questions
And give me answers three.
What is your ship? ' ' A British.'
' And where may Britain be? '
' Oh it lies north, dear lady;
It is a small country.'

' Yet you will know my lover,
Though you live far away:
And you will whisper where he has gone,
That lily boy to look upon
And whiter than the spray.'
' How should I know your lover,
Lady of the sea? '

'Alexander, Alexander,
The King of the World was he.'
'Weep not for him, dear lady,
But come aboard my ship.
So many years ago he died,
He 's dead as dead can be.'
'O base and brutal sailor
To lie this lie to me.
His mother was the foam-foot
Star-sparkling Aphrodite;
His father was Adonis
Who lives away in Lebanon,
In stony Lebanon, where blooms
His red anemone.
But where is Alexander,
The soldier Alexander,
My golden love of olden days
The King of the world and me? '

She sank into the moonlight
And the sea was only sea.

219   *The Old Ships*

I HAVE seen old ships sail like swans asleep
   Beyond the village which men still call Tyre,
With leaden age o'ercargoed, dipping deep
For Famagusta and the hidden sun
That rings black Cyprus with a lake of fire;
And all those ships were certainly so old
Who knows how oft with squat and noisy gun,
Questing brown slaves or Syrian oranges,
The pirate Genoese

226

Hell-raked them till they rolled
Blood, water, fruit and corpses up the hold.
But now through friendly seas they softly run,
Painted the mid-sea blue or shore-sea green,
Still patterned with the vine and grapes in gold.

But I have seen,
Pointing her shapely shadows from the dawn
And image tumbled on a rose-swept bay,
A drowsy ship of some yet older day;
And, wonder's breath indrawn,
Thought I — who knows — who knows — but in that
    same
(Fished up beyond Ææa, patched up new
— Stern painted brighter blue —)
That talkative, bald-headed seaman came
(Twelve patient comrades sweating at the oar)
From Troy's doom-crimson shore,
And with great lies about his wooden horse
Set the crew laughing, and forgot his course.

It was so old a ship — who knows, who knows?
— And yet so beautiful, I watched in vain
To see the mast burst open with a rose,
And the whole deck put on its leaves again.

220 *The Golden Journey to Samarkand*
PROLOGUE

WE who with songs beguile your pilgrimage
    And swear that Beauty lives though lilies die,
We Poets of the proud old lineage
    Who sing to find your hearts, we know not why, —

What shall we tell you?   Tales, marvellous tales
   Of ships and stars and isles where good men rest,
Where nevermore the rose of sunset pales,
   And winds and shadows fall toward the West:

And there the world's first huge white-bearded kings
   In dim glades sleeping, murmur in their sleep,
And closer round their breasts the ivy clings,
   Cutting its pathway slow and red and deep.

(*ii*)

And how beguile you?   Death has no repose
   Warmer and deeper than that Orient sand
Which hides the beauty and bright faith of those
   Who made the Golden Journey to Samarkand.

And now they wait and whiten peaceably,
   Those conquerors, those poets, those so fair:
They know time comes, not only you and I,
   But the whole world shall whiten, here or there;

When those long caravans that cross the plain
   With dauntless feet and sound of silver bells
Put forth no more for glory or for gain,
   Take no more solace from the palm-girt wells.

When the great markets by the sea shut fast
   All that calm Sunday that goes on and on:
When even lovers find their peace at last,
   And Earth is but a star, that once had shone.

228

GEOFFREY SCOTT

1884–1929

221 *From ' The Skaian Gate '*

HECTOR, the captain bronzed, from simple fight
Passing to herd his trembling pallid host,
Scorned a blind beggar in the Skaian Gate,
Rattled a blade, then flung his rags a gift.
And, turning his void eyes to the black sun,
In price of alms the beggar prayed — ' Long light,
Loud name attend, O captain, your stern ghost:
Blind prayers may not be lost,
For of each one
Zeus keeps the count and token.'

Homer blind
Filled the huge world with Hector like a wind.
Comely, clean of the crust
Of Earth like bud from a root,
Blade clear of its rust,
Smouldering crest afire,
Out of darkness.   From dust
Iron risen in ire;
To a lifted horn's long note
Hector 's afoot!

Words ghostly; the windy ones;
Thin tones: — outwearing stones
Tall Troy and Skaian Gate
Helen and Hector's hate —
Mouth of air; ghost of breath;
What a stone you have builded, what bronze
You have moulded, blown out of death!

222 *What was Solomon's Mind?*

WHAT was Solomon's mind?
If he was wise in truth,
'Twas something hard to find
And delicate: a mouse
Tingling, and small, and smooth,
Hid in vast haunted house.

By smallness quite beset —
Stillest when most alive —
Shrinking to smaller yet
And livelier, until,
Gladly diminutive,
Still smoother, and more still,

He centres to an Eye,
A clean expectancy,
That, from the narrow black
Safe velvet of his crack,
Quivering, quiet, dumb,
Drinks up the lighted room.

223 *All our Joy is enough*

ALL we make is enough
Barely to seem
A bee's din,
A beetle-scheme —
Sleepy stuff
For God to dream:
Begin.

GEOFFREY SCOTT

All our joy is enough
At most to fill
A thimble cup
A little wind puff
Can shake, can spill:
Fill it up;
Be still.

All we know is enough;
Though written wide,
Small spider yet
With tangled stride
Will soon be off
The page's side:
Forget.

Frutta di Mare

I AM a sea-shell flung
Up from the ancient sea;
Now I lie here, among
Roots of a tamarisk tree;
No one listens to me.

I sing to myself all day
In a husky voice, quite low,
Things the great fishes say
And you most need to know;
All night I sing just so.

But lift me from the ground,
And hearken at my rim,
Only your sorrow's sound
Amazed, perplexed and dim,
Comes coiling to the brim;

For what the wise whales ponder
Awaking out from sleep,
The key to all your wonder,
The answers of the deep,
These to myself I keep.

SIR JOHN SQUIRE

1884–

225   *Ballade of the Poetic Life*

THE fat men go about the streets,
    The politicians play their game,
The prudent bishops sound retreats
    And think the martyrs much to blame;
    Honour and love are halt and lame
And Greed and Power are deified,
    The wild are harnessed by the tame;
For this the poets lived and died.

Shelley 's a trademark used on sheets:
    Aloft the sky in words of flame
We read ' What porridge had John Keats?
    Why, Brown's!   A hundred years the same! '
    Arcadia 's an umbrella frame,
Milton 's a toothpaste; from the tide
    Sappho 's been dredged to rouge my Dame —
For this the poets lived and died.

And yet, to launch ideal fleets
    Lost regions in the stars to claim,
To face all ruins and defeats,
    To sing a beaten world to shame,
    To hold each bright impossible aim
Deep in the heart; to starve in pride
    For fame, and never know their fame —
For this the poets lived and died.

Envoi

    Princess, inscribe beneath my name
' He never begged, he never sighed,
    He took his medicine as it came ' —
For this the poets lived — and died.

WILLIAM FORCE STEAD

1884–

226   *How Infinite are Thy Ways*

I THOUGHT the night without a sound was falling;
    But standing still,
No stem or leaf I stirred,
And soon in the hedge a cricket chirred;
A robin filled a whole silence with calling;
An owl went hovering by,
Haunting the spacious twilight with tremulous cry;
Far off where the woods were dark
A ranging dog began to bark;
Down by the water-mill,
A cock, boasting his might,
Shouted a loud good-night;
A heifer lowed upon the lone-tree hill.

I had not known, were I not still,
How infinite are Thy ways.
I wondered what Thy life could be,
O Thou unknown Immensity:
Voice after voice, and every voice was Thine.
So I stood wondering,
Until a child began to sing,
Going late home, awed by the gathering haze. . . .
I said, Her life at one with Thine,
At one with mine.
But compassing Thy many voices now,
Lo I, somehow,
Am Thou.

227   *I closed my Eyes To-day and saw*

I CLOSED my eyes to-day and saw
A dark land fringed with flame,
A sky of grey with ochre swirls
Down to the dark land came.

No wind, no sound, no man, no bird,
No grass, no hill, no wood:
Tall as a pine amid the plain
One giant sunflower stood.

Its disk was large with ripened seed:
A red line on the grey,
The flames, as yet afar, I knew
Would gnaw the world away.

234

WILLIAM FORCE STEAD

In vain the seeds were ripe; the stem,
   With singed leaves hung around,
Relaxed; and all the big flower stooped
   And stared upon the ground.

DAVID HERBERT LAWRENCE
1885–1930

228   *Work*

THERE is no point in work
   unless it absorbs you
   like an absorbing game.

If it doesn't absorb you
if it 's never any fun,
   don't do it.

When a man goes out into his work
he is alive like a tree in spring,
he is living, not merely working.

When the Hindus weave thin wool into long, long lengths
   of stuff
with their thin dark hands and their wide dark eyes and
   their still souls absorbed
they are like slender trees putting forth leaves, a long white
   web of living leaf,
      the tissue they weave,
and they clothe themselves in white as a tree clothes itself in
   its own foliage.

235

As with cloth, so with houses, ships, shoes, wagons or cups or
 loaves.
Men might put them forth as a snail its shell, as a bird that
 leans
   its breast against its nest, to make it round,
as the turnip models his round root, as the bush makes
 flowers and gooseberries,
   putting them forth, not manufacturing them,
and cities might be as once they were, bowers grown out
 from the busy bodies of people.
And so it will be again, men will smash the machines.

At last, for the sake of clothing himself in his own leaf-like
 cloth
   tissued from his life,
and dwelling in his own bowery house, like a beaver's
 nibbled mansion
and drinking from cups that came off his fingers like flowers
 off their five-fold stem,
he will cancel the machines we have got.

229   *Hymn to Priapus*

M Y love lies underground
  With her face upturned to mine,
And her mouth unclosed in a last long kiss
That ended her life and mine.

 I dance at the Christmas party
 Under the mistletoe
 Along with a ripe, slack country lass
 Jostling to and fro.

DAVID HERBERT LAWRENCE

The big, soft country lass,
Like a loose sheaf of wheat
Slipped through my arms on the threshing floor
At my feet.

The warm, soft country lass,
Sweet as an armful of wheat
At threshing-time broken, was broken
For me, and ah, it was sweet!

Now I am going home
Fulfilled and alone,
I see the great Orion standing
Looking down.

He 's the star of my first beloved
Love-making.
The witness of all that bitter-sweet
Heart-aching.

Now he sees this as well,
This last commission.
Nor do I get any look
Of admonition.

He can add the reckoning up
I suppose, between now and then,
Having walked himself in the thorny, difficult
Ways of men.

He has done as I have done
No doubt:
Remembered and forgotten
Turn and about.

237

My love lies underground
With her face upturned to mine,
And her mouth unclosed in the last long kiss
That ended her life and mine.

She fares in the stark immortal
Fields of death;
I in these goodly, frozen
Fields beneath.

Something in me remembers
And will not forget.
The stream of my life in the darkness
Deathward set!

And something in me has forgotten,
Has ceased to care.
Desire comes up, and contentment
Is debonair.

I, who am worn and careful,
How much do I care?
How is it I grin then, and chuckle
Over despair?

Grief, grief, I suppose and sufficient
Grief makes us free
To be faithless and faithful together
As we have to be.

230   *Twilight*

DARKNESS comes out of the earth
    And swallows dip into the pallor of the west;
From the hay comes the clamour of children's mirth;
    Wanes the old palimpsest.

DAVID HERBERT LAWRENCE

The night-stock oozes scent,
    And a moon-blue moth goes flittering by:
All that the worldly day has meant
    Wastes like a lie.

The children have forsaken their play;
    A single star in a veil of light
Glimmers: litter of day
    Is gone from sight.

231   *Suburbs on a Hazy Day*

O STIFFLY shapen houses that change not,
    What conjurer's cloth was thrown across you, and raised
To show you thus transfigured, changed,
    Your stuff all gone, your menace almost rased?

Such resolute shapes so harshly set
    In hollow blocks and cubes deformed, and heaped
In void and null profusion, how is this?
    In what strong aqua regia now are you steeped?

That you lose the brick-stuff out of you
    And hover like a presentment, fading faint
And vanquished, evaporate away
    To leave but only the merest possible taint!

232   *Sorrow*

WHY does the thin grey strand
    Floating up from the forgotten
Cigarette between my fingers,
Why does it trouble me?

Ah, you will understand;
When I carried my mother downstairs,
A few times only, at the beginning
Of her soft-foot malady,

I should find, for a reprimand
To my gaiety, a few long grey hairs
On the breast of my coat; and one by one
I watched them float up the dark chimney.

233 *In Trouble and Shame*

I LOOK at the swaling sunset
And wish I could go also
Through the red doors beyond the black-purple bar.

I wish that I could go
Through the red doors where I could put off
    My shame like shoes in the porch,
    My pain like garments,
And leave my flesh discarded lying
Like luggage of some departed traveller
    Gone one knows not whither.

Then I would turn round,
And seeing my cast-off body lying like lumber,
    I would laugh with joy.

EZRA POUND

1885–

234 *The River-merchant's Wife: a Letter*

WHILE my hair was still cut straight across my fore-
    head
I played about the front gate, pulling flowers.
You came by on bamboo stilts, playing horse,
You walked about my seat, playing with blue plums.
And we went on living in the village of Chokan:
Two small people, without dislike or suspicion.

At fourteen I married My Lord you.
I never laughed, being bashful.
Lowering my head, I looked at the wall.
Called to, a thousand times, I never looked back.

At fifteen I stopped scowling,
I desired my dust to be mingled with yours
Forever and forever and forever.
Why should I climb the look out?

At sixteen you departed,
You went into far Ku-to-yen, by the river of swirling eddies,
And you have been gone five months.
The monkeys make sorrowful noise overhead.

You dragged your feet when you went out.
By the gate now, the moss is grown, the different mosses,
Too deep to clear them away!
The leaves fall early this autumn, in wind.
The paired butterflies are already yellow with August
Over the grass in the West garden;

They hurt me. I grow older.
If you are coming down through the narrows of the river
    Kiang,
Please let me know beforehand,
And I will come out to meet you
                As far as Cho-fu-Sa.
                     (From the Chinese of Rihaku.)

235   *From 'Homage to Sextus*
                Propertius'

WHEN, when, and whenever death closes our eyelids,
    Moving naked over Acheron
Upon the one raft, victor and conquered together,
Marius and Jugurtha together,
                one tangle of shadows.
Caesar plots against India,
Tigris and Euphrates shall, from now on, flow at his bidding,
Tibet shall be full of Roman policemen,
The Parthians shall get used to our statuary
                and acquire a Roman religion;

One raft on the veiled flood of Acheron,
        Marius and Jugurtha together.
Nor at my funeral either will there be any long trail,
            bearing ancestral lares and images;
No trumpets filled with my emptiness,
Nor shall it be on an Atalic bed;
        The perfumed cloths shall be absent.
A small plebeian procession.
        Enough, enough and in plenty
There will be three books at my obsequies
Which I take, my not unworthy gift, to Persephone.

You will follow the bare scarified breast
Nor will you be weary of calling my name, nor too weary
      To place the last kiss on my lips
When the Syrian onyx is broken.

      ' He who is now vacant dust
       ' Was once the slave of one passion: '
Give that much inscription
        ' Death why tardily come? '

You, sometimes, will lament a lost friend,
     For it is a custom:
This care for past men,

Since Adonis was gored in Idalia, and the Cytherean
Ran crying with out-spread hair,
     In vain, you call back the shade,
In vain, Cynthia. Vain call to unanswering shadow,
     Small talk comes from small bones.

236   *Canto XVII*

SO that the vines burst from my fingers
 And the bees weighted with pollen
Move heavily in the vine-shoots:
     chirr — chirr — chir-rikk — a purring sound,
And the birds sleepily in the branches.
     ZAGREUS! IO ZAGREUS!
With the first pale-clear of the heaven
And the cities set in their hills,
And the goddess of the fair knees
Moving there, with the oak-wood behind her,

The green slope, with white hounds
                leaping about her;
And thence down to the creek's mouth, until evening,
Flat water before me,
        and the trees growing in water,
Marble trunks out of stillness,
On past the palazzi,
                in the stillness,
The light now, not of the sun.
              Chrysoprase,
And the water green clear, and blue clear;
On, to the great cliffs of amber.

                      Between them,

Cave of Nerea,
      she like a great shell curved,
And the boat drawn without sound,
Without odour of ship-work,
Nor bird-cry, nor any noise of wave moving,
Nor splash of porpoise, nor any noise of wave moving,
Within her cave, Nerea,
                  she like a great shell curved
In the suavity of the rock,
                cliff green-gray in the far,
In the near, the gate-cliffs of amber,
And the wave
           green clear, and blue clear,
And the cave salt-white, and glare-purple,
        cool, porphyry smooth,
        the rock sea-worn.
No gull-cry, no sound of porpoise,
Sand as of malachite, and no cold there,
        the light not of the sun.

Zagreus, feeding his panthers,
        the turf clear as on hills under light.
And under the almond-trees, gods,
        with them, *choros nympharum*. Gods,
Hermes and Athene,
            As shaft of compass,
Between them, trembled —
To the left is the place of fauns,
        sylva nympharum;
The low wood, moor-scrub,
        the doe, the young spotted deer,
        leap up through the broom-plants,
           as dry leaf amid yellow.
And by one cut of the hills,
        the great alley of Memnons.
Beyond, sea, crests seen over dune
Night sea churning shingle,
To the left, the alley of cypress.

                A boat came,
One man holding her sail,
Guiding her with oar caught over gunwale, saying:
        ' There, in the forest of marble,
        the stone trees — out of water —
        the arbours of stone —
        marble leaf, over leaf,
        silver, steel over steel,
        silver beaks rising and crossing,
        prow set against prow,
        stone, ply over ply,
        the gilt beams flare of an evening '
Borso, Carmagnola, the men of craft, *i vitrei*,
Thither, at one time, time after time,

And the waters richer than glass,
Bronze gold, the blaze over the silver,
Dye-pots in the torch-light,
The flash of wave under prows,
And the silver beaks rising and crossing.
   Stone trees, white and rose-white in the darkness,
Cypress there by the towers,
   Drift under hulls in the night.

    ' In the gloom the gold
Gathers the light about it.' . . .

Now supine in burrow, half over-arched bramble,
One eye for the sea, through that peek-hole,
Gray light, with Athene.
Zothar and her elephants, the gold loin-cloth,
The sistrum, shaken, shaken,
   the cohort of her dancers.
And Aletha, by bend of the shore,
    with her eyes seaward,
    and in her hands sea-wrack
Salt-bright with the foam.
Koré through the bright meadow,
    with green-gray dust in the grass:
' For this hour, brother of Circe.'
Arm laid over my shoulder,
Saw the sun for three days, the sun fulvid,
As a lion lift over sand-plain;
     and that day,
And for three days, and none after,
Splendour, as the splendour of Hermes,
And shipped thence
    to the stone place,

EZRA POUND

Pale white, over water,
      known water,
And the white forest of marble, bent bough over bough,
The pleached arbour of stone,
Thither Borso, when they shot the barbed arrow at him,
And Carmagnola, between the two columns,
Sigismundo, after that wreck in Dalmatia.
  Sunset like the grasshopper flying.

ARTHUR WALEY

237   *The Temple*

AUTUMN: the ninth year of Yüan Ho;[1]
 The eighth month, and the moon swelling her arc;
It was then I travelled to the Temple of Wu-chēn,
A temple terraced on Wang Shun's Hill.
While still the mountain was many leagues away,
Of scurrying waters we heard the plash and fret.
From here the traveller, leaving carriage and horse,
Begins to wade through the shallows of the Blue Stream,
His hand pillared on a green holly-staff,
His feet treading the torrent's white stones.
A strange quiet stole on ears and eyes,
That knew no longer the blare of the human world.
From mountain-foot gazing at mountain-top,
Now we doubted if indeed it could be climbed;
Who had guessed that a path deep hidden there
Twisting and bending crept to the topmost brow?
Under the flagstaff we made our first halt;

    [1] A.D. 814.

Next we rested in the shadow of the Stone Shrine.[1]
The shrine-room was scarce a cubit long,
With doors and windows unshuttered and unbarred.
I peered down, but could not see the dead;
Stalactites hung like a woman's hair.
Waked from sleep, a pair of white bats
Fled from the coffin with a whirr of snowy wings.
I turned away, and saw the Temple gate —
Scarlet eaves flanked by steeps of green;
'Twas as though a hand had ripped the mountain-side
And filled the cleft with a temple's walls and towers.
Within the gate, no level ground;
Little ground, but much empty sky.
Cells and cloisters, terraces and spires
High and low, followed the jut of the hill.
On rocky plateaux with no earth to hold
Were trees and shrubs, gnarled and very lean.
Roots and stems stretched to grip the stone;
Humped and bent, they writhed like a coiling snake.
In broken ranks pine and cassia stood,
Through the four seasons forever shady-green.
On tender twigs and delicate branches breathing
A quiet music played like strings in the wind.
Never pierced by the light of sun or moon,
Green locked with green, shade clasping shade.
A hidden bird sometimes softly sings;
Like a cricket's chirp sounds its muffled song.

At the Strangers' Arbour a while we stayed our steps;
We sat down, but had no mind to rest.
In a little while we had opened the northern door.

[1] Where the mummified bodies of priests were kept, in
miniature temples.

Ten thousand leagues suddenly stretched at our feet!
Brushing the eaves, shredded rainbows swept;
Circling the beams, clouds spun and whirled.
Through red sunlight white rain fell;
Azure and storm swam in a blended stream.
In a wild green clustered grasses and trees,
The eye's orbit swallowed the plain of Ch'in.
Wei River was too small to see;
The Mounds of Han,[1] littler than a clenched fist.
I looked back; a line of red fence,
Broken and twisting, marked the way we had trod.
Far below, toiling one by one,
Later climbers straggled on the face of the hill.

Straight before me were many Treasure Towers,
Whose wind-bells at the four corners sang.
At door and window, cornice and architrave,
' Kap, kap,' the tinkle of gold and jade.
Some say that here the Buddha Kāśyapa [2]
Long ago quitted Life and Death.
Still they keep his iron begging-bowl,
With the furrow of his fingers chiselled deep at the base.
To the east there opens the Jade Image Hall,
Where white Buddhas sit like serried trees.
We shook from our garments the journey's grime and dust,
And bowing worshipped those faces of frozen snow
Whose white cassocks like folded hoar-frost hung,
Whose beaded crowns glittered like a shower of hail.
We looked closer; surely Spirits willed
This handicraft, never chisel carved!

[1] The tombs of the Han Emperors.
[2] Lived about 600,000,000,000 years ago and achieved
Buddhahood at the age of 20,000.

Next we climbed to the Chamber of Kuan-yin; [1]
From afar we sniffed its odours of sandal-wood.
At the top of the steps each doffed his shoes;
With bated stride we crossed the Jasper Hall.
The Jewelled Mirror on six pillars propped,
The Four Seats cased in hammered gold
Through the black night glowed with beams of their own,
Nor had we need to light candle or lamp.
These many treasures in concert nodded and swayed —
Banners of coral, pendants of cornaline.
When the wind came, jewels chimed and sang
Softly, softly like the music of Paradise.
White pearls like frozen dewdrops hanging;
Dark rubies spilt like clots of blood,
Spangled and sown on the Buddha's twisted hair,
Together fashioned his Sevenfold Jewel-crown.
In twin vases of pallid tourmaline
(Their colour colder than the waters of an autumn stream)
The calcined relics of Buddha's Body rest —
Rounded pebbles, smooth as the Specular Stone.
A jade flute, by angels long ago
Borne as a gift to the Garden of Jetavan! [2]
It blows a music sweet as the crane's song
That Spirits of Heaven earthward well might draw.

It was at autumn's height,
The fifteenth day and the moon's orbit full.
Wide I flung the three eastern gates;

[1] One of the self-denying Bodhisattvas who abstain from
entering Buddhahood in order better to assist erring humanity.
In Sanskrit, Avalokiteśvara.
[2] Near Benares; here Buddha preached most of his Sūtras
and the first monastery was founded.

A golden spectre walked at the chapel-door.
And jewel-beams now with moonbeams strove
In freshness and beauty darting a crystal light
That cooled the spirit and limbs of those it touched,
Nor all night-long needed they to rest.
At dawn I sought the road to the Southern Tope,
Where wild bamboos nodded in clustered grace.
In the lonely forest no one crossed my path;
Beside me faltered a cold butterfly.

Mountain fruits whose names I did not know
With their prodigal bushes hedged the pathway in;
The hungry here copious food had found;
Idly I plucked, to test sour and sweet.

South of the road, the Spirit of the Blue Dell,[1]
With his green umbrella and white paper pence!
When the year is closing, the people are ordered to grow,
As herbs of offering, marsil and motherwort;
So sacred the place, that never yet was stained
Its pure earth with sacrificial blood.

In a high cairn four or five rocks
Dangerously heaped, deep-scarred and heeling —
With what purpose did he that made the World
Pile them here at the eastern corner of the cliff?
Their slippery flank no foot has marked,
But mosses stipple like a flowered writing-scroll.
I came to the cairn, I climbed it right to the top;
Beneath my feet a measureless chasm dropped.
My eyes were dizzy, hand and knee quogged —
I did not dare bend my head and look.

[1] A native, non-Buddhist deity.

251

A boisterous wind rose from under the rocks,
Seized me with it and tore the ground from my feet.
My shirt and robe fanned like mighty wings,
And wide-spreading bore me like a bird to the sky.
High about me, triangular and sharp,
Like a cluster of sword-points many summits rose.
The white mist that struck them in its airy course
They tore asunder, and carved a patch of blue.

And now the sun was sinking in the north-west;
His evening beams from a crimson globe he shed,
Till far beyond the great fields of green
His sulphurous disk suddenly down he drove.

And now the moon was rising in the south-east;
In waves of coolness the night air flowed.
From the grey bottom of the hundred-fathom pool
Shines out the image of the moon's golden disk!
Blue as its name, the Lan River flows
Singing and plashing forever day and night.
I gazed down; like a green finger-ring
In winding circuits it follows the curves of the hill;
Sometimes spreading to a wide, lazy stream,
Sometimes striding to a foamy cataract.
Out from the deepest and clearest pool of all,
In a strange froth the Dragon's-spittle [1] flows.

I bent down; a dangerous ladder of stones
Paved beneath me a sheer and dizzy path.
I gripped the ivy, I walked on fallen trees,
Tracking the monkeys who came to drink at the stream.
Like a whirl of snowflakes the startled herons rose,
In damask dances the red sturgeon leapt.

[1] Ambergris.

For a while I rested, then plunging in the cool stream,
From my weary body I washed the stains away.
Deep or shallow, all was crystal clear;
I watched through the water my own thighs and feet.
Content I gazed at the stream's clear bed;
Wondered, but knew not, whence its waters flowed.

The eastern bank with rare stones is rife;
In serried courses the dusky chrysoprase,
That outward turns a smooth, glossy face;
In its deep core secret diamonds [1] lie.
Pien of Ch'u [2] died long ago,
And rare gems are often cast aside.
Sometimes a radiance leaks from the hill by night
To link its beams with the brightness of moon and stars.

At the central dome, where the hills highest rise,
The sky is pillared on a column of green jade;
Where even the spotty lizard cannot climb
Can I, a man, foothold hope to find?
In the top is hollowed the White-lotus lake;
With purple cusps the clear waves are crowned.
The name I heard, but the place I could not reach;
Beyond the region of mortal things it lies.

And standing here, a flat rock I saw,
Cubit-square, like a great paving-stone,
Midway up fastened in the cliff-wall;
And down below it, a thousand-foot drop.

[1] The stone mentioned (*yü-fan*), though praised by Confucius and used in the ceremonies of his native state, cannot be identified. Its name evokes vague ideas of rarity and beauty.

[2] Suffered mutilation because he had offered to his prince a gem which experts rejected. Afterwards it turned out to be genuine.

Here they say that a Master in ancient days
Sat till he conquered the concepts of Life and Death.
The place is called the Settled Heart Stone;
By aged men the tale is still told.

I turned back to the Shrine of Fairies' Tryst;
Thick creepers covered its old walls.
Here it was that a mortal [1] long ago
On new-grown wings flew to the dark sky;
Westward a garden of agaric and rue
Faces the terrace where his magic herbs were dried.
And sometimes still on clear moonlit nights
In the sky is heard a yellow crane's voice.

I turned and sought the Painted Dragon Hall,
Where the bearded figures of two ancient men
By the Holy Lectern at sermon-time are seen
In gleeful worship to nod their hoary heads;
Who, going home to their cave beneath the river,
Of weather-dragons the writhing shapes assume.
When rain is coming they puff a white smoke
In front of the steps, from a round hole in the stone.

Once a priest who copied the Holy Books
(Of purpose dauntless and body undefiled)
Loved yonder pigeons, that far beyond the clouds
Fly in flocks beating a thousand wings.
They came and dropped him water in his writing-bowl;
Then sipped afresh in the river under the rocks.
Each day thrice they went and came,
Nor ever once missed their wonted time.
When the Book was finished, he was named 'Holy Priest';
For like glory in vain his fellows vied.

[1] The wizard Wang Shun, after whom the hill is named.

He sang the hymns of the Lotus Blossom Book,[1]
Again and again, a thousand, a million times.
His body withered, but his mouth still was strong,
Till his tongue turned to a red lotus-flower.
   His bones no more are seen;
But the rock where he sat is still carved with his fame.

On a plastered wall are frescoes from the hand of Wu,[2]
Whose pencil-colours never-fading glow.
On a white screen is writing by the master Ch'u,[3]
The tones subtle as the day it first dried.

Magical prospects, monuments divine —
   Now all were visited.
Here we had tarried five nights and days;
Yet homeward now with loitering footsteps trod.
I, that a man of the wild hills was born,
Floundering fell into the web of the World's net.
Caught in its trammels, they forced me to study books;
Twitched and tore me down the path of public life.
Soon I rose to be Bachelor of Arts;
In the Record Office, in the Censorate I sat.
My simple bluntness did not suit the times;
A profitless servant, I drew the royal pay.
The sense of this made me always ashamed,
And every pleasure a deep brooding dimmed.
To little purpose I sapped my heart's strength,
Till seeming age shrank my youthful frame.
From the very hour I doffed belt and cap
I marked how with them sorrow slank away.

[1] The verses of the Saddharmapundarīka Sūtra, *Sacred Books of the East*, vol. 21.

[2] The great eighth-century painter, Wu Tao-tzŭ.

[3] The calligrapher, Ch'u Sui-liang, A.D. 596–658.

But now that I wander in the freedom of streams and hills
My heart to its folly comfortably yields.
Like a wild deer that has torn the hunter's net
I range abroad by no halters barred.
Like a captive fish loosed into the Great Sea
To my marble basin I shall not ever return.
My body girt in the hermit's single dress,
My hand holding the Book of Chuang Chou,
On these hills at last I am come to dwell,
Loosed forever from the shackles of a trim world.
I have lived in labour forty years and more;
If Life's remnant vacantly I spend,
Seventy being our span, then thirty years
Of idleness are still left to live.

(From the Chinese of Po Chü-i.)

FRANCES CORNFORD

1886–

238 *A Glimpse*

O GRASSES wet with dew, yellow fallen leaves,
  Smooth-shadowed waters Milton loved, green banks,
Arched bridges, rooks, and rain-leaved willow-trees,
Stone, serious familiar colleges,
For ever mine.
The figure of a scholar carrying back
Books to the library — absorbed, content,
Seeming as everlasting as the elms
Bark-wrinkled, puddled round their roots, the bells,
And the far shouting in the football fields.

The same since I was born, the same to be
When all my children's children grow old men.

256

FRANCES CORNFORD

239   *London Despair*

THIS endless gray-roofed city, and each heart —
   Each with its problems, urgent and apart —
And hearts unborn that wait to come again,
Each to its problems, urgent, and such pain.

Why cannot all of us together — why? —
Achieve the one simplicity: to die?

240   *Near an old Prison*

WHEN we would reach the anguish of the dead,
   Whose bones alone, irrelevant, are dust,
Out of ourselves it seems we must, we must
To some obscure but ever-bleeding thing
Unreconciled, a needed solace bring,
Like a resolving chord, like daylight shed.

Or through thick time must we reach back in vain
To inaccessible pain?

241   *To a Fat Lady seen from the Train*

O WHY do you walk through the fields in gloves,
   Missing so much and so much?
O fat white woman whom nobody loves,
Why do you walk through the fields in gloves,
When the grass is soft as the breast of doves
     And shivering-sweet to the touch?
O why do you walk through the fields in gloves,
     Missing so much and so much?

1886–

242 *When I'm alone*

'WHEN I'm alone' — the words tripped off his tongue
    As though to be alone were nothing strange.
'*When I was young,*' he said; '*when I was young. . . .*'

I thought of age, and loneliness, and change.
I thought how strange we grow when we're alone,
And how unlike the selves that meet, and talk,
And blow the candles out, and say good-night.
Alone . . . The word is life endured and known.
It is the stillness where our spirits walk
And all but inmost faith is overthrown.

243 *Grandeur of Ghosts*

WHEN I have heard small talk about great men
    I climb to bed; light my two candles; then
Consider what was said; and put aside
What Such-a-one remarked and Someone-else replied.

They have spoken lightly of my deathless friends,
(Lamps for my gloom, hands guiding where I stumble,)
Quoting, for shallow conversational ends,
What Shelley shrilled, what Blake once wildly muttered. . . .

How can they use such names and be not humble?
I have sat silent; angry at what they uttered.
The dead bequeathed them life; the dead have said
What these can only memorize and mumble.

258

244   *On Passing the New Menin Gate*

WHO will remember, passing through this Gate,
　　The unheroic Dead who fed the guns?
Who shall absolve the foulness of their fate, —
Those doomed, conscripted, unvictorious ones?
　　Crudely renewed, the Salient holds its own.
　　Paid are its dim defenders by this pomp;
　　Paid, with a pile of peace-complacent stone,
　　The armies who endured that sullen swamp.

Here was the world's worst wound. And here with pride
' Their name liveth for ever,' the Gateway claims.
Was ever an immolation so belied
As these intolerably nameless names?
Well might the Dead who struggled in the slime
Rise and deride this sepulchre of crime.

245   *The Power and the Glory*

LET *there be life*, said God. And what He wrought
　　Went past in myriad marching lives, and brought
This hour, this quiet room, and my small thought
Holding invisible vastness in its hands.

Let there be God, say I. And what I've done
Goes onward like the splendour of the sun
And rises up in rapture and is one
With the white power of conscience that commands.

Let life be God. . . . What wail of fiend or wraith
Dare mock my glorious angel where he stands
To fill my dark with fire, my heart with faith?

RUPERT BROOKE

246   *Clouds*

DOWN the blue night the unending columns press
   In noiseless tumult, break and wave and flow,
   Now tread the far South, or lift rounds of snow
Up to the white moon's hidden loveliness.
Some pause in their grave wandering comradeless,
   And turn with profound gesture vague and slow,
   As who would pray good for the world, but know
Their benediction empty as they bless.

They say that the Dead die not, but remain
   Near to the rich heirs of their grief and mirth.
      I think they ride the calm mid-heaven, as these,
In wise majestic melancholy train,
      And watch the moon, and the still-raging seas,
And men, coming and going on the earth.

EDITH SITWELL

1887–

247   *From 'The Sleeping Beauty'*
            To OSBERT

WHEN we come to that dark house,
   Never sound of wave shall rouse
The bird that sings within the blood
Of those who sleep in that deep wood,
For in that house the shadows now
Seem cast by some dark unknown bough.

EDITH SITWELL

The gardener plays his old bagpipe
To make the melons' gold seeds ripe;
The music swoons with a sad sound —
' Keep, my lad, to the good safe ground!
For once, long since, there was a felon
With guineas gold as the seeds of a melon,
And he would sail for a far strand
To seek a waking, clearer land, —
A land whose name is only heard
In the strange singing of a bird.
The sea was sharper than green grass,
The sailors would not let him pass,
For the sea was wroth and rose at him
Like the turreted walls of Jerusalem,
Or like the towers and gables seen
Within a deep-boughed garden green.
And the sailors bound and threw him down
Among those wrathful towers to drown.
And oh, far best,' the gardener said,
' Like fruits to lie in your kind bed, —
To sleep as snug as in the grave
In your kind bed, and shun the wave,
Nor ever sigh for a strange land
And songs no heart can understand.'

I hunted with the country gentlemen
Who, seeing Psyche fly, thought her a hen

And aimed at her; the mocking wingèd one
Laughed at their wingless state, their crooked gun.

Then on the water — green and jewelled leaves
Hiding ripe fruitage — every sportsman grieves,

EDITH SITWELL

Sitting and grumbling in their flat boat edged
With the soft feathers of the foam, scarce fledged.

But I will seek again the palace in the wood,
Where never bird shall rouse our sleepy blood

Within the bear-dark forests, far beyond
This hopeless hunting, or Time's sleepy bond.

The wicked fay descended, mopping, mowing
In her wide-hooped petticoat, her water-flowing

Brightly-perfumed silks. . . . ' Ah, ha, I see
You have remembered all the fays but me! '

(She whipped her panthers, golden as the shade
Of afternoon in some deep forest glade.)

' I am very cross because I am old,
And my tales are told,
And my flames jewel-cold.

' I will make your bright birds scream,
I will darken your jewelled dream,
I will spoil your thickest cream.

' I will turn the cream sour,
I will darken the bower,
I will look through the darkest shadows and lour, —

' And sleep as dark as the shade of a tree
Shall cover you. . . . Don't answer me!
For if the Princess prick her finger
Upon a spindle, then she shall be lost.'

*   *   *   *

DO, do,
Princess, do,
Like a tree that drips with gold you flow
With beauty ripening very slow.
Soon beneath that peaceful shade
The whole world dreaming will be laid.
Do, do,
Princess, do,
The years like soft winds come and go.

Do, do,
Princess, do,
How river-thick flow your fleecèd locks
Like the nymphs' music o'er the rocks. . . .
From satyr-haunted caverns drip
These lovely airs on brow and lip.
Do, do,
Princess, do,
Like a tree that drips with gold you flow.

248 *The Hambone and the Heart*
(*To* PAVEL TCHELITCHEW)
A Girl speaks:

HERE in this great house in the barrack square,
The plump and heart-shaped flames all stare
Like silver empty hearts in wayside shrines.
No flame warms ever, shines,
Nor may I ever tire.

Outside, the dust of all the dead,
Thick on the ground is spread
Covering the tinsel flowers
And pretty dove-quick hours,

Among the round leaves, Cupid-small
Upon the trees so wise and tall.
O dust of all the dead, my heart has known
That terrible Gehenna of the bone
Deserted by the flesh, — with Death alone!

Could we foretell the worm within the heart,
That holds the households and the parks of heaven,
Could we foretell that land was only earth,
Would it be worth the pain of death and birth,
Would it be worth the soul from body riven?

For here, my sight, my sun, my sense,
In my gown white as innocence,
I walked with you.   Ah, that my sun
Loved my heart less than carrion.

Alas!   I dreamed that the bare heart could feed
One who with death's corruption loved to breed, —
This Dead, who fell, that he might satisfy
The hungry grave's blind need, —

That Venus stinking of the Worm!
Deep in the grave, no passions storm:
The worm 's a pallid thing to kiss;
She is the hungering grave that is

Not filled, that is not satisfied!
Not all the sunken Dead that lies
Corrupt there, chills her luxuries.

And fleet, and volatile her kiss,
For all the grave's eternities!
And soon another Dead shall slake
Her passion, till that dust, too, break.

EDITH SITWELL

Like little pigeons small dove-breasted flowers,
Were cooing of far-off bird-footed showers,
My coral neck was pink as any rose
Or like the sweet pink honey-wax that grows,
Or the fresh coral beams of clear moonlight,
Where leaves like small doves flutter from our sight.

Beneath the twisted rose-boughs of the heat
Our shadows walked like little foreigners,
Like small unhappy children dressed in mourning,
They listened by the serres-chaudes waterfalls
But could not understand what we were saying,
Nor could we understand their whispered warning, —
There by the waterfalls we saw the Clown,
As tall as Heaven's golden town,
And in his hands, a Heart, and a Hambone
Pursued by loving vermin; but deserted, lone,
The Heart cried to my own:

The Heart speaks:

Young girl, you dance and laugh to see,
The thing that I have come to be.
Oh, once this heart was like your own.
Go, pray that yours may turn to stone.

This is the murdered heart of one
Who bore and loved an only son.
For him, I worked away mine eyes,
My starved breast could not still his cries.

My little lamb, of milk bereft . . .
My heart was all that I had left.
Ah, could I give thee this for food,
My lamb, thou knowest that I would.

265

Yet lovely was the summer light
Those days . . . I feel it through this night.
Once Judas had a childish kiss,
And still his mother knows but this.

He grew to manhood.   Then one came,
False-hearted as Hell's blackest shame
To steal my child from me, and thrust
The soul I loved down to the dust.

Her hungry wicked lips were red
As that dark blood my son's hand shed;
Her eyes were black as Hell's own night;
Her ice-cold breast was winter-white.

I had put by a little gold
To bury me when I was cold.
That fangèd wanton kiss to buy,
My son's love willed that I should die.

The gold was hid beneath my bed, —
So little, and my weary head
Was all the guard it had.   They lie
So quiet and still who soon must die.

He stole to kill me while I slept,
The little son who never wept,
But that I kissed his tears away
So fast, his weeping seemed but play.

So light his footfall.   Yet I heard
Its echo in my heart and stirred
From out my weary sleep to see
My child's face bending over me.

The wicked knife flashed serpent-wise,
Yet I saw nothing but his eyes
And heard one little word he said,
Go echoing down among the Dead.

      *   *   *   *

They say the Dead may never dream.
But yet I heard my pierced heart scream
His name within the dark.   They lie
Who say the Dead can ever die.

For in the grave I may not sleep,
For dreaming that I hear him weep.
And in the dark, my dead hands grope
In search of him.   O barren hope!

I cannot draw his head to rest,
Deep down upon my wounded breast;
He gave the breast that fed him well
To suckle the small worms of Hell.

The little wicked thoughts that fed
Upon the weary helpless Dead,
They whispered o'er my broken heart, —
They struck their fangs deep in the smart.

' The child she bore with bloody sweat
And agony has paid his debt.
Through that bleak face the stark winds play,
The crows have chased his soul away, —

' His body is a blackened rag
Upon the tree, — a monstrous flag,'
Thus one worm to the other saith,
Those slow mean servitors of Death,

They chuckling, said: ' Your soul grown blind
With anguish, is the shrieking wind
That blows the flame that never dies
About his empty lidless eyes.'

I tore them from my heart, I said:
' The life-blood that my son's hand shed —
That from my broken heart outburst,
I'd give again to quench his thirst.

' He did no sin.   But cold blind earth
The body was that gave him birth.
All mine, all mine the sin.   The love
I bore him was not deep enough.'

*   *   *   *

The Girl speaks:

O crumbling heart, I too, I too have known
The terrible Gehenna of the bone
Deserted by the flesh. . . . I too have wept
Through centuries like the deserted bone
To all the dust of all the Dead to fill
That place. . . . It would not be the dust I loved.

For underneath the lime-tree's golden town
Of Heaven, where he stood, the tattered Clown
Holding the screaming Heart and the Hambone,
You saw the Clown's thick hambone, life-pink carrion,
That Venus perfuming the summer air.
Old pigs, starved dogs, and long worms of the grave
Were rooting at it, nosing at it there.
Then you, my sun, left me and ran to it
Through pigs, dogs, grave-worms' ramparted tall waves.

*   *   *   *

268

I know that I must soon have the long pang
Of grave-worms in the heart. . . . You are so changed,
How shall I know you from the other long
Anguishing grave-worms? I can but foretell
The worm where once the kiss clung, and that last less chasm-
    deep farewell.

249 The Lament of Edward Blastock

For RICHARD ROWLEY

NOTE. — I took this story from the ' Newgate Calendar.'
Edward Blastock suffered at Tyburn on the 26th of May,
1738. Being in the direst want, and seeing his sister and
her children in an equal misery, he yielded to the solicita-
tions of his sister's husband, and joined with him in becom-
ing highwaymen. They went so far as to rob a gentleman
of a few shillings. Then Edward Blastock, finding a war-
rant was out against him, took refuge in his sister's house.

    She betrayed him to his death.

THE pang of the long century of rains,
   Melting the last flesh from the bone,
Cries to the heart: ' At least the bone remains, —
If this alone.'

My bone cries to my mother's womb:
Why were you not my tomb?
Why was I born from the same womb as she
Who sold my heart, my blood, who stole even my grave from
    me?

I crept to steal in the rich man's street
That my sister's starving babes might eat —

(Death, you have known such rags as hold
The starved man's heart together, — Death, you have
    known such cold!)

I crept to hide in my sister's room,
And dreamed it safe as my mother's womb:

But there was a price upon the head
Of one who stole that her babes might feed,

So my sister said, ' I must go to buy
Us bread with this pence . . .' And, for this, I die
— Beyond my Death . , . with no grave to lie

In, hide my heart deep down in that hole.
For my sister went to sell her soul

And my heart, and my life, and the love I gave . . .
She went to rob me of my grave.

And I would, I would the heart I gave
Were dead and mouldering in that grave,

I would my name were quite forgot,
And my death dead beneath Death's rot.

But I'd give the last rag of my flesh
About my heart to the endless cold
Could I know again the childish kiss
My Judas gave of old —
Oh, Christ that hung between two men like me, —
Could I but know she was not this, — not this!

250   *Colonel Fantock*

    THUS spoke the lady underneath the trees:
      I was a member of a family
  Whose legend was of hunting — (all the rare
  And unattainable brightness of the air) —

EDITH SITWELL

A race whose fabled skill in falconry
Was used on the small song-birds and a winged
And blinded Destiny. . . . I think that only
Winged ones know the highest eyrie is so lonely.

There in a land, austere and elegant,
The castle seemed an arabesque in music;
We moved in an hallucination born
Of silence, which like music gave us lotus
To eat, perfuming lips and our long eyelids
As we trailed over the sad summer grass,
Or sat beneath a smooth and mournful tree.

And Time passed, suavely, imperceptibly.

But Dagobert and Peregrine and I
Were children then; we walked like shy gazelles
Among the music of the thin flower-bells.
And life still held some promise, — never ask
Of what, — but life seemed less a stranger, then,
Than ever after in this cold existence.
I always was a little outside life, —
And so the things we touch could comfort me;
I loved the shy dreams we could hear and see —
For I was like one dead, like a small ghost,
A little cold air wandering and lost.

All day within the straw-roofed arabesque
Of the towered castle and the sleepy gardens wandered
We; those delicate paladins the waves
Told us fantastic legends that we pondered.

And the soft leaves were breasted like a dove,
Crooning old mournful tales of untrue love.

When night came, sounding like the growth of trees,
My great-grandmother bent to say good night,
And the enchanted moonlight seemed transformed
Into the silvery tinkling of an old
And gentle music-box that played a tune
Of Circean enchantments and far seas;
Her voice was lulling like the splash of these.
When she had given me her good-night kiss,
There, in her lengthened shadow, I saw this
Old military ghost with mayfly whiskers, —
Poor harmless creature, blown by the cold wind,
Boasting of unseen unreal victories
To a harsh unbelieving world unkind, —
For all the battles that this warrior fought
Were with cold poverty and helpless age —
His spoils were shelters from the winter's rage.
And so for ever through his braggart voice,
Through all that martial trumpet's sound, his soul
Wept with a little sound so pitiful,
Knowing that he is outside life for ever
With no one that will warm or comfort him. . . .
He is not even dead, but Death's buffoon
On a bare stage, a shrunken pantaloon.
His military banner never fell,
Nor his account of victories, the stories
Of old apocryphal misfortunes, glories
Which comforted his heart in later life
When he was the Napoleon of the schoolroom
And all the victories he gained were over
Little boys who would not learn to spell.

All day within the sweet and ancient gardens
He had my childish self for audience —

Whose body flat and strange, whose pale straight hair
Made me appear as though I had been drowned —
(We all have the remote air of a legend) —
And Dagobert my brother whose large strength,
Great body and grave beauty still reflect
The Angevin dead kings from whom we spring;
And sweet as the young tender winds that stir
In thickets when the earliest flower-bells sing
Upon the boughs, was his just character;
And Peregrine the youngest with a naïve
Shy grace like a faun's, whose slant eyes seemed
The warm green light beneath eternal boughs.
His hair was like the fronds of feathers, life
In him was changing ever, springing fresh
As the dark songs of birds . . . the furry warmth
And purring sound of fires was in his voice
Which never failed to warm and comfort me.

And there were haunted summers in Troy Park
When all the stillness budded into leaves;
We listened, like Ophelia drowned in blond
And fluid hair, beneath stag-antlered trees;
Then, in the ancient park the country-pleasant
Shadows fell as brown as any pheasant,
And Colonel Fantock seemed like one of these.
Sometimes for comfort in the castle kitchen
He drowsed, where with a sweet and velvet lip
The snapdragons within the fire
Of their red summer never tire.
And Colonel Fantock liked our company;
For us he wandered over each old lie,
Changing the flowering hawthorn, full of bees,

Into the silver helm of Hercules,
For us defended Troy from the top stair
Outside the nursery, when the calm full moon
Was like the sound within the growth of trees.
But then came one cruel day in deepest June,
When pink flowers seemed a sweet Mozartian tune,
And Colonel Fantock pondered o'er a book.
A gay voice like a honeysuckle nook, —
So sweet, — said, ' It is Colonel Fantock's age
Which makes him babble.' . . . Blown by winter's rage
The poor old man then knew his creeping fate,
The darkening shadow that would take his sight
And hearing; and he thought of his saved pence
Which scarce would rent a grave . . . that youthful voice
Was a dark bell which ever clanged ' Too late ' —
A creeping shadow that would steal from him
Even the little boys who would not spell, —
His only prisoners. . . . On that June day
Cold Death had taken his first citadel.

251   *Ass-face*

ASS-FACE drank
      The asses' milk of the stars . . .
The milky spirals as they sank
From heaven's saloons and golden bars,
Made a gown
For Columbine,
Spirting down
On sands divine
By the asses' hide of the sea
(With each tide braying free).

274

And the beavers building Babel
Beneath each tree's thin beard,
Said, ' Is it Cain and Abel
Fighting again we heard? '
It is Ass-face, Ass-face,
Drunk on the milk of the stars,
Who will spoil their houses of white lace —
Expelled from the golden bars!

252   *From ' Gold Coast Customs '*

In Ashantee, a hundred years ago, the death of any rich or important person was followed by several days of national ceremonies, during which the utmost licence prevailed, and slaves and poor persons were killed that the bones of the deceased might be laved with human blood. These ceremonies were called Customs.

O NE fantee wave
    Is grave and tall
As brave Ashantee's
Thick mud wall.
Munza rattles his bones in the dust,
Lurking in murk because he must.

Striped black and white
Is the squealing light;
The dust brays white in the market place,
Dead powder spread on a black skull's face.

Like monkey skin
Is the sea — one sin
Like a weasel is nailed to bleach on the rocks
Where the eyeless mud screeched fawning, mocks

EDITH SITWELL

At a negro that wipes
His knife . . . dug there
A bugbear bellowing
Bone dared rear —
A bugbear bone that bellows white
As the ventriloquist sound of light,

*   *   *   *

It rears at his head-dress of felted black hair
The one humanity clinging there —
His eyeless face whitened like black and white bones
And his beard of rusty
Brown grass cones.

Hard blue and white
Cowrie shells (the light
Grown hard) outline
The leopardskin musty
Leaves that shine
With an animal smell both thick and fusty.

One house like a ratskin
Mask flaps fleet
In the sailor's tall
Ventriloquist street
Where the rag houses flap —
Hiding a gap.

Here, tier on tier,
Like a black box rear
In the flapping slum
Beside Death's docks.

276

I did not know this meaner Death
Meant this: that the bunches of nerves still dance
And caper among these slums, and prance.

*   *   *   *

Can a planet tease
With its great gold train,
Walking beside the pompous main —
That great gold planet the heat of the Sun
Where we saw black Shadow, a black man, run,
So a negress dare
Wear long gold hair?
The negress Dorothy one sees
Beside the caverns and the trees
Where her parasol
Throws a shadow tall
As a waterfall —
The negress Dorothy still feels
The great gold planet tease her brain.

And dreaming deep within her blood
Lay Africa like the dark in the wood;
For Africa is the unhistorical
Unremembering, unrhetorical
Undeveloped spirit involved
In the conditions of nature — Man,
That black image of stone hath delved
On the threshold where history began.

Now under the cannibal
Sun is spread
The black rhinoceros-hide of the mud
For endlessness and timelessness . . . dead
Grass creaks like a carrion-bird's voice, rattles,

EDITH SITWELL

Squeaks like a wooden shuttle.   Battles
Have worn this deserted skeleton black
As empty chain armour . . . lazily back
With only the half of its heart it lies,
With the giggling mud devouring its eyes,
Naught left to fight
But the black clotted night
In its heart, and ventriloquist squealing light.

*   *   *   *

So Lady Bamburgher's Shrunken Head,
Slum hovel, is full of the rat-eaten bones
Of a fashionable god that lived not
Ever, but still has bones to rot:
A bloodless and an unborn thing
That cannot wake, yet cannot sleep,
That makes no sound, that cannot weep,
That hears all, bears all, cannot move —
It is buried so deep
Like a shameful thing
In that plague-spot heart, Death's last dust-heap.

THOMAS STEARNS ELIOT

1888–

253   *Preludes*

(*i*)

THE winter evening settles down
With smell of steaks in passageways.
Six o'clock.
The burnt-out ends of smoky days.
And now a gusty shower wraps
The grimy scraps

278

Of withered leaves about your feet
And newspapers from vacant lots;
The showers beat
On broken blinds and chimney-pots,
And at the corner of the street
A lonely cab-horse steams and stamps.
And then the lighting of the lamps.

(ii)

The morning comes to consciousness
Of faint stale smells of beer
From the sawdust-trampled street
With all its muddy feet that press
To early coffee-stands.
With the other masquerades
That time resumes,
One thinks of all the hands
That are raising dingy shades
In a thousand furnished rooms.

(iii)

You tossed a blanket from the bed,
You lay upon your back, and waited;
You dozed, and watched the night revealing
The thousand sordid images
Of which your soul was constituted;
They flickered against the ceiling.
And when all the world came back
And the light crept up between the shutters,
And you heard the sparrows in the gutters,
You had such a vision of the street
As the street hardly understands;

Sitting along the bed's edge, where
You curled the papers from your hair,
Or clasped the yellow soles of feet
In the palms of both soiled hands.

(iv)

His soul stretched tight across the skies
That fade behind a city block,
Or trampled by insistent feet
At four and five and six o'clock;
And short square fingers stuffing pipes,
And evening newspapers, and eyes
Assured of certain certainties,
The conscience of a blackened street
Impatient to assume the world.

I am moved by fancies that are curled
Around these images, and cling:
The notion of some infinitely gentle
Infinitely suffering thing.

Wipe your hand across your mouth, and laugh;
The worlds revolve like ancient women
Gathering fuel in vacant lots.

254   *The Hippopotamus*

' *And when this epistle is read among you, cause that it be
read also in the church of the Laodiceans.*'

THE broad-backed hippopotamus
Rests on his belly in the mud;
Although he seems so firm to us
He is merely flesh and blood.

Flesh and blood is weak and frail,
Susceptible to nervous shock;
While the True Church can never fail
For it is based upon a rock.

The hippo's feeble steps may err
In compassing material ends,
While the True Church need never stir
To gather in its dividends.

The 'potamus can never reach
The mango on the mango-tree;
But fruits of pomegranate and peach
Refresh the Church from over sea.

At mating time the hippo's voice
Betrays inflexions hoarse and odd,
But every week we hear rejoice
The Church, at being one with God.

The hippopotamus's day
Is passed in sleep; at night he hunts;
God works in a mysterious way —
The Church can sleep and feed at once.

I saw the 'potamus take wing
Ascending from the damp savannas,
And quiring angels round him sing
The praise of God, in loud hosannas.

Blood of the Lamb shall wash him clean
And him shall heavenly arms enfold,
Among the saints he shall be seen
Performing on a harp of gold.

He shall be washed as white as snow,
By all the martyr'd virgins kist,
While the True Church remains below
Wrapt in the old miasmal mist.

255 *Whispers of Immortality*

WEBSTER was much possessed by death
And saw the skull beneath the skin;
And breastless creatures under ground
Leaned backward with a lipless grin.

Daffodil bulbs instead of balls
Stared from the sockets of the eyes!
He knew that thought clings round dead limbs
Tightening its lusts and luxuries.

Donne, I suppose, was such another
Who found no substitute for sense;
To seize and clutch and penetrate,
Expert beyond experience,

He knew the anguish of the **marrow**
The ague of the skeleton;
No contact possible to flesh
Allayed the fever of the bone.

* * * *

Grishkin is nice: her Russian eye
Is underlined for emphasis;
Uncorseted, her friendly bust
Gives promise of pneumatic bliss.

THOMAS STEARNS ELIOT

The couched Brazilian jaguar
Compels the scampering marmoset
With subtle effluence of cat;
Grishkin has a maisonette;

The sleek Brazilian jaguar
Does not in its arboreal gloom
Distil so rank a feline smell
As Grishkin in a drawing-room.

And even the Abstract Entities
Circumambulate her charm;
But our lot crawls between dry ribs
To keep our metaphysics warm.

256 *Sweeney among the Nightingales*

(ὤμοι, πέπληγμαι καιρίαν πληγὴν ἔσω.)

APENECK SWEENEY spreads his knees
Letting his arms hang down to laugh,
The zebra stripes along his jaw
Swelling to maculate giraffe.

The circles of the stormy moon
Slide westward toward the River Plate,
Death and the Raven drift above
And Sweeney guards the horned gate.

Gloomy Orion and the Dog
Are veiled; and hushed the shrunken seas;
The person in the Spanish cape
Tries to sit on Sweeney's knees

THOMAS STEARNS ELIOT

Slips and pulls the table cloth
Overturns a coffee-cup,
Reorganized upon the floor
She yawns and draws a stocking up;

The silent man in mocha brown
Sprawls at the window-sill and gapes;
The waiter brings in oranges
Bananas figs and hothouse grapes;

The silent vertebrate in brown
Contracts and concentrates, withdraws;
Rachel *née* Rabinovitch
Tears at the grapes with murderous paws;

She and the lady in the cape
Are suspect, thought to be in league;
Therefore the man with heavy eyes
Declines the gambit, shows fatigue,

Leaves the room and reappears
Outside the window, leaning in,
Branches of wistaria
Circumscribe a golden grin;

The host with someone indistinct
Converses at the door apart,
The nightingales are singing near
The Convent of the Sacred Heart,

And sang within the bloody wood
When Agamemnon cried aloud,
And let their liquid siftings fall
To stain the stiff dishonoured shroud.

257

The Hollow Men

(*A Penny for the Old Guy*)

(*i*)

WE are the hollow men
　　We are the stuffed men
Leaning together
Headpiece filled with straw.　Alas!
Our dried voices, when
We whisper together
Are quiet and meaningless
As wind in dry grass
Or rats' feet over broken glass
In our dry cellar

Shape without form, shade without colour,
Paralysed force, gesture without motion;

Those who have crossed
With direct eyes, to death's other Kingdom
Remember us — if at all — not as lost
Violent souls, but only
As the hollow men
The stuffed men.

(*ii*)

Eyes I dare not meet in dreams
In death's dream kingdom
These do not appear:
There, the eyes are
Sunlight on a broken column

THOMAS STEARNS ELIOT

There, is a tree swinging
And voices are
In the wind's singing
More distant and more solemn
Than a fading star.

Let me be no nearer
In death's dream kingdom
Let me also wear
Such deliberate disguises
Rat's coat, crowskin, crossed staves
In a field
Behaving as the wind behaves
No nearer —

Not that final meeting
In the twilight kingdom

(*iii*)

This is the dead land
This is cactus land
Here the stone images
Are raised, here they receive
The supplication of a dead man's hand
Under the twinkle of a fading star.

Is it like this
In death's other kingdom
Waking alone
At the hour when we are
Trembling with tenderness
Lips that would kiss
Form prayers to broken stone.

THOMAS STEARNS ELIOT

(iv)

The eyes are not here
There are no eyes here
In this valley of dying stars
In this hollow valley
This broken jaw of our lost kingdoms

In this last of meeting places
We grope together
And avoid speech
Gathered on this beach of the tumid river

Sightless, unless
The eyes reappear
As the perpetual star
Multifoliate rose
Of death's twilight kingdom
The hope only
Of empty men.

(v)

Here we go round the prickly pear
Prickly pear prickly pear
Here we go round the prickly pear
At five o'clock in the morning.

Between the idea
And the reality
Between the motion
And the act
Falls the Shadow
              For Thine is the Kingdom

Between the conception
And the creation
Between the emotion
And the response
Falls the Shadow
                    Life is very long

Between the desire
And the spasm
Between the potency
And the existence
Between the essence
And the descent
Falls the Shadow
                    For Thine is the Kingdom

For Thine is
Life is
For Thine is the

This is the way the world ends
This is the way the world ends
This is the way the world ends
Not with a bang but a whimper.

258   *Journey of the Magi*

A COLD coming we had of it,
    Just the worst time of the year
For a journey, and such a long journey:
The ways deep and the weather sharp,
The very dead of winter.'
And the camels galled, sore-footed, refractory,
Lying down in the melting snow.

288

There were times we regretted
The summer palaces on slopes, the terraces,
And the silken girls bringing sherbet.
Then the camel men cursing and grumbling
And running away, and wanting their liquor and women,
And the night-fires going out, and the lack of shelters,
And the cities hostile and the towns unfriendly
And the villages dirty and charging high prices:
A hard time we had of it.
At the end we preferred to travel all night,
Sleeping in snatches,
With the voices singing in our ears, saying
That this was all folly.
Then at dawn we came down to a temperate valley,
Wet, below the snow line, smelling of vegetation;
With a running stream and a water-mill beating the dark-
        ness,
And three trees on the low sky,
And an old white horse galloped away in the meadow.

Then we came to a tavern with vine-leaves over the lintel,
Six hands at an open door dicing for pieces of silver,
And feet kicking the empty wine-skins.
But there was no information, and so we continued
And arrived at evening, not a moment too soon
Finding the place; it was (you may say) satisfactory.

All this was a long time ago, I remember,
And I would do it again, but set down
This set down
This: were we led all that way for
Birth or Death? There was a Birth, certainly,
We had evidence and no doubt. I had seen birth and death,

But had thought they were different; this Birth was
Hard and bitter agony for us, like Death, our death.
We returned to our places, these Kingdoms,
But no longer at ease here, in the old dispensation,
With an alien people clutching their gods.
I should be glad of another death.

259   *From 'The Rock'*

THE Eagle soars in the summit of Heaven,
    The Hunter with his dogs pursues his circuit.
O perpetual revolution of configured stars,
O perpetual recurrence of determined seasons,
O world of spring and autumn, birth and dying!
The endless cycle of idea and action,
Endless invention, endless experiment,
Brings knowledge of motion, but not of stillness;
Knowledge of speech, but not of silence;
Knowledge of words, and ignorance of the Word.
All our knowledge brings us nearer to our ignorance,
All our ignorance brings us nearer to death,
But nearness to death no nearer to God.
Where is the Life we have lost in living?
Where is the wisdom we have lost in knowledge?
Where is the knowledge we have lost in information?
The cycles of Heaven in twenty centuries
Bring us farther from God and nearer to the Dust.

1888–1915

260   *Into Battle*

THE naked earth is warm with spring,
    And with green grass and bursting trees
Leans to the sun's gaze glorying,
    And quivers in the sunny breeze;
And life is colour and warmth and light,
    And a striving evermore for these;
And he is dead who will not fight;
    And who dies fighting has increase.

The fighting man shall from the sun
    Take warmth, and life from the glowing earth;
Speed with the light-foot winds to run,
    And with the trees to newer birth;
And find, when fighting shall be done,
    Great rest, and fullness after dearth.

All the bright company of Heaven
    Hold him in their high comradeship,
The Dog-Star, and the Sisters Seven,
    Orion's Belt and sworded hip.

The woodland trees that stand together,
    They stand to him each one a friend;
They gently speak in the windy weather;
    They guide to valley and ridge's end.

The kestrel hovering by day,
    And the little owls that call by night,
Bid him be swift and keen as they,
    As keen of ear, as swift of sight.

JULIAN GRENFELL

The blackbird sings to him, ' Brother, brother,
  If this be the last song you shall sing,
Sing well, for you may not sing another;
  Brother, sing.'

In dreary, doubtful, waiting hours,
  Before the brazen frenzy starts,
The horses show him nobler powers;
  O patient eyes, courageous hearts!

And when the burning moment breaks,
  And all things else are out of mind,
And only joy of battle takes
  Him by the throat, and makes him blind,

Through joy and blindness he shall know,
  Not caring much to know, that still
Nor lead nor steel shall reach him, so
  That it be not the Destined Will.

The thundering line of battle stands,
  And in the air death moans and sings;
But Day shall clasp him with strong hands,
  And Night shall fold him in soft wings.

WALTER JAMES TURNER

1889–

261   *Epithalamium*

CAN the lover share his soul,
  Or the mistress show her mind;
Can the body beauty share,
  Or lust satisfaction find?

Marriage is but keeping house,
    Sharing food and company,
What has this to do with love
    Or the body's beauty?

If love means affection, I
    Love old trees, hats, coats and things,
Anything that 's been with me
    In my daily sufferings.

That is how one loves a wife —
    There 's a human interest too,
And a pity for the days
    We so soon live through.

What has this to do with love,
    The anguish and the sharp despair,
The madness roving in the blood
    Because a girl or hill is fair?

I have stared upon a dawn
    And trembled like a man in love,
A man in love I was, and I
    Could not speak and could not move.

262   *Romance*

WHEN I was but thirteen or so
    I went into a golden land,
Chimborazo, Cotopaxi
    Took me by the hand.

My father died, my brother too,
    They passed like fleeting dreams.
I stood where Popocatapetl
    In the sunlight gleams.

I dimly heard the Master's voice
   And boys far-off at play,
Chimborazo, Cotopaxi
   Had stolen me away.

I walked in a great golden dream
   To and fro from school —
Shining Popocatapetl
   The dusty streets did rule.

I walked home with a gold dark boy
   And never a word I'd say,
Chimborazo, Cotopaxi
   Had taken my speech away:

I gazed entranced upon his face
   Fairer than any flower —
O shining Popocatapetl
   It was thy magic hour:

The houses, people, traffic seemed
   Thin fading dreams by day,
Chimborazo, Cotopaxi
   They had stolen my soul away!

263   *A Love-song*

THE beautiful, delicate bright gazelle
   That bounds upon Night's hills
Has not more lovely, silken limbs
   Than she who my heart fills.

But though this loveliness I lose
   When I shall lie with her,
I do but pass that Image on
   For new eyes to discover.

294

264 *The Dancer*

THE young girl dancing lifts her face
   Passive among the drooping flowers;
The jazz band clatters sticks and bones
   In a bright rhythm through the hours.

The men in black conduct her round;
   With small sensations they are blind:
Thus Saturn's Moons revolve embraced
   And through the cosmos wind.

But Saturn has not that strange look
   Unhappy, still, and far away,
As though upon the face of Night
   Lay the bright wreck of day.

265 *In Time like Glass*

IN Time like glass the stars are set,
   And seeming-fluttering butterflies
Are fixèd fast in Time's glass net
With mountains and with maids' bright eyes.

Above the cold Cordilleras hung
The wingèd eagle and the Moon:
The gold, snow-throated orchid sprung
From gloom where peers the dark baboon:

The Himalayas' white, rapt brows;
The jewel-eyed bear that threads their caves;
The lush plains' lowing herds of cows;
That Shadow entering human graves:

All these like stars in Time are set,
They vanish but can never pass;
The Sun that with them fades is yet
Fast-fixed as they in Time like glass.

266 *The Navigators*

I SAW the bodies of earth's men
  Like wharves thrust in the stream of time
Whereon cramped navigators climb
And free themselves in the warm sun:

With outflung arms and shouts of joy
  Those spirits tramped their human planks;
  Then pressing close, reforming ranks,
They pushed off in the stream again:

Cold darkly rotting lay the wharves,
  Decaying in the stream of time;
  Slow winding silver tracks of slime
Showed bright where came back none.

267 *Men fade like Rocks*

ROCK-LIKE the souls of men
  Fade, fade in time.
Falls on worn surfaces,
  Slow chime on chime,

  Sense, like a murmuring dew,
    Soft sculpturing rain,
  Or the wind that blows hollowing
    In every lane.

Smooth as the stones that lie
Dimmed, water-worn,
Worn of the night and day,
In sense forlorn,

Rock-like the souls of men
Fade, fade in time;
Smoother than river-rain
Falls chime on chime.

268 *Tragic Love*

WHO shall invoke when we are gone
The glory that we knew,
Can we not carve To-Day in stone,
In diamond this Dawn's dew?

The song that heart to heart has sung
Write fadeless on the air;
Expression in eyes briefly hung
Fix in a planet's stare?

Alas, all beauty flies in *Time*
And only as it goes
Upon death's wind its fleeting chime
Into sad memory blows.

Is this but presage of re-birth
And of another Day
When what within our hearts we said
We once again shall say?

Oh, no! we never could repeat
Those numbered looks we gave;
But some pure lustre from their light
All future worlds shall have.

269 *Reflection*

IS it not strange that men can die
  Before their bodies do,
And women's souls fade from their eyes?
  'Tis strange, but it is so.

Where have they gone and what were they,
  Those gleams of tenderer light
Than falls from mere quick shining limbs
  And eyeballs merely bright?

Undying fires removing far
  Their unseen presence show,
Leaving their brightness on dead moons
  As suns less heavenly do.

270   *From 'The Seven Days of the Sun'*

(*i*)

I HAD watched the ascension and decline of the Moon
  And did not realize that it moved only in my own mind.

Or that its distance of 240,000 miles
Could also be .240,000 of an inch.

But now I know that the solar system and the constellations
    of stars
Are contained within me.
Nothing exists outside me. . . .

Death and Birth —
Strange and beautiful Appearances —
Like the Cypress and the Lily
Beside the amaranthine sea,

WALTER JAMES TURNER

Where the dark Orange Tree
With its gold suns
Hangs like a solar universe!

Myriads of fading faces

The flowering of the same meadow!

(ii)

That is the last time
I shall call upon that Ancient **Mariner**,
The God of my youth.

Seated among the stars
I saw Him,
With his hand on the tiller.

Is he not a Graven Image,
A Stone Figure?

Are not the stars
Frozen on his garment?

Is not the Universe
The fixed Expression of his **Face**?

Henceforth I do not pretend
To know God.

(iii)

If God kept a terrarium
Our world religions
Would be child's guides to the **Zoo**.

Our scientific textbooks
Catalogues for collectors —
' Many plates missing '!

But in what guide or textbook
Shall *That* which looks out from the eye of the leopard be
    found?

If God were a Baptist
He would keep an aquarium.

(*iv*)

What is the meaning of this Ideal
That haunts my intelligence
And charms my senses?

I cannot create her.
Did Rosalind, Cleopatra and Miranda
Satisfy Shakespeare?

Or the Dark Lady of the Sonnets?

Where did *she* come from?

Since they were all emanations of his own mind,
Forms of his creative imagination,
Why did she affect him as flesh and blood?

Yet no doubt he was aware of the flesh of Rosalind:
It was cooler and more white.
And Cleopatra!
He was aware of her warm blood.

Yet ' The Dark Lady ' was a different sensation
She was what is called ' real.'

WALTER JAMES TURNER

I have met ' The Dark Lady '
And I assure you she is no more real than Rosalind.

But we get intangled in a confusion of sensations.
When past present and future are mixed in a certain way
The intelligence is bewildered;
And being unanalysed the effect is given a meaningless
    name —
Reality.

Reality is bewilderment. . . .

Only in a state of ' complete confusion ' can I beget a
    daughter.
Not from Rosalind, Cleopatra and Miranda
But from ' The Dark Lady.'

Evidently there is a difference in these phantoms!

But a daughter is merely the continuation of my bewilder-
    ment,
Another ' Dark Lady.'

Are there different kinds of ' complete confusion '?
Is every ' Dark Lady ' the same?

Let me tell of The Dark Lady
With whom I lay down in a corner of my brain!

(v)

Dian, Isis, Artemis, whate'er thy name
Thou ghost, thou principle, can thy white stags
Move and beget themselves, eclipse a tree?
Are they not white, the Moon's transparent rags,
Mere insubstantial light! But O how bright,
How milk-opaque, how concrete to the sight —
Chaste negatives, washwhites of chastity!

WALTER JAMES TURNER

(vi)

Spirits walking everywhere,
Thrown up like fountains
Then sinking into the ground,
Walking among the trees
That seem fast
So slowly do they well up
And sink down.

But to me the landscape is like a sea
the waves of the hills
and the bubbles of bush and flower
and the springtide breaking into white **foam**!

It is a slow sea,
Mare tranquillum,
And a thousand years of wind
Cannot raise a dwarf billow to the moonlight.

But the bosom of the landscape lifts and falls
With its own leaden tide,
That tide whose sparkles are the lilliputian stars.

It is that slow sea
That sea of adamantine languor,
Sleep!

(vii)

I have seen mannequins,
As white and gold as lilies,
Swaying their tall bodies across the burnished floor
Of *Reville* or *Paquin*;
Writhing in colour and line,
Curved tropical flowers
As bright as thunderbolts.

302

Or hooded in dark furs
The sun's pale splash
In English autumn woods.

And I have watched these soft explosions of life
As astronomers watch the combustion of stars.

The violence of supernatural power
Upon their faces,
White orbits
Of incalculable forces.

And I have had no desire for their bodies
But have felt the whiteness of a lily
Upon my palate;
And the solidity of their slender curves
Like a beautiful mathematical proposition
In my brain.

But in the expression of their faces
Terror.

Cruelty in the eyes, nostrils and lips —

Pain
thou passion-flower, thou wreath, thou orbit,
thou spiritual rotation,
thou smile upon a pedestal
Peony of the garden of paradise!

(*viii*)

What is this tempest
This rumbling of drums!
These yellow stripes of the tiger
Through the dark green leaves!

WALTER JAMES TURNER

It is only the Sun
Walking along the river bank.

Can you not hear the *pad pad* of the sunbeams
Through the trees?

And the noiseless hurry of the water?

You would not think they were chained —
Vibrating in the stillness of adamant!

(*ix*)

Beneath a thundery glaze
The raindrops fall.

What is this new oppression of my heart?

Have I not looked upon this scene before!
These leafy dromedaries
Dark green,
Painted upon that wall
Of livid sky
Where vacancy's bright silent spiders crawl!

The hills' pure outlined contours on that light
Empty my soul.
I watch those spidery lines
Bright violet.

And there 's a poisonous cloud as dark as jet
Pouring from heaven.

271   *The Word made Flesh?*

HOW often does a man need to see a woman?
    Once!
Once is enough, but a second time will confirm if it be she,
She who will be a fountain of everlasting mystery,
Whose glance escaping hither and thither
Returns to him who troubles her.

This happens rarely when a man is young;
For the lusts of the young are full of universal gladness
They have no sadness of disillusioning error
But only earth's madness of thunder
And its fading bright crackle of lightning.

But when a man is old, married, and in despair
Has slept with the bodies of many women,
And many women have attempted him vainly;

Then if he meet a woman whose loveliness
Is young and yet troubled with power;
Of the earth and yet not of the earth, homeless
He will find her chained by distance.

No light travelling through space-time immeasurable
Can leap so great a distance as their eyes;
Naked together their spirits commingling
Stir the seed in their genitals —
Like a babe never to be born that leaps up crying.

The children of the flesh are sweet and fair
But sweeter and fairer
Are the children of no flesh but of the spirit,
They are like an ever-living fever

Of the perishable blood
Driving the dark brood of men and women
Who because of these phantoms cannot come to rest in one
    another.

For the blood of a man when he is old,
Old and full of power,
Is no longer like the blood of a young man, inflammable,
It is like a serpent and an eagle,
A bull violent and immovable,
And a burning that is without flame or substance.

Terrible is the agony of an old man
The agony of incommunicable power
Holding his potency like a rocket that is full of stars
But his countenance is like a sky;

Or the tranquil countenance of the moon,
The stars like jewels set in everlasting adamant
Transparent as diamond:
Drought, calm, serene, eternal!

His hairs crisp, like a Gorgon,
They are the serpents of the spirit
Curled like the hairs of a chaste body
Emblem of a God who is not creative
Who never from an Adam of dust
Took that white bone, woman.

This the everlasting youth of an old man
For whom there is no illusion.

This it is to be excluded from the bliss
Of the men and women that He made in His image;
But his are the children of the spirit,

Sweeter and fairer are they than the children of the flesh
But they are born solitary
And agony is their making-kiss.

272   *Hymn to her Unknown*

IN despair at not being able to rival the creations of God
I thought on her
Whom I saw on the twenty-fourth of August nineteen
    thirty-four
Having tea on the fifth story of Swan and Edgar's
In Piccadilly Circus.

She sat facing me with an older woman and a younger
And a little boy aged about five;
I could see that she was his mother,
Also she wore a wedding-ring and one set with diamonds.

She was about twenty-five years old,
Slim, graceful, disciplined;
She had none of the mannerisms of the suburbs,
No affectations, a low clear speech, good manners,
Hair thick and undyed.

She knew that she was beautiful and exceedingly attractive,
Every line of her dress showed it;
She was cool and determined and laughed heartily,
A wide mouth with magnificent teeth.

And having said this I come to the beginning of my despair,
Despair that I in no way can describe her
Or bring before the eyes of the present or the future
This image that I saw.

WALTER JAMES TURNER

Hundreds and hundreds of women do I see
But rarely a woman on whom my eyes linger
As the eyes of Venus lingered on Adonis.

What is the use of being a poet?
Is it not a farce to call an artist a creator,
Who can create nothing, not even re-present what his eyes
      have seen?

She never showed a sign that she saw me
But I knew and she knew that I knew —
Our eyes fleeting past, never meeting directly
Like that vernal twinkling of butterflies
To which Coleridge compared Shakespeare's *Venus and
      Adonis*.

And, like Venus, I lavished my love upon her
I dallied with her hair, her delicate skin and smooth limbs,
On her arms were heavy thick bangles
Like the ropes of my heart's blood.

Could I express the ecstasy of my adoration?
Mating with her were itself a separation!
Only our bodies fusing in a flame of crystal
Burning in an infinite empyrean
Until all the blue of the limitless heaven were drunken
In one globe of united perfection
Like a bubble that is all the oceans of the world ascending
To the fire that is the fire of fires, transcending
The love of God, the love of God, the love of God —
Ah! my pitiful efforts now ending
I remember a bough of coral
Flower of the transparent sea

WALTER JAMES TURNER

Delicate pink as though a ray of the sun descending
Pathless into the ocean
Printed the foot of Venus
Where bloomed this asphodel.

DOROTHY WELLESLEY

1889–

273   *Fire*

(' *Does not our life consist of the four elements?* '
— SHAKESPEARE.)

THE great stone hearth has gone.
   An oblong electric tube is set in the wall
Like a cheap jewel.
Men converge no more to the fire,
Men are one with the isolation:
The pride of science stands, and the final desolation.

No smoke, no danger, you tell me with veneration:
Much dies with the fire, young man,
More than one generation:
Man has known fire more than one generation.

Modern man! the mystical
Core of life, and the carnal
Are one with that you have slain,
One with the fire, Cain!
Truth, Passion, Pain,
And regeneration eternal.

Life ends where life began:
Adam delved and Eve span.

DOROTHY WELLESLEY

Age-ago beside the hearth,
Son of man, you lay at birth:
When a cave-man carved a horn,
By the cave fire you were born.

The Ionian conceives,
His fraternity declare
(Living with Shelley, plants and leaves,
Their thoughts flowers of the atmosphere)
Life is Water, Fire, and Air.

Empedocles he added Earth
To the elements.

Life ends where life began,
At the death or birth.
' Is it son or daughter, man? '
' Earth, Air, Fire and Water! '

Man, the earth shall grow the bread:
In the dead behold the quick.
In the quick behold the dead.

Thales counted Water,
Aristotle tells,
In the elements.
Thales saw in wells and brine
Some intelligence divine.

Water then for purge of blood,
Man's first purge of flesh is so.
(Put the pan upon the hob

DOROTHY WELLESLEY

Put the tub beside the fire,
Bathe him so!)
Belly-ache and sweat of blood
Whether we will or no.

Anaxágoras added Air
To the elements.

But where is here the envoy
Of the infinite Air?

(All Man's soul the Air conceives,
All was Air till God began
To mould the gladsome god, the Pan
Who lives among the leaves.)

The Infinite fails you at your birth,
Sorely fails you, man, on earth.
He will fail in direst love,
He'll betray with curse and scorn,
Fame and Substance, Style and Place:
The Infinite fails when you are born.

Fire will never fail you, Man,
Whether you fever or tire.
Adam butchered, but Eve span
For the new life by the fire.

Heraclitus added Fire
To the elements.

Man, at leaping of the wood-ash,
Shaken with desire
Take her, slim with silver flanks:
Heraclitus added Fire.

DOROTHY WELLESLEY

Woman, you will muse by wood-ash
When your young man sleeps beside:
Mother now of all creation,
Guardian, you, of reincarnation,
Who so lately was a bride.

Woman, by the whitening wood-ash
Is it girl or son?
Have you wedded flesh to spirit?
Carnal in the incarnate
In this new soul begun?

For the Greek he added
Half ethereal Fire.

Butcher, baker, candlestick-maker,
Blood, and bread, and taper,
Meat, and wheat, and light,
Along with Jones the draper
The wife finds these in the little shops
On the right of the undertaker.

Empedocles he added Earth
To the elements.

Heat the meat then, bake the bread,
Woman, as you desire.
Fire's the fellow for board and bed,
But light the candles at your prayers
For him you lech with, or will wed:
Heraclitus added Fire.

DOROTHY WELLESLEY

Make the fire up, he is cold.
Dawns are cold in spring.
Easter comes, but he is old
At February-fill-dyke when the water
Is blossoming everything,
Here by fireside sits grand-daughter
Sewing for the coming child.

' Was it son or daughter, Midwife? '
In the roof the rents
Let the years in with the doctor,
And another shouldering past,
Death the tall one come at last!
Entering with men's memories,
Entering with the elements,
With the wind and water,
With the sorrow and snow.
' Woman, was it son or daughter
Eighty years ago? '

Fire was once his crony:
Now his flame 's at fag-end,
Now his fire 's at goal.
Women, sheet him so!
Set the tapers spick-and-spanly,
Candles burn erect and manly
For that whimpering brat the soul!

Doctor, Undertaker, Death,
Mother, Gamp and Sire:
What 's a man at moment's birth?
What 's a man at moment's death?
' Earth, Air, Water, Fire! '

Fire was fierce, dead man, in love,
And in the dread conception.
Fire was truth through passion known
By sweat of blood, by rebel bone;
Fire, sear the last deception!

Send him forth into the night
Alone and unattended.
Send him out alone to Fire,
His rude dignity of man
Untended and unfriended.

Run with torches, blaze the pyre,
Far from town and street:
Burn his body on the shore
Where Earth, Air and Water meet,
As all poets know,
As all dead men know.

Death's the first and everlasting,
Life the lean time and the fasting,
Birth the end and everlasting,
Whether we will or no.

274 *Horses*

(*Newmarket or St. Leger*)

WHO, in the garden-pony carrying skeps
    Of grass or fallen leaves, his knees gone slack,
Round belly, hollow back,
Sees the Mongolian Tarpan of the Steppes?
Or, in the Shire with plaits and feathered feet,
The war-horse like the wind the Tartar knew?
Or, in the Suffolk Punch, spells out anew
The wild grey asses fleet

314

DOROTHY WELLESLEY

With stripe from head to tail, and moderate ears?
In cross sea-donkeys, sheltering as storm gathers,
The mountain zebras maned upon the withers,
With round enormous ears?

And who in thoroughbreds in stable garb
Of blazoned rug, ranged orderly, will mark
The wistful eyelashes so long and dark,
And call to mind the old blood of the Barb?
And that slim island on whose bare campaigns
Galloped with flying manes,
For a king's pleasure, churning surf and scud,
A white Arabian stud?

That stallion, teaser to Hobgoblin, free
And foaled upon a plain of Barbary:
Godolphin Barb, who dragged a cart for hire
In Paris, but became a famous sire,
Covering all lovely mares; and she who threw
Rataplan to the Baron, loveliest shrew;
King Charles's royal mares; the Dodsworth Dam;
And the descendants: Yellow Turk, King Tom;
And Lath out of Roxana, famous foal;
Careless; Eclipse, unbeaten in the race,
With white blaze on his face;
Prunella who was dam to Parasol.

Blood Arab, pony, pedigree, no name,
All horses are the same:
The Shetland stallion stunted by the damp,
Yet filled with self-importance, stout and small;
The Cleveland slow and tall;
New Forests that may ramp

Their lives out, being branded, breeding free
When bluebells turn the Forest to a sea,
When mares with foal at foot flee down the glades,
Sheltering in bramble coverts
From mobs of corn-fed lovers;
Or, at the acorn harvest, in stockades
A round-up being afoot, will stand at bay,
Or, making for the heather clearings, splay
Wide-spread towards the bogs by gorse and whin,
Roped as they flounder in
By foresters.

But hunters as day fails
Will take the short-cut home across the fields;
With slackened rein will stoop through darkening wealds;
With creaking leathers skirt the swedes and kales;
Patient, adventuring still,
A horse's ears bob on the distant hill;
He starts to hear
A pheasant chuck or whirr, having the fear
In him of ages filled with war and raid,
Night gallop, ambuscade;
Remembering adventures of his kin
With giant winged worms that coiled round mountain bases,
And Nordic tales of young gods riding races
Up courses of the rainbow; here, within
The depth of Hampshire hedges, does he dream
How Athens woke, to hear above her roofs
The welkin flash and thunder to the hoofs
Of Dawn's tremendous team?

275

Asian Desert

HERE the hills are earth's bones,
Jutting up out of her,
Here she died long since,
Here fell to decay,
Demolished by storm and rain,
Her skeleton hardened to stones
That grow not the flesh again.

There is her spine, dark, rack-a-bones,
Iron-stone ranges her limbs
Zigzagging the sky,
Cleansed and eased is her sex,
Pure, bitter, and rank
The hollow, the dearth of her flank,
Here lies the mother of men.

Here she gave birth, brought forth,
Stretched awry in an acid dawn,
Came here, crowding, trampling, hating,
Came forth her spawn.

Her spawn have abandoned her.
Here is left nothing,
Nothing but bone.

I am in love with her.
No appurtenances are hers;
No trappings are hers, only stone,
Fossil stone she has grown;
No flesh tint is here. The winds blow
Always from Asia, retrieved her flesh
Of ecstasy, long ago.

Here is she old, old.
Here is her structure, her core;
Here the slate, and the surface scree is washed down
Into platforms of shale;
Here she died with her heart bled brown:
No blood coursed from her more.

Here she has no heart,
Lies not as the earth in the other lands
With her limbs apart.

Here strongly the sap is outwrung,
Here the memory divine
Of an old woman is mine,
So old she was never young.

Ah, but see, is she not beautiful?
Hank of stone, wrinkle of rock,
Pared, seared, stark with age?
Is she not tenderer far than when she allures
Man on his pilgrimage?

276   *Fishing*

I WILL go with the first air of morning
To the land of Palestine.

Once, far from oasis,
Where dates grow costly and fine,
Men gathered the shining shoals,
That rippled up the road to the moon,
The road of the moonshine.

Lovely the mercury, the flutter of the sea,
And the squares of the quicksilver nets,
And the drops of the sea divine,

318

DOROTHY WELLESLEY

As the fishes took the road to death;
Little waifs, little souls,
Lovely in their living and dying ever,
For luminous are their fins as feathers in the sun,
Sunny their scales as the sheen of the jay,
— When, silly tomboy, in sunshine he screams —
For inwardly lit are they;
Inwardly lit of their own light it seems,
Knowing a clarity ungiven to the day,
As on the branching reefs undersea they alight and sway
To the swell like swarming starlings in a windy tree.
Yet intimate with shadows that in air cannot be,
Dark are they, brooding, knowing, yet gay,
Shaft of sunlight theirs, deeps the lark never knows,
No, nor even the nightingale crucified
On the spine of the rose!

Beautiful their world, having no purpose, being for ever un-
      seen.
None know that beauty for beauty's sake made,
Alone, content in the depth for ever it dwells;
Unstable as beech-leaves in May that eternal green,
The shifting, tremulous purple and brown of the rock-shade,
The frail light on the shallows,
And the young travelling shells
Like angels gently moving their wings
Over the dappled wells,
Rising and dipping as they swim in the sunlight;
And the waving, wooing anemones like hedgerow mallows,
And the Horned Iridescent whose life and death is a sleep.

Let me learn the wonder
Of those then who dwelt in the deep,

When Jesus went fishing.
When they by Jesus were lifted from the sea;
From the fast-flowing moonlight with His hands hauled He,
Singing a sailor's tune;
A tune men forgot, having short memory,
Or tired òf knowing too well all the handcraft songs:
Potter's plaint or huckster's croon.

But a lilt that He knew
When making cork floats at Madonna's knee,
And singing now where sagged the barque side,
Tumbling black oval in the spate of the moon;
With Matthew, Mark, Luke, and the little John behind
    Him,
While gaped the rest of the crew;
While broke in hissing bubbles the eternal road of fire,
So the eyes were dazzled looking overside,
From His fingers fled the phosphorus away,
To the road no man may pursue.

For up that road went the feet of the Messiah,
Out of the horizon walked He,
Slim between the fishing smacks glancing not aside,
Gentle in His going, bornè slightly on the tide,
Preaching gravely as He went to the groups of gaping fishes,
In the waters of Galilee.

277   *From 'Lenin'*

    S O I came down the steps to Lenin.
      With a herd of peasants before
      And behind me, I saw
      A room stained scarlet, and there
      A small wax man in a small glass case.

Two sentinels at his feet, and one at his head,
Two little hands on his breast:
Pious spinster asleep; and I said
' Many warrants these delicate hands have signed.'
A lamp shone, red,
An aureole over him, on his red hair;
His uniform clothed him still.

Greedy of detail I saw,
In those two minutes allowed,
The man was not wax, as they said,
But a corpse, for a thumb nail was black,
The thing was Lenin.

Then a woman beside me cried
With a strange voice, foreign, loud.
And I, who fear not life nor death, and those who have died
Only a little, was inwardly shaken with fear,
For I stood in the presence of God;
The voice I heard was the voice of all generations
Acclaiming new faiths, horrible, beautiful faiths;
I knew that the woman wailed as women wailed long ago
For Christ in the sepulchre laid.
Christ was a wax man too,
When they carried Him down to the grave.

278   *From ' Matrix '*

THE spiritual, the carnal, are one.
    For when love is greatly found,
It outcries, as men cry
When in pain to be laid on the ground;
As men in pain moan for the grave;
Hear: how in love the lips moan,

321

DOROTHY WELLESLEY

For Man must pursue
Love the lamp back to darkness again;
Is not this death too?

*   *   *   *

Earth, back to the earth.

Out of her beauty at birth,
Out of her I came
To lose all that I knew:
Though somehow at birth I died,
One night she will teach me anew:
Peace?   The same,
As a woman's, a mother's
Breast undenied, to console
The small bones built in the womb,
The womb that loathed the bones,
And cast out the soul.

279   *The Buried Child*

(Epilogue to 'Deserted House')

HE is not dead nor liveth
The little child in the grave,
And men have known for ever
That he walketh again;
They hear him November evenings,
When acorns fall with the rain.

Deep in the hearts of men
Within his tomb he lieth,
And when the heart is desolate
He desolate sigheth.

Teach me then the heart of the dead child,
Who, holding a tulip, goeth
Up the stairs in his little grave-shift,
Sitting down in his little chair
By his biscuit and orange,
In the nursery he knoweth.

Teach me all that the child who knew life
And the quiet of death,
To the croon of the cradle-song
By his brother's crib
In the deeps of the nursery dusk
To his mother saith.

280   *The Morning after*

BARABBAS, Judas Iscariot,
The night after He died,
The night after He cried
' They know not what they do,'
What did you do?
You two.

Chaste, and sober from prison,
You went to a tavern, Barabbas,
You drank the night through,
You shared thirty pieces of silver,
Judas Iscariot and you.

Barabbas disorderly,
Bawdy Barabbas,
Drank, stole, and swore;
Next day was back in the prison!
By word of a whore.

DOROTHY WELLESLEY

Judas Iscariot, sun half arisen,
Went out in the gloom.
Beautiful Judas Tree,
April in bloom.

HUGH M'DIARMID

1892–

281 *Parley of Beasts*

AULD Noah was at hame wi' them a',
The lion and the lamb,
Pair by pair they entered the Ark
And he took them as they cam'.

If twa a' ilka beist there is
Into this room s'ud come,
Wad I could welcome them like him,
And no' stand gowpin' dumb!

Be chief wi' them and they wi' me
And a' wi' ane anither
As Noah and his couples were
There in the Ark thegither.

It 's fain I'd mell wi' tiger and tit,
Wi' elephant and eel,
But noo-a'days e'en wi' ain's sel
At hame it 's hard to feel.

282 *O Wha 's been here afore me, Lass*

O WHA 'S been here afore me, lass,
And hoo did he get in?
— *A man that deed or I was born*
This evil thing has din.

324

And left as it were on a corpse
Your maidenheid to me?
— *Nae lass, gudeman, sin' Time began*
'S hed ony mair to gi'e.

But I can gi'e ye kindness, lad,
And a pair o' willin' hands,
And you sall ha'e my briests like stars,
My limbs like willow wands;

And on my lips ye'll heed nae mair,
And in my hair forget,
The seed o' a' the men that in
My virgin womb ha'e met.

283   *Cattle Show*

I SHALL go among red faces and virile voices,
See stylish sheep, with fine heads and well-wooled,
And great bulls mellow to the touch,
Brood mares of marvellous approach, and geldings
With sharp and flinty bones and silken hair.

And through th' enclosure draped in red and gold
I shall pass on to spheres more vivid yet
Where countesses' coque feathers gleam and glow
And, swathed in silks, the painted ladies are
Whose laughter plays like summer lightning there.

284   *The Skeleton of the Future*
              (*At Lenin's Tomb*)

RED granite and black diorite, with the blue
Of the labradorite crystals gleaming like precious stones
In the light reflected from the snow; and behind them
The eternal lightning of Lenin's bones.

English Girl

I THAT lived ever about you
Never touched you, Lilian;
You came from far away
And devils with twitching faces
Had all their will of you
For gold.
But I saw your little feet in your bedroom,
Your little heathen shoes I kept so bright.
For they regarded not your feet, Lilian,
But I regarded.
Your little heathen stockings were mine to carry
And to set out and to wash.
They regarded not your feet,
But I that lived ever about you
Never touched you, Lilian.
Their faces twitch more this frosty morning;
They have put you in a heathen box
And hidden your feet and carried you out in the frosty
    morning.
They have passed with you over the foggy brook
And look like big blue men in the mist on the other side.
Now only the mist and the water remain.
They never regarded your feet,
But I regarded, Lilian.
Their faces ever twitched,
But for the seven years since I saw you
My face did not change.
They never regarded your warm feet,
But I regarded.

(From the Chinese, 19th century.)

VIVIAN DE SOLA PINTO

1895–

286   *At Piccadilly Circus*

I WANDER through a crowd of women,
   Whose hair and teeth are false,
Whose lips and cheeks have artificial colours,
Whose dress is artificial silk and velvet,
Whose talk is mainly lies.

And I remember
How once I dreamed of Truth:
It was a fair green tree,
Growing in an open grassy place
Beside cool flowing water . . .

They have cut down the tree.
Its sap is dried up long ago.
Perhaps some fragment of it still remains
Embedded in an ugly garish building.

But most of it is turn'd to poisonous dust,
Blown through the stifling streets of slums.

VICTORIA SACKVILLE–WEST

1892–

287   *The Greater Cats*

THE greater cats with golden eyes
   Stare out between the bars.
Deserts are there, and different skies,
And night with different stars.
They prowl the aromatic hill,
And mate as fiercely as they kill,

And hold the freedom of their will
To roam, to live, to drink their fill;
But this beyond their wit know I:
Mān loves a little, and for long shall die.

Their kind across the desert range
Where tulips spring from stones,
Not knowing they will suffer change
Or vultures pick their bones.
Their strength 's eternal in their sight,
They rule the terror of the night,
They overtake the deer in flight,
And in their arrogance they smite;
But I am sage, if they are strong:
Man's love is transient as his death is long.

Yet oh what powers to deceive!
My wit is turned to faith,
And at this moment I believe
In love, and scout at death.
I came from nowhere, and shall be
Strong, steadfast, swift, eternally:
I am a lion, a stone, a tree,
And as the Polar star in me
Is fixed my constant heart on thee.
Ah, may I stay forever blind
With lions, tigers, leopards, and their kind.

288   *On the Lake*

A CANDLE lit in darkness of black waters,
   A candle set in the drifting prow of a boat,
And every tree to itself a separate shape,
Now plumy, now an arch; tossed trees

VICTORIA SACKVILLE–WEST

Still and dishevelled; dishevelled with past growth,
Forgotten storms; left tufted, tortured, sky-rent,
Even now in stillness; stillness on the lake,
Black, reflections pooled, black mirror
Pooling a litten candle, taper of fire;
Pooling the sky, double transparency
Of sky in water, double elements,
Lying like lovers, light above, below;
Taking, from one another, light; a gleaming,
A glow reflected, fathoms deep, leagues high,
Two distances meeting at a film of surface
Thin as a membrane, sheet of surface, fine
Smooth steel; two separates, height and depth,
Able to touch, giving to one another
All their profundity, all their accidents,
— Changeable mood of clouds, permanent stars, —
Like thoughts in the mind hanging a long way off,
Revealed between lovers, friends.   Peer in the water
Over the boat's edge; seek the sky's night-heart;
Are they near, are they far, those clouds, those stars
Given, reflected, pooled? are they so close
For a hand to clasp, to lift them, feel their shape,
Explore their reality, take a rough possession?
Oh no! too delicate, too shy for handling,
They tilt at a touch, quiver to other shapes,
Dance away, change, are lost, drowned, scared;
Hands break the mirror, speech's crudity
The surmise, the divining;
Such things so deeply held, so lightly held,
Subtile, imponderable, as stars in water
Or thoughts in another's thoughts.
Are they near, are they far, those stars, that knowledge?

VICTORIA SACKVILLE–WEST

Deep? shallow? solid? rare?   The boat drifts on,
And the litten candle single in the prow,
The small, immediate candle in the prow,
Burns brighter in the water than any star.

EDWARD SHANKS

1892–

289   *Sleeping Heroes*

OLD Barbarossa
   Sleeps not alone
With his beard flowing over
   The gray mossy stone.

Arthur is with him
   And Charlemain.   The three
Wait for awaking,
   Wait to be free.

When the raven calls them
   They'll rise all together
And gird their three swords on
   And look at the weather.

Arthur will swear it is
   A very cold morning:
Charlemain says a red sunrise
   Is the shepherd's warning.

Barbarossa says nothing
   But feels in every bone
A pang of rheumatism
   From sleeping on wet stone.

330

Then from the gray heaven
    Comes a mist of faint rain
    And the three sleeping heroes
    Turn to sleep again.

290   *Drilling in Russell Square*

THE withered leaves that drift in Russell Square
    Will turn to mud and dust and moulder there
And we shall moulder in the plains of France
Before these leaves have ceased from their last dance.

The hot sun triumphs through the fading trees,
The fading houses keep away the breeze
And the autumnal warmth strange dreams doth breed
As right and left the faltering columns lead.
Squad, 'shun! Form fours. . . . And once the France we
    knew
Was a warm distant place with sun shot through,
A happy land of gracious palaces,
And Paris! Paris! Where twice green the trees
Do twice salute the all delightful year!
(Though the sun lives, the trees are dying here.)
And Germany we thought a singing place,
Where in the hamlets dwelt a simple race,
Where th' untaught villager would still compose
Delicious things upon a girl or rose.
Well, I suppose all I shall see of France
Will be most clouded by an Uhlan's lance,
Red fields from cover glimpsed be all I see
Of innocent, singing, peasant Germany.

Form four-rs! Form two deep! We wheel and pair
And still the brown leaves drift in Russell Square.

291   *Going in to Dinner*

BEAT the knife on the plate and the fork on the can,
For we're going in to dinner, so make all the noise you
  can,
Up and down the officer wanders, looking blue,
Sing a song to cheer him up, he wants his dinner too.

March into the village-school, make the tables rattle
Like a dozen dam' machine-guns in the bloody battle,
Use your forks for drumsticks, use your plates for drums,
Make a most infernal clatter, here the dinner comes!

292   ' *High Germany* '

NO more the English girls may go
    To follow with the drum,
But still they flock together
    To see the soldiers come;
For horse and foot are marching by
    And the bold artillery:
They're going to the cruel wars
    In Low Germany.

They're marching down by lane and town
    And they are hot and dry,
But as they marched together
    I heard the soldiers cry:
' O all of us, both horse and foot
    And the proud artillery,
We're going to the merry wars
    In Low Germany.'

RICHARD CHURCH

1893–

293   *On Hearing the First Cuckoo*

O H Menelaus,
  Oh my poor friend,
You have heard the news?
I know! I know! They all betray us.
Sooner or later there comes an end
To kindness; and the winds of abuse
Nip the bud, shrivel the bloom.
Then marriage, with the promise of the bed,
Is a disgusting memory of betrayal,
Shame in the heart for words once said
With a bride now clasped to another groom.
Not the flesh, but the mind, Menelaus, is frail.

THOMAS McGREEVY

1893–

294   *Aodh Ruadh O Domhnaill*

To STIEFÁN MACENNA

J UAN de Juni the priest said,
  Each J becoming H;

Berruguette, he said,
And the G was aspirate;

Ximenez, he said then
And aspirated first and last.

But he never said
And — it seemed odd — he

333

THOMAS McGREEVY

Never had heard
The aspirated name
Of the centuries-dead
Bright-haired young man
Whose grave I sought.

All day I passed
In greatly built gloom
From dusty gilt tomb
Marvellously wrought
To tomb
Rubbing
At mouldy inscriptions
With fingers wetted with spit
And asking
Where I might find it
And failing.
Yet when
Unhurried —
    Not as at home
    Where heroes, hanged, are buried
    With non-commissioned officers' bored
      maledictions
    Quickly in the gaol-yard —

They brought
His blackening body
Here
To rest
Princes came
Walking
Behind it

And all Valladolid knew
And out to Simancas all knew
Where they buried Red Hugh.

NOTE

Aodh Ruadh O Domhnaill

*Aodh Ruadh O Domhnaill, 'Red' Hugh O'Donnell, Prince
of Tirconaill, went to Spain to consult with King Philip III
after the defeat of the Irish and Spanish at Kinsale in 1601.
He was lodged in the castle of Simancas during the negotiations
but, poisoned by a certain James Blake, a Norman-Irish crea-
ture of the Queen of England (Elizabeth Tudor), he died there.
As a member of the Third Order of Saint Francis, he was
buried in the church of San Francisco at Valladolid. This
church was destroyed during the nineteenth century and none
of the tombs that were in it seem to have been preserved.*

295   *Homage to Jack Yeats*

GREYER than the tide below, the tower;
   The day is grey above;
About the walls
A curlew flies, calls;
Rain threatens, west;
This hour,
Driving,
I thought how this land, so desolate,
Long, long ago, was rich in living,
More reckless, consciously, in strife,
More conscious daring-delicate
In love.

And then the tower veered
Greyly to me,
Passed . . .
I meditated,

335

THOMAS M^cGREEVY

Feared
The thought experience sent,
That the gold years
Of Limerick life
Might be but consecrated
Lie,
Heroic lives
So often merely meant
The brave stupidity of soldiers,
The proud stupidity of soldiers' wives.

ROBERT NICHOLS

1893–1944

296 *To D'Annunzio: Lines from the Sea*

LOUDENS the sea-wind, downward plunge the bows,
Glass-green she takes it, staggers, rolls and checks,
Then sheers, and as she buffets back the blows
There comes a thundering along the decks.

The surf-smoke flies, the tatter'd cloud-wings haste,
And the white sun, sheeted or glaring cold,
Whirrs a harsh sword upon the spumy waste —
Now ancient grey, now weltering dizzy gold.

This is the Adriatic; and I gaze
In vain toward the north horizon's round,
To where behind the threshes' driving haze,
Beyond the glittering wilderness's bound,

There stands that man, target of Europe's eyes,
Who in unholy honour her decree
Defied; whom now the unbending Fates chastise
With their most biting scourge: bare memory.

336

ROBERT NICHOLS

D'Annunzio, upon the further shore
Of this bleak Adriatic, while the brine
Whitens the tunic which the shrapnel tore,
From which you have ripped your valour's golden sign,

They say you wander, and the shrewd sun's glance
Mocks you with starving warmth, the cruel cold
Hail compasses you with its ironic dance —
You, halt, bald, blind; you, shivering, beaten, old.

Thus do they say; and that you sometimes cast
Hands that entreat towards the thunderous waves,
As if to summon from the gorgeous past,
And those black depths, such galleons and such braves

As throned your Venice, in republican state,
Regent of every sun-filled sea that stirs
Between the Sicilian's rosy sundown gate
And the Cathayan's dawn-dark ridge of firs.

But vainly, quite in vain! the breaker's crest
Shrieks as the wind stoops on the tortured seas
To tear the brown weed from its cloven breast. . . .
And suddenly you fall upon your knees,

When there is broken from your desolate heart
So loud, so bitter, long and lost a cry
That those who watch you secretly apart
For sudden pity do not dare draw nigh.

They pity — but not I! Were pity priced
So low, how spare true misery a tear?
What though you bear the cross of Antichrist,
It is in very truth a cross you bear;

337

ROBERT NICHOLS

And we, to whom no certain faith is given
With which in desperate act to gauge our worth,
Or, having faith, are granted not of heaven
Fierce hours to bear its crown or cross on earth,

We envy you.   Whose is a happier lot
Than his, who of all contraries aware
Dares to believe, and when hell rages hot
Is given an hour for that belief to dare?

He, who in face of contradiction's spite
Has with his doubt so wrought he can aver
That he believes, has to his soul a right;
And he whom not a world's odds can deter

From making trial of belief so won
Has known his soul; but he who best and last
Fights till belief be lost or he undone
Has given the world a soul, and holds his fast.

Therefore, D'Annunzio, gazing on your sea,
I hail you, and I lift to heaven this prayer:
Mine be such faith, mine such a foe as he,
That, when my hour strikes, I, as he, may dare!

> The Adriatic, a half-gale
> from the NE., January, 1921.

338

ROBERT NICHOLS

From 'Sonnets to Aurelia'

(i)

WHEN the proud World does most my world despise,
  Vaunting what most my human heart must grieve,
Choosing what most I value to disprize,
  Deriding most that which I most believe —
When the proud World, I say, does most offend
  The artless passion of my patient heart,
Till I despair the morrow make amend,
  And before sunset from the sun would part:
Then in my ruin's hour remembrance brings
  Faith to my doubt, to my intention grace,
Reminding me how feebly fall such stings
  On one whose eyes dared once your eyes to face,
  And read in them, what no ill can remove,
  The love that to the lover said, '*I love*'.

298   *(ii)*

THOUGH to your life apparent stain attach,
  Yet to my eyes more fair shines its hid fame;
Though tongues repeat what deceived eyes may catch,
  Yet to my ears your praise grows, not your blame;
Though of yourself, yourself make ill report,
  The voice that speaks, so speaking, counters you;
Though to your heart, your heart impute false sport,
  Yet by its height I know it calm and true.

I grow love-wise that was but worldly-wise,
  My sight is healed by my own bitter tears,
My truth more proved by these disprovèd lies,
  My faith more firm for these unfounded fears;
  For now I know you never shall deceive
  Till my belief your truth shall misbelieve.

299   (*iii*)

BUT piteous things we are — when I am gone,
    Dissolved in the detritus of the pits,
And you, poor drivelling disregarded crone,
    Bide blinking at memory between drowsy fits,
Within the mouldering ball-room of your brain,
    That once was filled fantastically bright
With dancers eddying to a frantic strain,
    What ghosts will haunt the last hours of the light?

Among the mothlike shadows you will mark
    Two that most irk you, that with gesture human
Yet play out passion heedless of the dark:
    A desperate man and a distracted woman,
    And you mayhap will vaguely puzzle, ' Who
    Is she? and he? why do they what they do? '

300   (*iv*)

COME, let us sigh a requiem over love
    That we ourselves have slain in love's own bed,
Whose hearts that had courage to drink enough
    Lacked courage to forbid the taste they bred,
Which body captained soon, till, in disgust,
    These very hearts of bodily surfeit died,
Poisoned by that sweet overflow of lust
    Whose past delight our substance deified.

No courage, no, nor pleasure have we now,
    To our own frantic bodies are we tossed,
Only sometimes exhaustion will allow
    Us peace to observe the image of love's ghost,
    With torturing voice and with hid face return
    Faintly, as even now, to bid us mourn.

340

ROBERT NICHOLS

301   *Aurelia*

WHEN within my arms I hold you,
   Motionless in long surrender,
Then what love-words can I summon,
Tender as my heart is tender?

When within your arms you hold me,
And kisses speak your love unspoken,
Then my eyes with tears run over,
And my very heart is broken.

302   *From 'The Flower of Flame'*

BEFORE I woke I knew her gone,
   Though nothing nigh had stirred;
Now by the curtain inward blown
   She stood, not seen, but heard,
Where the faint moonlight dimmed or shone . . .
   And neither spoke a word.

One hand against her mouth she pressed,
   But could not stanch its cry;
The other knocked upon her breast
   Impotently . . . while I
Glared rigid, labouring, possessed,
   And dared not ask her why.

303 *The Moon behind high tranquil Leaves*

THE moon behind high tranquil leaves
   Hides her sad head;
The dwindled water tinkles and grieves
In the stream's black bed;
     And where now, where are you sleeping?

ROBERT NICHOLS

The shadowy nightjar, hawking gnats,
Flickers or floats;
High in still air the flurrying bats
Repeat their wee notes;
    And where now, where are you sleeping?

Silent lightning flutters in heaven,
Where quiet crowd
By the toil of an upper whirlwind driven
Dark legions of cloud;
    In whose arms now are you sleeping?
The cloud makes, lidding the sky's wan hole,
The world a tomb;
Far out at sea long thunders roll
From gloom to dim gloom;
    In whose arms now are you sleeping?

Rent clouds, like boughs, in darkness hang
Close overhead;
The foreland's bell-buoy begins to clang
As if for the dead;
    Awake they where you are sleeping?
The chasms crack; the heavens revolt;
With tearing sound
Bright bolt volleys on flaring bolt,
Wave and cloud clash; through deep, through vault,
Huge thunders rebound!
    But they wake not where you are sleeping.

ROBERT NICHOLS

304   *Don Juan's Address to the Sunset*

EXQUISITE stillness!   What serenities
Of earth and air!   How bright atop the wall
The stonecrop's fire, and beyond the precipice
How huge, how hushed the primrose evenfall!
How softly, too, the white crane voyages
Yon honeyed height of warmth and silence, whence
He can look down on islet, lake and shore
And crowding woods and voiceless promontories,
Or, further grazing, view the magnificence
Of cloud-like mountains and of mountainous cloud
Or ghostly wrack below the horizon rim
Not even his eye has vantage to explore.
Now, spirit, find out wings and mount to him,
Wheel where he wheels, where he is soaring soar,
Hang where now he hangs in the planisphere —
Evening's first star and golden as a bee
In the sun's hair — for happiness is here!

HERBERT READ

1893–

305   *The End of a War*

'*In former days we used to look at life, and sometimes from
a distance, at death, and still further removed from us, at
eternity. To-day it is from afar that we look at life, death is
near us, and perhaps nearer still is eternity.*' — JEAN BOUVIER,
a French subaltern, February 1916.

ARGUMENT

In the early days of November 1918, *the Allied Forces had
for some days been advancing in pursuit of the retreating
German Army. The advance was being carried out accord-*

ing to a schedule. Each Division was given a line to which it must attain before nightfall; and this meant that each battalion in a division had to reach a certain point by a certain time. The schedule was in general being well adhered to, but the opposition encountered varied considerably at different points.

On November 10th, a certain English Battalion had been continuously harassed by machine-gun fire, and late in the afternoon was still far from its objective. Advancing under cover, it reached the edge of a plantation from which stretched a wide open space of cultivated land, with a village in front about 500 yards away. The officer in charge of the scouts was sent ahead with a corporal and two men to reconnoitre, and this little party reached the outskirts of the village without observing any signs of occupation. At the entrance of the village, propped against a tree, they found a German officer, wounded severely in the thigh. He was quite conscious and looked up calmly as Lieut. S— approached him. He spoke English, and when questioned, intimated that the village had been evacuated by the Germans two hours ago.

Thereupon Lieut. S— signalled back to the battalion, who then advanced along the road in marching formation. It was nearly dusk when they reached the small place in front of the church, and there they were halted. Immediately from several points, but chiefly from the tower of the church, a number of machine-guns opened fire on the massed men. A wild cry went up, and the men fled in rage and terror to the shelter of the houses, leaving a hundred of their companions and five officers dead or dying on the pavement. In the houses and the church they routed out the ambushed Germans and mercilessly bayoneted them.

The corporal who had been with Lieut. S— ran to the entrance of the village, to settle with the wounded officer who had betrayed them. The German seemed to be expecting him; his face did not flinch as the bayonet descended.

When the wounded had been attended to, and the dead gathered together, the remaining men retired to the schoolhouse to rest for the night. The officers then went to the château of the village, and there in a gardener's cottage, searching for fuel, the corporal already mentioned found the naked body of a young girl. Both legs were severed, and one severed arm was found in another room. The body itself was covered with bayonet wounds. When the discovery was reported to Lieut. S.—, he went to verify the strange crime, but there was nothing to be done; he was, moreover, sick and tired. He found a bed in another cottage near the château, where some old peasants were still cowering behind a screen. He fell into a deep sleep, and did not wake until the next morning, the 11th of November, 1918.

I. MEDITATION OF THE DYING GERMAN OFFICER

ICH sterbe . . . Life ebbs with an easy flow
and I've no anguish now. This failing light
is the world's light: it dies like a lamp
flickering for want of oil. When the last jump comes
and the axe-head blackness slips through flesh
that welcomes it with open but unquivering lips
then I shall be one with the Unknown
this Nothing which Heinrich made his argument
for God's existence: a concept beyond the mind's reach.
But why embody the Unknown: why give to God

345

anything but essence, intangible, invisible, inert?
The world is full of solid creatures — these
are the mind's material, these we must mould
into images, idols to worship and obey:
the Father and the Flag, and the wide Empire
of our creative hands.   I have seen
the heart of Europe send its beating blood
like a blush over the world's pallid sphere
calling it to one life, one order and one living.
For that dream I've given my life and to the last
fought its listless enemies.   Now Chaos intervenes
and I leave not gladly but with harsh disdain
a world too strong in folly for the bliss of dreams.

I fought with gladness.   When others cursed the day
this stress was loosed
and men were driven into camps, to follow
with wonder, woe, or base delirium
the voiceless yet incessant surge
then I exulted: but with not more
than a nostril's distension, an eager eye
and fast untiring step.

                          The first week
I crossed the Fatherland, to take my place
in the swift-winged swoop that all but ended
the assay in one wild and agile venture.
I was blooded then, but the wound
seared in the burning circlet of my spirit
served only to temper courage
with scorn of action's outcome.
Blooded but not beaten I left the ranks
to be a leader.   Four years

HERBERT READ

I have lived in the ecstasy of battle.
The throbbing of guns, growing yearly,
has been drum music to my ears
the crash of shells the thrill of cymbals
bayonets fiddlers' bows and the crack of rifles
plucked harp strings.   Now the silence
is unholy.   Death has no deeper horror
than diminishing sound — ears that strain
for the melody of action, hear
only the empty silence of retreating life.
Darkness will be kinder.

I die —

But still I hear a distant gunfire, stirring in my ear
like a weary humming nerve.   I will cling to that sound
and on its widening wave
lapse into eternity.   Heinrich, are you near?
Best friend, but false to my faith.
Would you die doubtfully with so calm a gaze?
Mind above battles, does your heart resign
love of the Fatherland in this hour of woe?
No drum will beat in your dying ears, and your God
will meet you with a cold embrace.
The void is icy: your Abstraction
freezes the blood at death: no calm
bound in such a barren law.   The bond between
two human hearts is richer.   Love can seal
the anguished ventricles with subtle fire
and make life end in peace, in love
the love we shared in all this strife.
Heinrich, your God has not this power, or he would heal
the world's wounds and create the empire
now left in the defeated hands of men.

HERBERT READ

At Valenciennes I saw you turn
swiftly into an open church. I followed
stood in the shadow of the aisle
and watched you pray. My impulse then
was to meet you in the porch and test
my smile against your smile, my peace against yours
and from your abashment pluck a wilder hope.
But the impulse died in the act: your face was blank
drained of sorrow as of joy, and I was dumb
before renunciation's subtler calm.
I let you pass, and into the world
went to deny my sight, to seal my lips
against the witness of your humble faith.
For my faith was action: is action now!
In death I triumph with a deed
and prove my faith against your passive ghost.

Faith in self comes first, from self we build
the web of friendship, from friends to confederates
and so to the State. This web has a weft
in the land we live in, a town, a hill
all that the living eyes traverse. There are lights
given by the tongue we speak, the songs we sing,
the music and the magic of our Fatherland.
This is a tangible trust. To make it secure
against the tempests of inferior minds
to build it in our blood, to make our lives
a tribute to its beauty — there is no higher aim.
This good achieved, then to God we turn
for a crown on our perfection: God we create
in the end of action, not in dreams.

God dies in this dying light.   The mists receive
my spent spirit: there is no one to hear
my last wish.   Already my thoughts
rebound in a tenement whose doors
are shut: strange muscles clench my jaws
these limbs are numb.   I cannot lift
a finger to my will.   But the mind
rises like a crystal sphere above the rigid wreck
is poised there, perhaps to fall into the void
still dreaming of an Empire of the West.
And so still feels no fear!   Mind triumphs over flesh
ordering the body's action in direst danger.
Courage is not born in men, but born of love
love of life and love of giving, love
of this hour of death, which all love seeks.

I die, but death was destined.   My life was given
my death ordained when first my hand
held naked weapons in this war.   The rest
has been a waiting for this final hour.
In such a glory I could not always live.

My brow falls like a shutter of lead, clashes
on the clenched jaw.   The curtain of flesh
is wreathed about these rigid lines
in folds that have the easy notion of a smile.
So let them kiss earth and acid corruption:
extinction of the clod.   The bubble is free
to expand to the world's confines or to break
against the pricking stars.   The last lights shine
across its perfect crystal: rare ethereal glimmer
of mind's own intensity.   Above the clod
all things are clear, and what is left

HERBERT READ

is petulant scorn, implanted passions,
everything not tensely ideal.   Blind emotions
wreck the image with their blundering wings.
Mind must define before the heart intrigues.
Last light above the world, wavering in the darkest
void of Nothing — how still and tenuous
no music of the spheres — and so break with a sigh
against the ultimate
shores of this world
so finite
so small
Nichts

II.   DIALOGUE BETWEEN THE BODY AND THE SOUL OF THE MURDERED GIRL

Body

I speak not from my pallid lips
but from these wounds.

Soul

Red lips that cannot tell
a credible tale.

Body

In a world of martyred men
these lips renounce their ravage:
The wounds of France
roused their fresh and fluid voices.

Soul

War has victims beyond the bands
bonded to slaughter.   War moves with armoured wheels
across the quivering flesh and patient limbs
of all life's labile fronds.

350

HERBERT READ

Body

France was the garden I lived in.
Amid these trees, these fields, petals fell
flesh to flesh; I was a wilder flower.

Soul

Open and innocent. So is the heart
laid virgin to my voice. I filled
your vacant ventricles with dreams
with immortal hopes and aspirations that exalt
the flesh to passion, to love and hate.
Child-radiance then is clouded, the light
that floods the mind is hot with blood
pulse beats to the vibrant battle-cry
the limbs are burnt with action.

Body

This heart had not lost its innocence so soon
but for the coming of that day when men
speaking a strange tongue, wearing strange clothes
armed, flashing with harness and spurs
carrying rifles, lances or spears
followed by rumbling waggons, shrouded guns
passed through the village in endless procession
swift, grim, scornful, exulting.

Soul

You had not lost your innocence so soon
but for the going of men from the village
your father gone, your brother
only the old left, and the very young
the women sad, the houses shuttered

351

suspense of school, even of play
the eager search for news, the air
of universal doubt, and then the knowledge
that the wavering line of battle now was fixed
beyond this home.   The soil was tilled
for visionary hate.

Body

Four years was time enough
for such a seedling hate to grow
sullen, close, intent;
To wait and wonder
but to abate
no fervour in the slow passage of despair.

Soul

The mind grew tense.

Body

My wild flesh was caught
in the cog and gear of hate.

Soul

I lay coiled, the spring
of all your intricate design.

Body

You served me well.   But still I swear
Christ was my only King.

Soul

France was your Motherland:
To her you gave your life and limbs.

HERBERT READ

Body

I gave these hands and gave these arms
I gave my head of ravelled hair.

Soul

You gave your sweet round breasts
like Agatha who was your Saint.

Body

Mary Aegyptiaca
is the pattern of my greatest loss.

Soul

To whom in nakedness and want
God sent a holy man.
Who clothed her, shrived her, gave her peace
before her spirit left the earth.

Body

My sacrifice was made to gain
the secrets of these hostile men.

Soul

I hover round your fameless features
barred from Heaven by light electric.

Body

All men who find these mauled remains
will pray to Mary for your swift release.

Soul

The cry that left your dying lips
was heard by God.

353

HERBERT READ

Body

I died for France.

Soul

A bright mantle fell across your bleeding limbs.
Your face averted shone with sacred fire.
So be content.   In this war
many men have perished not blessed
with faith in a cause, a country or a God
not less martyrs than Herod's Victims, Ursula's Virgins
or any massed innocents massacred.

Body

Such men give themselves not to their God but to their fate
die thinking the face of God not love but hate.

Soul

Those who die for a cause die comforted and coy;
believing their cause God's cause they die with joy.

III.   MEDITATION OF THE WAKING
ENGLISH OFFICER

I wake: I am alive: there is a bell
sounding with the dream's retreating surf
O catch the lacey hem dissolved in light
that creeps along the healing tendrils of a mind
still drugged with sleep.   Why must my day
kill my dreams?   Days of hate.   But yes a bell
beats really on this air, a mad bell.
The peasants stir behind that screen.
Listen: they mutter now: they sing

354

in their old cracked voices, intone
a litany. There are no guns
only these voices of thanksgiving. Can it be?
Yes yes yes: it is peace, peace!
The world is very still, and I am alive!
Look: I am alive, alive, alive.
O limbs, your white radiance
no longer to stand against bloody shot
this heart secure, to live and worship
to go God's way, to grow in faith
to fight with and not against the will!
That day has come at last! Suspended life
renews its rhythmic beat. I live!
Now can I love and strive, as I have dreamt.

Lie still, and let this litany
of simple voices and the jubilant bell
ease rebirth. First there are the dead to bury
O God, the dead. How can God's bell
ring out from that unholy ambush?
That tower of death! In excess of horror
war died. The nerve was broken
frayed men fought obscenely then: there was no fair joy
no glory in the strife, no blessed wrath.
Man's mind cannot excel
mechanic might except in savage sin.
Our broken bodies oiled the engines: mind was grit.

Shall I regret my pact? Envy that friend
who risked ignominy, insult, gaol
rather than stain his hands with human blood?
And left his fellow men. Such lonely pride

was never mine. I answered no call
there was no call to answer. I felt no hate
only the anguish of an unknown fate
a shot, a cry: then armies on the move
the sudden lull in daily life
all eyes wide with wonder, past surprise:
our felt dependence on a ruling few:
the world madness: the wild plunge:
the avalanche and I myself a twig
torn from its mother soil
and to the chaos rendered.

Listless

I felt the storm about me; its force
too strong to beat against; in its swirl
I spread my sapling arms, tossed on its swell
I rose, I ran, I down the dark world sped
till death fell round me like a rain of steel
and hope and faith and love coiled in my inmost cell.

Often in the weariness of watching
warding weary men, pitched against
the unmeaning blackness of the night, the wet fog,
the enemy blanketed in mystery, often
I have questioned my life's inconstant drift;
God not real, hate not real, the hearts of men
insentient engines pumping blood
into a spongy mass that cannot move
above the indignity of inflicted death:
the only answer this: the infinite is all
and I, a finite speck, no essence even
of the life that falls like dew
from the spirit breathed on the fine edge

of matter, perhaps only that edge
a ridge between eternal death and life eternal,
a moment of time, temporal.
The universe swaying between Nothing and Being
and life faltering like a clock's tick
between a pendulum's coming and going.
The individual lost: seventy years
seventy minutes have no meaning.
Let death, I cried, come from the forward guns
let death come this moment, swift and crackling
tick-tock, tick-tock — moments that pass
not reckoned in the infinite.

Then I have said: all is that must be.
There is no volition, even prayer
dies on lips compressed in fear.
Where all must be, there is no God
for God can only be the God of prayer
an infinitely kind Father whose will
can mould the world, who can
in answer to my prayer mould me.
But whilst I cannot pray, I can't believe
but in this frame of machine necessity
must renounce not only God, but self.
For what is the self without God?
A moment not reckoned in the infinite.
My soul is less than nothing, lost,
unless in this life it can build
a bridge to life eternal.

In a warm room, by the flickering fire
in friendly debate, in some remote
sheltered existence, even in the hermit's cell

357

easy it is to believe in God: extend the self
to communion with the infinite, the eternal.
But haggard in the face of death
deprived of all earthly comfort, all hope of life,
the soul a distilled essence, held
in a shaking cup, spilled
by a spit of lead, saved
by chance alone
very real
in its silky bag of skin, its bond of bone,
so little and so limited,
there's no extenuation then.
Fate is in facts: the only hope
an unknown chance.

So I have won through.   What now?
Will faith rise triumphant from the wreck
despair once more evaded in a bold
assertion of the self: self to God related
self in God attained, self a segment
of the eternal circle, the wheel
of Heaven, which through the dust of days
and stagnant darkness steadily revolves?
The bells of hell ring ting-a-ling
for you but not for me — for you
whose gentian eyes stared from the cold
impassive alp of death.   You betrayed us
at the last hour of the last day
playing the game to the end
your smile the only comment
on the well-done deed.   What mind
have you carried over the confines?

HERBERT READ

Your fair face was noble of its kind
some visionary purpose cut the lines
clearly on that countenance.
But you are defeated: once again
the meek inherit the kingdom of God.
No might can win against this wandering
wavering grace of humble men.
You die, in all your power and pride:
I live, in my meekness justified.

When first this fury caught us, then
I vowed devotion to the rights of men
would fight for peace once it came again
from this unwilled war pass gallantly
to wars of will and justice.
That was before I had faced death
day in day out, before hope had sunk
to a little pool of bitterness.
Now I see, either the world is mechanic force
and this the last tragic act, portending
endless hate and blind reversion
back to the tents and healthy lusts
of animal men: or we act
God's purpose in an obscure way.
Evil can only to the Reason stand
in scheme or scope beyond the human mind.
God seeks the perfect man, planned
to love him as a friend: our savage fate
a fire to burn our dross
to temper us to finer stock
man emerging in some inconceivèd span
as something more than remnant of a dream.

HERBERT READ

To that end worship God, join the voices
heard by these waking ears. God is love:
in his will the meek heart rejoices
doubting till the final grace a dove
from Heaven descends and wakes the mind
in light above the light of human kind
in light celestial
infinite and still
eternal
bright

It was necessary for my poetic purpose to take an incident
from the War of 1914–18 which would serve as a focus for
feeling and sentiments otherwise diffuse. The incident is true,
and can be vouched for by several witnesses still living. But
its horrors do not accuse any particular nation; they are rep-
resentative of war and of human nature in war. It is not my
business as a poet to condemn war (or, to be more exact, mod-
ern warfare). I only wish to present the universal aspects of
a particular event. Judgement may follow, but should never
precede or become embroiled with the act of poetry. It is for
this reason that Milton's attitude to his Satan has so often
been misunderstood.

SYLVIA TOWNSEND WARNER
1893–

306   *The Sailor*

I HAVE a young love —
A landward lass is she —
And thus she entreated:
' O tell me of the sea
That on thy next voyage
My thoughts may follow thee.'

360

SYLVIA TOWNSEND WARNER

I took her up a hill
And showed her hills green,
One after other
With valleys between:
So green and gentle, I said,
Are the waves I've seen.

I led her by the hand
Down the grassy way,
And showed her the hedgerows
That were white with May:
So white and fleeting, I said,
Is the salt sea-spray.

I bade her lean her head
Down against my side,
Rising and falling
On my breath to ride:
Thus rode the vessel, I said,
On the rocking tide.

For she so young is, and tender,
I would not have her know
What it is that I go to
When to sea I must go,
Lest she should lie awake and tremble
When the great storm-winds blow.

1896–

307   *In Festubert*

NOW every thing that shadowy thought
    Lets peer with bedlam eyes at me
From alley-ways and thoroughfares
    Of cynic and ill memory
Lifts a gaunt head, sullenly stares,
    Shuns me as a child has shunned
A whizzing dragon-fly that daps
    Above his mudded pond.

Now bitter frosts, muffling the morn
    In old days, crunch the grass anew;
There where the floods made fields forlorn
    The glinzy ice grows thicker through.
The pollards glower like mummies when
    Thieves break into a pyramid,
Inscrutable as those dead men
    With painted mask and balm-cloth hid;

And all the old delight is cursed
    Redoubling present undelight.
Splinter, crystal, splinter and burst;
    And sear no more with second sight.

1916

308   *Forefathers*

HERE they went with smock and crook,
    Toiled in the sun, lolled in the shade,
Here they mudded out the brook
    And here their hatchet cleared the glade:
Harvest-supper woke their wit,
Huntsman's moon their wooings lit.

EDMUND BLUNDEN

From this church they led their brides,
　　From this church themselves were led
Shoulder-high; on these waysides
　　Sat to take their beer and bread.
Names are gone — what men they were
These their cottages declare.

Names are vanished, save the few
　　In the old brown Bible scrawled;
These were men of pith and thew,
　　Whom the city never called;
Scarce could read or hold a quill,
Built the barn, the forge, the mill.

On the green they watched their sons
　　Playing till too dark to see,
As their fathers watched them once,
　　As my father once watched me;
While the bat and beetle flew
On the warm air webbed with dew.

Unrecorded, unrenowned,
　　Men from whom my ways begin,
Here I know you by your ground
　　But I know you not within —
There is silence, there survives
Not a moment of your lives.

Like the bee that now is blown
　　Honey-heavy on my hand,
From his toppling tansy-throne
　　In the green tempestuous land —
I'm in clover now, nor know
Who made honey long ago.

EDMUND BLUNDEN

Almswomen

A^T Quincey's moat the squandering village ends,
   And there in the alms-house dwell the dearest friends
Of all the village, two old dames that cling
As close as any true-loves in the spring.
Long, long ago they passed three-score-and-ten,
And in this doll's house lived together then;
All things they have in common being so poor,
And their one fear, Death's shadow at the door.
Each sundown makes them mournful, each sunrise
Brings back the brightness in their failing eyes.

How happy go the rich fair-weather days
When on the roadside folk stare in amaze
At such a honeycomb of fruit and flowers
As mellows round their threshold; what long hours
They gloat upon their steepling hollyhocks,
Bee's balsams, feathery southernwood and stocks,
Fiery dragon's-mouths, great mallow leaves
For salves, and lemon-plants in bushy sheaves,
Shagged Esau's-hands with five green finger-tips.
Such old sweet names are ever on their lips.

As pleased as little children where these grow
In cobbled pattens and worn gowns they go,
Proud of their wisdom when on gooseberry shoots
They stuck egg shells to fright from coming fruits
The brisk-billed rascals; scanning still to see
Their neighbour owls saunter from tree to tree,
Or in the hushing half-light mouse the lane
Long-winged and lordly.

EDMUND BLUNDEN

> But when those hours wane
Indoors they ponder, scared by the harsh storm
Whose pelting saracens on the window swarm,
And listen for the mail to clatter past
And church-clock's deep bay withering on the blast;
They feed the fire that flings its freakish light
On pictured kings and queens grotesquely bright,
Platters and pitchers, faded calendars
And graceful hour-glass trim with lavenders.

Many a time they kiss and cry and pray
That both be summoned in the selfsame day,
And wiseman linnet tinkling in his cage
End too with them the friendship of old age,
And all together leave their treasured room
Some bell-like evening when the May's in bloom.

1920

310   *Mole Catcher*

WITH coat like any mole's, as soft and black,
     And hazel bows bundled beneath his arm,
With long-helved spade and rush-bag on his back,
The trapper plods alone about the farm:
And spies new mounds in the ripe pasture-land,
And where the lob-worms writhe up in alarm
And easy sinks the spade, he takes his stand
Knowing the moles' dark high-road runs below:
Then sharp and square he chops the turf, and day
Gloats on the opened turnpike through the clay.

Out from his wallet hurry pin and prong,
And trap, and noose to tie it to the bow;
And then his grand arcanum, oily and strong,
Found out by his forefather years ago

365

To scent the peg and witch the moles along.
The bow is earthed and arched ready to shoot
And snatch the death-knot fast round the first mole
Who comes and snuffs well pleased and tries to root
Past the sly nose peg; back again is put
The mould, and death left smirking in the hole.
The old man goes and tallies all his snares
And finds the prisoners there and takes his toll.

And moles to him are only moles; but hares
See him afield and scarcely cease to nip
Their dinners, for he harms not them; he spares
The drowning fly that of his ale would sip
And throws the ant the crumbs of comradeship.
And every time he comes into his yard
Grey linnet knows he brings the groundsel sheaf,
And clatters round the cage to be unbarred,
And on his finger whistles twice as hard. —
What his old vicar says is his belief,
In the side pew he sits and hears the truth;
And never misses once to ring his bell
On Sundays night and morn, nor once since youth
Has heard the chimes afield, but has heard tell
There 's not a peal in England sounds so well.

311   *The Survival*

TO–DAY'S house makes to-morrow's road;
    I knew these heaps of stone
When they were walls of grace and might,
The country's honour, art's delight
That over fountained silence showed
    Fame's final bastion.

366

Inheritance has found fresh work,
  Disunion union breeds;
Beauty the strong, its difference lost,
Has matter fit for flood and frost.
Here 's the true blood that will not shirk
  Life's new-commanding needs.

With curious costly zeal, O man,
  Raise orrery and ode;
How shines your tower, the only one
Of that especial site and stone!
And even the dream's confusion can
  Sustain to-morrow's road.

312   *Report on Experience*

I HAVE been young, and now am not too old;
  And I have seen the righteous forsaken,
His health, his honour and his quality taken.
  This is not what we were formerly told.

I have seen a green country, useful to the race,
Knocked silly with guns and mines, its villages vanished,
Even the last rat and last kestrel banished —
  God bless us all, this was peculiar grace.

I knew Seraphina; Nature gave her hue,
Glance, sympathy, note, like one from Eden.
I saw her smile warp, heard her lyric deaden;
  She turned to harlotry; — this I took to be new.

Say what you will, our God sees how they run.
These disillusions are His curious proving
That He loves humanity and will go on loving;
  Over there are faith, life, virtue in the sun.

367

FREDERICK ROBERT HIGGINS
1896–

313   *The Little Clan*

OVER their edge of earth
    They wearily tread,
Leaving the stone-grey dew —
    The hungry grass;
Most proud in their own defeat,
    These last men pass
This labouring grass that bears them
    Little bread.

Too full their spring-tide flowed,
    And ebbing then
Has left each hooker deep
    Within salt grass;
All ebbs, yet lives in their song;
    Song shall not pass
With these most desperate,
    Most noble men!

Then, comfort your own sorrow;
    Time has heard
One groping singer hold
    A burning face;
You mourn no living Troy,
    Then mourn no less
The living glory of
    Each Gaelic word!

FREDERICK ROBERT HIGGINS

314 *Father and Son*

ONLY last week, walking the hushed fields
Of our most lovely Meath, now thinned by November,
I came to where the road from Laracor leads
To the Boyne river — that seemed more lake than river,
Stretched in uneasy light and stript of reeds.

And walking longside an old weir
Of my people's, where nothing stirs — only the shadowed
Leaden flight of a heron up the lean air —
I went unmanly with grief, knowing how my father,
Happy though captive in years, walked last with me there.

Yes, happy in Meath with me for a day
He walked, taking stock of herds hid in their own breathing;
And naming colts, gusty as wind, once steered by his hand;
Lightnings winked in the eyes that were half shy in greeting
Old friends — the wild blades, when he gallivanted the
　　　　land.

For that proud, wayward man now my heart breaks —
Breaks for that man whose mind was a secret eyrie,
Whose kind hand was sole signet of his race,
Who curbed me, scorned my green ways, yet increasingly
　　　　loved me
Till death drew its grey blind down his face.

315 *The Old Jockey*

HIS last days linger in that low attic
That barely lets out the night,
With its gabled window on Knackers' Alley,
Just hoodwinking the light.

He comes and goes by that gabled window
And then on the window-pane
He leans, as thin as a bottled shadow —
A look and he 's gone again:

Eyeing, maybe, some fine fish-women
In the best shawls of the Coombe
Or, maybe, the knife-grinder plying his treadle,
A run of sparks from his thumb!

But, O you should see him gazing, gazing,
When solemnly out on the road
The horse-drays pass overladen with grasses,
Each driver lost in his load;

Gazing until they return; and suddenly,
As galloping by they race,
From his pale eyes, like glass breaking,
Light leaps on his face.

316 *Padraic O'Conaire — Gaelic Storyteller*

(Died in the Fall of 1928)

THEY'VE paid the last respects in sad tobacco
And silent is this wake-house in its haze;
They've paid the last respects; and now their whisky
Flings laughing words on mouths of prayer and praise;
And so young couples huddle by the gables,
O let them grope home through the hedgy night —
Alone I'll mourn my old friend, while the cold dawn
Thins out the holy candlelight.

370

FREDERICK ROBERT HIGGINS

Respects are paid to one loved by the people;
Ah, was he not — among our mighty poor —
The sudden wealth cast on those pools of darkness,
Those bearing, just, a star's faint signature;
And so he was to me, close friend, near brother,
Dear Padraic of the wide and sea-cold eyes —
So lovable, so courteous and noble,
The very West was in his soft replies.

They'll miss his heavy stick and stride in Wicklow —
His story-talking down Winetavern Street,
Where old men sitting in the wizen daylight
Have kept an edge upon his gentle wit;
While women on the grassy streets of Galway,
Who hearken for his passing — but in vain,
Shall hardly tell his step as shadows vanish
Through archways of forgotten Spain.

Ah, they'll say: Padraic 's gone again exploring;
But now down glens of brightness, O he'll find
An ale-house overflowing with wise Gaelic
That 's braced in vigour by the bardic mind,
And there his thoughts shall find their own forefathers —
In minds to whom our heights of race belong,
In crafty men, who ribbed a ship or turned
The secret joinery of song.

Alas, death mars the parchment of his forehead;
And yet for him, I know, the earth is mild —
The windy fidgets of September grasses
Can never tease a mind that loved the wild;

So drink his peace — this grey juice of the barley
Runs with a light that ever pleased his eye —
While old flames nod and gossip on the hearthstone
And only the young winds cry.

317   *Song for the Clatter Bones*

GOD rest that Jewy woman,
   Queen Jezebel, the bitch
Who peeled the clothes from her shoulder-bones
Down to her spent teats
As she stretched out of the window
Among the geraniums, where
She chaffed and laughed like one half daft
Titivating her painted hair —

King Jehu he drove to her,
She tipped him a fancy beck;
But he from his knacky side-car spoke
'Who'll break that dewlapped neck?'
And so she was thrown from the window;
Like Lucifer she fell
Beneath the feet of the horses and they beat
The light out of Jezebel.

That corpse wasn't planted in clover;
Ah, nothing of her was found
Save those grey bones that Hare-foot Mike
Gave me for their lovely sound;
And as once her dancing body
Made star-lit princes sweat
So I'll just clack: though her ghost lacks a back
There's music in the old bones yet.

FREDERICK ROBERT HIGGINS

318   *The Ballad of O'Bruadir*

WHEN first I took to cutlass, blunderbuss and gun,
        Rolling glory on the water;
With boarding and with broadside we made the Dutchmen run,
        Rolling glory on the water;
Then down among the captains in their green skin shoes,
I sought for Hugh O'Bruadir and got but little news
Till I shook him by the hand in the bay of Santa Cruz,
        Rolling glory on the water.

O'Bruadir said kindly, ' You're a fresh blade from Mayo,
        Rolling glory on the water,
But come among my captains, to Achill back we go,
        Rolling glory on the water;
Although those Spanish beauties are dark and not so dear,
I'd rather taste in Mayo, with April on the year,
One bracing virgin female; so swing your canvas here,
        Rolling glory on the water! '

' There 's no man,' said a stranger, ' whose hand I'd sooner
        grip
        Rolling glory on the water.'
' Well I'm your man,' said Bruadir, ' and you're aboard my
        ship
        Rolling glory on the water.'
They drank to deeper friendship in ocean roguery;
And rolled ashore together, but between you and me
We found O'Bruadir dangling within an airy tree,
        Ghosting glory from the water!

373

LEONARD ALFRED GEORGE STRONG
1896–

319   *Two Generations*

I TURNED and gave my strength to woman,
    Leaving untilled the stubborn field.
Sinew and soul are gone to win her,
    Slow, and most perilous, her yield.

The son I got stood up beside me,
    With fire and quiet beauty filled;
He looked upon me, then he looked
    Upon the field I had not tilled.

He kissed me, and went forth to labour.
    Where lonely tilth and moorland meet
A gull above the ploughshare hears
    The ironic song of our defeat.

320   *The Old Man at the Crossing*

I SWEEP the street and lift me hat
    As persons come and persons go,
Me lady and me gentleman:
I lift me hat — but you don't know!

I've money by against I'm dead:
A hearse and mourners there will be!
And every sort of walking man
Will stop to lift his hat to me!

374

LEONARD ALFRED GEORGE STRONG

321   *The knowledgeable Child*

I ALWAYS see, — I don't know why, —
If any person's going to die.

That 's why nobody talks to me.
There was a man who came to tea,

And when I saw that he would die
I went to him and said ' Good-bye,

' I shall not see you any more.'
He died that evening. Then, next **door**,

They had a little girl: she died
Nearly as quick, and Mummy cried

And cried, and ever since that day
She 's made me promise not to say.

But folks are still afraid of me,
And, where they've children, nobo**dy**

Will let me next or nigh to them
For fear I'll say good-bye to them.

SACHEVERELL SITWELL
1897–

322   *Agamemnon's Tomb*

TOMB
A hollow hateful word
A bell, a leaden bell the dry lips mock,
Though the word is as mud or clay in its own sound;
A hollow noise that echoes its own emptiness,
Such is this awful thing, this cell to hold the box.
It is breathless, a sink of damp and mould, that 's all,

375

Where bones make dust and move not otherwise;
Who loves the spider or the worm, for this,
That they starve in there, but are its liveliness?
The grave-cloth, coldest and last night-gown,
That 's worn for ever till its rags are gone,
This comes at the end when every limb is straight,
When mouth and eyes are shut in mockery of sleep.
Much comes before this, for the miser hand
That clutches at an edge of wood, a chair, a table,
Must have its fingers broken, have its bones cracked back,
It 's the rigor mortis, death struggle out of life,
A wrestling at the world's edge for which way to go.

There are all other deaths, but all are sisters;
What dreams must they have who die so quiet in sleep,
What dread pursuings into arms of terror,
Feared all through life, gigantic in dark corridors,
A giant in a wood, or a swirling of deep waters;
This may be worst of all, for pain is material,
And it has lulls, or you may pray for them,
While, when the pain is worst, you pray for death,
For swift delivery from heart and lungs,
The tyrant machinery, the creaking engine,
Lungs like wheezing bellows, heart like a clock that stops;
To die frightened, with a scream that never comes
That shivers with no shape out of the dumb dry lips,
This is worse than pain, and worse than death, awake,
For with that cry you're in the tomb already,
There 's its arch above you, there 's its hand upon your
        mouth,
Knock, knock, knock, these are the nails of the coffin,
They go in easy, but must be wrenched out,

For no strength can break them from the walled night
    within;
They are little shining points, they are cloves that have no
    scent,
But the dead are kept in prison by such little things,
Though little does it help them when that guard is gone.
It is night, endless night, with not a chink of day,
And if the coffin breaks there is no hope in that,
The bones tumble out and only dogs will steal them;
There is no escape, no tunnel back to life,
And, soon, no person digging at the other end,
For the living soon forget, but soon will join you there;
The dead are but dead, there is no use for them,
But who can realize that it ends with breath,
That the heart is not a clock and will not wind once more?
There is something in mortality that will not touch on death,
That keeps the mind from it, that hides the coffin;
And, if this were not so, there would be nought else,
No other thing to think of; the skull would be the altar,
There could be no prayer save rest for the skeleton
That has jagged bones and cannot lie at comfort;
The sweetest flowers soon wither there, they love it not.
Who pondered too much on this would lie among the bones
And sleep and wake by little contrast there,
Finding them no different but always cold;
The hermit's only plaything was the death's head in his cell,
That he was long used to, that never stared at night
Through eyes without lids, kissed away by something,
With a mouth below that, bare and lipless,
Eaten by the dust, quite burned away;
But the hermit was not frightened, he had grown accus-
    tomed,

For it is one sort of logic to be living with the dead,
It's so slight a difference, a stone dropped from the hand
Picked up not long ago, now dropped again;
This is one remedy, to know the dead from near,
But it ends at nothing, there's no more than that,
The fright of death goes, but not the dreading of its dull-
    ness;
It is endless, dull, and comfortless, it never stops
There is no term to it, no first nor last,
There is no mercy in that dark land of death.
Think of death's companions, the owl, the bat, the spider,
And they can only enter when the tomb is broken,
They live in that darkness, in that lair of treachery,
And crawl, and spin their webs, and shake their speckled
    wings,
And come out in the double night, the night that's dark out-
    side,
So they bring no light back on their fattened bodies.
The spider, with its eight legs, runs and crawls,
With dreadful stomach, hairy paunch in air,
While the bat hangs, asleep, with gripping claws above
Holding to the stone ledge fouled by it;
He'll wake, when it's night outside, and wave his skinny
    wings,
And fly out through the crevice where the spider weaves
    anew,
Her silk will choke and fill it when the bat comes back,
And the bat, more clumsy, rends the webs asunder.
Such are death's companions and their twilit lives,
They keep by dry bones and yet they profit by them,
Living on death's bounties, on his dying portion,
Paid like marriage money, or the fees for school;

SACHEVERELL SITWELL

This, in stone or marble, is the home of others,
For they share it, but too soon, and it is theirs no more.
There is nothing at the other end, no door at which to listen,
There is nothing, nothing, not a breath beyond,
Give up your hopes of it, you'll wake no more.
The poor are fast forgotten,
They outnumber the living, but where are all their bones?
For every man alive there are a million dead,
Has their dust gone into earth that it is never seen?
There should be no air to breathe, with it so thick,
No space for wind to blow, or rain to fall;
Earth should be a cloud of dust, a soil of bones,
With no room, even, for our skeletons;
It is wasted time to think of it, to count its grains,
When all are alike and there's no difference in them;
They wait in the dark corridors, in earth's black galleries,
But the doors never open; they are dead, dead, dead.
Ah! Seek not the difference in king or beggar:
The King has his gold with him, that will not buy,
It is better to have starved and to be used to it.
Is there no comfort down the long dead years,
No warmth in prison, no love left for dead bones;
Does no one come to kiss them?   Answer, none, none, none.
Yet that was their longing, to be held and given,
To be handed to death while held in arms that loved them,
For his greater care, who saw that they were loved
And would take note of it and favour them in prison;
But, instead, he stood more near to them, his chill was in
      them,
And the living were warm, the last of love was warm;
Oh! One more ray of it, one beam before the winter,
Before they were unborn, beyond the blind, unborn,

379

More blind and puny, carried back into the dark,
But without rumour, with no fate to come,
Nothing but waiting, waiting long for nothing.
It was too late to weep, this was the last of time,
The light flickered, but tears would dim it more:
It was better to be calm and keep the taste of life;
But a sip or two of life, and then, for ever, death.
Oh! The cold, the sinking cold, the falling from the edge
Where love was no help and could not hold one back,
Falling, falling, falling into blackest dark,
Falling while hands touched one, while the lips felt warm,
If one was loved, and was not left alone.

Now it was so little that a babe was more,
No more of self, a little feeble thing
That love could not help,
That none could love for what it was;
It looked, and love saw it, but it could not answer:
Life's mystery was finished, only death was clear,
It was sorry for the living, it was glad to die,
Death was its master, it belonged to death.

O kiss it no more, it is so cold and pale,
It is not of this world, it is no part of us;
Not the soul we loved, but something pitiful
The hands should not touch. Oh! Leave it where it lies;
Let the dead where they die; come out among the living;
Weep not over dead bones; your tears are wasted.

There 's no escape, there is no subterfuge,
Death is decay; nor was it any better,
The mummied dead body, with brain pulled through the
    nose,

SACHEVERELL SITWELL

With entrails cut out, and all the mutilation
Wrapped in sweet bandages, bound up with herbs:
Death is not aromatic, it is false with flowers,
It has no ferment, it is always bitter;
The Egyptians live for ever, but not like themselves,
They are clenched, tortured, stifled, not the portrait on the
    lid;
They'd be better as old bones, and then might lie at peace.

All is degradation in the chambers of dead bones,
Nor marble, nor porphyry, but make it worse
For the mind sees, inside it, to the stained wet shroud
Where all else is dry, and only that is fluid,
So are carven tombs in the core to their cool marble,
The hollowed out heart of it, the inner cell,
All is degradation in the halls of the dead;
I never thought other things of death, until
The climb to Mycenae, when the wind and rain
Stormed at the tombs, where the rocks were as clouds
Struck still in the hurricane, driven to the hillside,
And rain poured in torrents, all the air was water.
The wet grey Argolide wept below,
The winds wailed and tore their hair,
The plain of Argos mourned and was in mist,
In mist tossed and shaken, in a sea of wrack;
This was the place of weeping, the day of tears,
As if all the dead were here, in all their pain,
Not stilled, nor assuaged, but aching to the bone:
It was their hell, they had no other hope than this,
But not alone, it was not nothingness:
The wind shrieked, the rain poured, the steep wet stones
Were a cliff in a whirlwind, by a raging sea,

SACHEVERELL SITWELL

Hidden by the rain-storm pelting down from heaven
To that hollow valley loud with melancholy;
But the dark hill opened.   And it was the tomb.
A passage led unto it, cut through the hill,
Echoing, rebounding with the million-ringing rain,
With walls, ever higher, till the giant lintel
Of huge stone, jagged and immense, rough-hewn
That held up the mountain: it was night within:
Silence and peace, nor sound of wind nor rain,
But a huge dome, glowing with the day from out
Let in by the narrow door, diffused by that,
More like some cavern under ocean's lips,
Fine and incredible, diminished in its stones,
For the hand of man had fitted them, of dwindling size,
Row after row, round all the hollow dome,
As scales of fish, as of the ocean's fins,
Pinned with bronze flowers that were, now, all fallen,
But the stones kept their symmetry, their separate shape
To the dome's high cupola of giant stone:
All was high and solemn in the cavern tomb:
If this was death, then death was poetry,
First architecture of the man-made years,
This was peace for the accursed Atridae:
Here lay Agamemnon in a cell beyond,
A little room of death, behind the solemn dome
Not burnt, nor coffined, but laid upon the soil
With a golden mask upon his dead man's face
For a little realm of light within that shadowed room:
And ever the sun came, every day of life,
Though less than star-point in that starry sky,
To the shadowed meridian, and sloped again,
Nor lit his armour, nor the mask upon his face,

SACHEVERELL SITWELL

For they burned in eternal night, they smouldered in it;
Season followed season, there was summer in the tomb,
Through hidden crevice, down that point of light,
Summer of loud wings and of the ghosts of blossom;
One by one, as harvesters, all heavy laden,
The bees sought their corridor into the dome
With honey of the asphodel, the flower of death,
Or thyme, rain-sodden, and more sweet for that;
Here was their honeycomb, high in the roof,
I heard sweet summer from their drumming wings,
Though it wept and rained and was the time of tears;
They made low music, they murmured in the tomb,
As droning nuns through all a shuttered noon,
Who prayed in this place of death, and knew it not.

How sweet such death, with honey from the flowers,
A little air, a little light, and drone of wings,
To long monotony, to prison of the tomb!
But he did not know it. His bones, picked clean,
Were any other bones. The trick is in our mind:
They love not a bed, nor raiment for their bones,
They are happy on cold stone or in the aching water,
And neither care, nor care not, they are only dead.
It once was Agamemnon, and we think him happy:
O false, false hope! How empty his happiness,
All for a fine cavern and the hum of bees.

I went again to him, another year,
And still it stormed, the corn-ripe Argolide
Rattled in dust, in burning grain of sand,
Earth lay in fever by the tombed Atridae.
O happy, happy death, and only happiness of that,
There is none other, where it ever weeps

SACHEVERELL SITWELL

In the ripened corn and round the silent cavern,
First, and best building of the man-made years.
O happy Agamemnon, who was luckless, living,
Happy in death, in the hollow haunted room,
Your very name is the treading of a spectre:
O speak to us of death, tell us of its mysteries,
Not here, not here, not in the hollow tomb,
But at the Muse's fountain, the Castalian spring,
By the plane-trees you planted, in the sacred shade;
The leaves speak in syllables, the live-long hours,
Their leaves are your leaves, and their shade is yours;
Listen, listen, listen to the voice of water
Alive and living, more than Agamemnon,
Whose name is sound of footsteps on the shaking boards,
A tragedian's ghost, a shadow on the rocks.
You are dead, you are dead, and all the dead are nothing to us,
There's nothing, nothing, nothing, not a breath beyond:
O give up every hope of it, we'll wake no more,
We are the world and it will end with us:
The heart is not a clock, it will not wind again,
The dead are but dead, there is no use for them,
They neither care, nor care not, they are only dead.

EDWARD DAVISON

1898–

323   *In this Dark House*

I SHALL come back to die
  From a far place at last,
After my life's carouse
In the old bed to lie
Remembering the past
  In this dark house.

384

EDWARD DAVISON

Because of a clock's chime
In the long waste of night
I shall awake and wait
At that calm, lonely time
Each sound and smell and sight
Mysterious and innate:

Some shadow on the wall
When curtains by the door
Move in a draught of wind;
Or else a light footfall
In a near corridor;
Even to feel the kind
Caress of a cool hand
Smoothing the draggled hair
Back from my shrunken brow,
And strive to understand
The woman's presence there,
And whence she came, and how.

What gust of wind that night
Will mutter her lost name
Through windows open wide,
And twist the flickering light
Of a sole candle's flame
Smoking from side to side,
Till the last spark it blows
Sets a moth's wings aflare
As the faint flame goes out?

Some distant door may close;
Perhaps a heavy chair
On bare floors dragged about

O'er the low ceiling sound,
And the thin twig of a tree
Knock on my window-pane
Till all the night around
Is listening with me,
While like a noise of rain
Leaves rustle in the wind.

Then from the inner gloom
The scratching of a mouse
May echo down my mind
And sound around the room
    In this dark house.

The vague scent of a flower,
Smelt then in that warm air
From gardens drifting in,
May slowly overpower
The vapid lavender,
Till feebly I begin
To count the scents I knew
And name them one by one,
And search the names for this.

Dreams will be swift and few
Ere that last night be done,
And gradual silences
In each long interim
Of halting time awake
All conscious sense confuse;
Shadows will grow more dim,
And sound and scent forsake
The dark, ere dawn ensues.

EDWARD DAVISON

In the new morning then,
So fixed the stare and fast,
The calm unseeing eye
Will never close again.

I shall come back at last
In this dark house to die.

RICHARD HUGHES

1900—

324   *The Sermon*

LIKE gript stick
    Still I sit:
Eyes fixed on far small eyes,
Full of it:
On the old, broad face,
The hung chin;
Heavy arms, surplice
Worn through and worn thin.
Probe I the hid mind
Under the gross flesh:
Clutch at poetic words,
Follow their mesh
Scarce heaving breath.
Clutch, marvel, wonder,
Till the words end.

Stilled is the muttered thunder:
The hard few people wake,
Gather their books, and go.
— Whether their hearts could break
How can I know?

325 *Felo de Se*

IF I were stone dead and buried under,
Is there a part of me would still wander,
Shiver, mourn, and cry Alack,
With no body to its back?

When brain grew mealy, turned to dust,
Would lissom Mind, too, suffer rust?
Immortal Soul grow imbecile,
Having no brain to think and feel?

— Or grant it be as priests say,
And growth come on my death-day:
Suppose Growth came: would Certainty?
Or would Mind still a quester be,

Frame deeper mysteries, not find them out,
And wander in a larger doubt?
— Alas! If to mind's petty stir
Death prove so poor a silencer:

Through veins when emptied a few hours
Of this hot blood, might suckle flowers:
From spiritual flames that scorch me
Never, never were I free!

Then back, Death, till I call thee!
Hast come too soon!
— Thou silly worm, gnaw not
Yet thine intricate cocoon.

326   *Old Cat Care*

Outside the Cottage

GREEN–EYED Care
May prowl and glare
And poke his snub, be-whiskered nose:
But Door fits tight
Against the Night:
Through criss-cross cracks no evil goes.

Window is small:
No room at all
For Worry and Money, his shoulder-bones:
Chimney is wide,
But Smoke 's inside
And happy Smoke would smother his moans.

Be-whiskered Care
May prowl out there:
But I never heard
He caught the Blue Bird.

327   *Glaucopis*

JOHN FANE DINGLE
By Rumney Brook
Shot a crop-eared owl,
   For pigeon mistook:

Caught her by the lax wing.
   — She, as she dies,
Thrills his warm soul through
   With her deep eyes.

389

Corpse-eyes are eerie:
  Tiger-eyes fierce:
John Fane Dingle found
  Owl-eyes worse.

Owl-eyes on night-clouds,
  Constant as Fate:
Owl-eyes in baby's face:
  On dish and plate:

Owl-eyes, without sound.
  — Pale of hue
John died, of no complaint,
  With owl-eyes too.

328   *The Walking Road*

THE World is all orange-round:
  The sea smells salt between:
The strong hills climb on their own backs,
Coloured and damascene,
Cloud-flecked and sunny-green;
Knotted and straining up,
Up, with still hands and cold:
Grip at the slipping sky,
Yet cannot hold:
Round twists old Earth, and round,
Stillness not yet found.

Plains like a flat dish, too,
Shudder and spin:
Roads in a pattern crawl
Scratched with a pin

390

RICHARD HUGHES

Across the fields' dim shagreen:
— Dusty their load:
But over the craggy hills
Wanders the walking road.

Broad as the hill 's broad,
Rough as the world 's rough, too:
Long as the Age is long,
Ancient and true,
Swinging, and broad, and long,
Craggy, strong.

Gods sit like milestones
On the edge of the Road, by the Moon's sill;
Man has feet, feet that swing, pound the high hill
Above and above, until
He stumble and widely spill
His dusty bones.

Round twists old Earth, and round,
Stillness not yet found.

329   *The Image*

DIM the light in your faces: be passionless in the room.
Snuffed are the tapers, and bitterly hang on the flow-
    erless air:
See: and this is the image of her they will lay in the tomb;
Clear, and waxen, and cooled in the mass of her hair.

Quiet the tears in your voices: feel lightly, finger, for finger
In love: then see how like is the image, but lifelessly fash-
    ioned
And sightless, calm, unloving. Who is the Artist? Linger
And ponder whither has flitted his sitter impassioned.

RICHARD HUGHES

330   *Winter*

SNOW wind-whipt to ice
    Under a hard sun:
Stream-runnels curdled hoar
    Crackle, cannot run.

Robin stark dead on twig,
    Song stiffened in it:
Fluffed feathers may not warm
    Bone-thin linnet:

Big-eyed rabbit, lost,
    Scrabbles the snow,
Searching for long-dead grass
    With frost-bit toe:

Mad-tired on the road
    Old Kelly goes;
Through crookt fingers snuffs the air
    Knife-cold in his nose.

Hunger-weak, snow-dazzled,
    Old Thomas Kelly
Thrusts his bit hands, for warmth,
    'Twixt waistcoat and belly.

331   *The Ruin*

GONE are the coloured princes, gone echo, gone laughter:
    Drips the blank roof: and the moss creeps after.

Dead is the crumbled chimney: all mellowed to rotting
The wall-tints, and the floor-tints, from the spotting
Of the rain, from the wind and slow appetite
Of patient mould: and of the worms that bite
At beauty all their innumerable lives.

    392

— But the sudden nip of knives,
The lady aching for her stiffening lord,
The passionate-fearful bride,
And beaded Pallor clamped to the torment-board,
Leave they no ghosts, no memories by the stairs?
No sheeted glimmer treading floorless ways?
No haunting melody of lovers' airs,
Nor stealthy chill upon the noon of days?

No: for the dead and senseless walls have long forgotten
What passionate hearts beneath the grass lie rotten.

Only from roofs and chimneys pleasantly sliding
Tumbles the rain in the early hours:
Patters its thousand feet on the flowers,
Cools its small grey feet in the grasses.

ROY CAMPBELL

1902–

332 *The Serf*

HIS naked skin clothed in the torrid mist
That puffs in smoke around the patient hooves,
The ploughman drives, a slow somnambulist,
And through the green his crimson furrow grooves.
His heart, more deeply than he wounds the plain,
Long by the rasping share of insult torn,
Red clod, to which the war-cry once was rain
And tribal spears the fatal sheaves of corn,
Lies fallow now. But as the turf divides
I see in the slow progress of his strides
Over the toppled clods and falling flowers,
The timeless, surly patience of the serf
That moves the nearest to the naked earth
And ploughs down palaces, and thrones, and towers.

ROY CAMPBELL

The Zulu Girl

WHEN in the sun the hot red acres smoulder,
    Down where the sweating gang its labour plies,
A girl flings down her hoe, and from her shoulder
Unslings her child tormented by the flies.

She takes him to a ring of shadow pooled
By thorn-trees: purpled with the blood of ticks,
While her sharp nails, in slow caresses ruled,
Prowl through his hair with sharp electric clicks,

His sleepy mouth, plugged by the heavy nipple,
Tugs like a puppy, grunting as he feeds:
Through his frail nerves her own deep languors ripple
Like a broad river sighing through its reeds.

Yet in that drowsy stream his flesh imbibes
An old unquenched unsmotherable heat —
The curbed ferocity of beaten tribes,
The sullen dignity of their defeat.

Her body looms above him like a hill
Within whose shade a village lies at rest,
Or the first cloud so terrible and still
That bears the coming harvest in its breast.

The Sisters

AFTER hot loveless nights, when cold winds stream
    Sprinkling the frost and dew, before the light,
Bored with the foolish things that girls must dream
Because their beds are empty of delight,

Two sisters rise and strip.   Out from the night
Their horses run to their low-whistled pleas —
Vast phantom shapes with eyeballs rolling white
That sneeze a fiery steam about their knees:

Through the crisp manes their stealthy prowling hands,
Stronger than curbs, in slow caresses rove,
They gallop down across the milk-white sands
And wade far out into the sleeping cove:

The frost stings sweetly with a burning kiss
As intimate as love, as cold as death:
Their lips, whereon delicious tremors hiss,
Fume with the ghostly pollen of their breath.

Far out on the grey silence of the flood
They watch the dawn in smouldering gyres expand
Beyond them: and the day burns through their blood
Like a white candle through a shuttered hand.

335   *Autumn*

I LOVE to see, when leaves depart,
   The clear anatomy arrive,
Winter, the paragon of art,
   That kills all forms of life and feeling
Save what is pure and will survive.

Already now the clanging chains
Of geese are harnessed to the moon:
Stripped are the great sun-clouding planes:
And the dark pines, their own revealing,
Let in the needles of the noon.

ROY CAMPBELL

Strained by the gale the olives whiten
Like hoary wrestlers bent with toil
And, with the vines, their branches lighten
To brim our vats where summer lingers
In the red froth and sun-gold oil.

Soon on our hearth's reviving pyre
Their rotted stems will crumble up:
And like a ruby, panting fire,
The grape will redden on your fingers
Through the lit crystal of the cup.

MICHAEL ROBERTS

1902–

336   *Les Planches-en-Montagnes*

WHERE I go are flowers blooming
And the foaming waters fuming
Where in defiles stubborn boulders
Set in rubble hunch their shoulders.

At each crevice root and branches
Grip the gully's weathered haunches,
Though I go where bluebells ringing
Swell cicadas' ceaseless singing.

Far above, the insulators,
Hiss and spark like commutators,
For I go where bees are humming
And dynamic turbines drumming.

Rocks and boulders are abolished
Under engines brightly polished;
Angular detritus is
Crushed to concrete terraces.

Roses bloom in pillared gardens;
Spindrift blown to rainbow hardens
Cool cement in fashioned fountains;
Sunlit pools reflect the mountains.

Here untended roar machines
In mastery of black ravines.

337   ## Midnight

I HAVE thrown wide my window
  And looked upon the night,
And seen Arcturus burning
    In chaos, proudly bright.

The powdered stars above me
    Have littered heaven's floor —
A thousand I remember;
    I saw a myriad more.

I have forgotten thousands,
    For deep and deep between,
My mind built up the darkness
    Of space, unheard, unseen.

I held my hands to heaven
    To hold perfection there,
But through my fingers streaming
    Went time, as thin as air;

And I must close my window
    And draw a decent blind
To screen from outer darkness
    The chaos of the mind.

FRANK O'CONNOR
1903–

338   *The Old Woman of Beare regrets*
Lost Youth

(i)

I, THE old woman of Beare,
Once a shining shift would wear,
Now and since my beauty's fall
I have scarce a shift at all.

Plump no more I sigh for these,
Bones bare beyond belief.
Ebbtide is all my grief;
I am ebbing like the seas.

It is pay
And not men ye love to-day,
But when we were young, ah then
We gave all our hearts to men.

Men most dear,
Horseman, huntsman, charioteer.
We gave them love with all our will
But the measure did not fill;

When to-day men ask you fair,
And get little for their care,
And the mite they get from you
Leaves their bodies bent in two.

And long since the foaming steed,
And the chariot with its speed,
And the charioteer went by —
God be with them all, say I.

FRANK O'CONNOR

Luck has left me, I go late
To the dark house where they wait,
When the Son of God thinks fit
Let Him call me home to it.

Oh, my hands when they are seen
Are so bony and so thin
That a boy might start in dread
Feeling them about his head.

(*ii*)

Girls are gay
When the year draws on to May,
But for me, so poor am I,
Sun will never light the day.

Though I care
Nothing now to bind my hair;
I had headgear bright enough
When the kings for love went bare.

'Tis not age that makes my pain
But the eye that sees so plain
That when all I love decays
Femon's ways are gold again.

Femon, Bregon, sacring stone,
Sacring stone and Ronan's throne
Storms have sacked so long that now
Tomb and sacring stone are one.

Where are they? Ah! well I know
Old and toiling bones that row
Alma's flood, or by its deep
Sleep in cold that slept not so.

Welladay
Every child outlives its play,
Year on year has worn my flesh
Since my fresh sweet strength went grey.

And, my God
Once again for ill or good
Spring will come and I shall see
Everything but me renewed.

Summer sun and autumn sun,
These I knew and these are gone,
And the winter time of men
Comes and these come not again.

(*iii*)

And ' Amen! ' I cry and ' Woe '
That the boughs are shaken bare,
And that candle-light and feast
Leave me to the dark and prayer.

I that had my day with kings,
And drank deep of mead and wine
Drink whey-water with old hags,
Sitting in their rags, and pine.

' That my cups be cups of whey! '
' That Thy will be done,' I pray,
But the prayer Oh Living God,
Stirs up madness in my blood.

And I shout ' Thy locks are grey! '
At the mantle that I stroke,
Then I grieve and murmur ' Nay
I am grey and not my cloak.'

FRANK O'CONNOR

And of eyes that loved the sun
Age my grief has taken one,
And the other too will take
Soon for good proportion's sake.

Floodtide!
Flood or ebb upon the strand?
What to thee the flood had brought
Ebbtide sweeps from out thy hand.

Floodtide!
And the swifter tides that fall,
All have reached me ebb and flow,
Ay, and now I know them all.

Happy Island of the sea,
Tide on tide shall come to thee,
But to me no waters fare
Though the beach is stark and bare.

Passing I can hardly say
' Here is such a place.' To-day
What was water far and wide
Changes with the ebbing tide.
> Ebbtide.
> > (*From the Irish.*)

339   *Autumn*

WOMAN full of wile,
  Take your hand away,
Nothing tempts me now,
  Sick for love you pray?

401

FRANK O'CONNOR

See this hair how grey,
    See this flesh how weak,
See this blood gone cold —
    Tell me what you seek.

Think me not perverse,
    Never bow your head;
Let love last as now,
    Slender witch, instead.

Take your mouth from mine,
    Kissing 's bitterer still;
Flesh from flesh must part
    Lest of warmth come will.

Your twined branching hair,
    Your grey eye dew-bright,
Your rich rounded breast
    Turn to lust the sight.

All but fill the bed
    Now that grey hairs fall,
Woman full of wile
    I would give you all!

               (From the Irish.)

340   *A Learned Mistress*

TELL him the tale is a lie!
    I love him as much as my life,
So why be jealous of me?
    I love him and loathe his wife.

FRANK O'CONNOR

If he kill me through jealousy now
　　His wife will perish of spite,
He will die of grief for his wife,
　　So three shall die in a night.

All blessings from heaven to earth
　　On the head of the woman I hate,
And the man I love as my life,
　　Sudden death be his fate!

　　　　　　　　　　(From the Irish.)

341 *Prayer for the Speedy End of Three*
Great Misfortunes

THERE be three things seeking my death,
　　All at my heels run wild —
Hang them, oh God, all three! —
　　Devil, maggot and child.

So much does each of them crave
　　The morsel that falls to his share
He cares not a thraneen what
　　Falls to the other pair.

If the devil, that crafty man,
　　Can capture my sprightly soul,
My money may go to my children,
　　My flesh to the worm in the hole.

My children think more of the money
　　That falls to them when I die,
Than a soul that they could not spend,
　　A body that none would buy.

403

FRANK O'CONNOR

And how would the maggots fare
   On a soul too thin to eat
And money too tough to chew?
   They must have my body for meat.

Christ, speared by a fool that was blind,
   Christ, nailed to a naked tree,
Since these three are waiting my end,
   Hang them, oh Christ, all three!

(From the Irish.)

342   *The Student*

THE student's life is pleasant,
   And pleasant is his labour,
Search all Ireland over
   You'll find no better neighbour.

Nor lords nor petty princes
   Dispute the student's pleasure,
Nor chapter stints his purse
   Nor stewardship his leisure.

None orders early rising,
   Calf-rearing or cow-tending,
Nor nights of toilsome vigil,
   His time is his for spending.

He takes a hand at draughts,
   And plucks a harp-string bravely,
And fills his nights with courting
   Some golden-haired light lady.

And when spring-time is come,
    The ploughshaft 's there to follow,
A fistful of goosequills,
    And a straight deep furrow!

(From the Irish.)

343   *A Grey Eye weeping*

'*Having gone with a poem to Sir Valentine Brown and
    gotten from him nothing but denial, rejection and
    flat refusal, the poet made these lines extempore.*'

THAT my old mournful heart was pierced in this black
  doom,
That foreign devils have made our land a tomb,
That the sun that was Munster's glory has gone down,
Has made me travel to seek you, Valentine Brown.

That royal Cashel is bare of house and guest,
That Brian's turreted home is the otter's nest,
That the kings of the land have neither land nor crown,
Has made me travel to seek you, Valentine Brown.

That the wild deer wanders afar, that it perishes now,
That alien ravens croak on the topmost bough,
That fish are no more in stream or streamlet lit by the sun,
Has made me travel to seek you, Valentine Brown.

Dernish away in the west — and her master banned;
Hamburg the refuge of him that has lost his land;
Two old grey eyes that weep; great verse that lacks renown,
Have made me travel to seek you, Valentine Brown.

(From the Irish of Egan O'Rahilly.)

405

344 *Kilcash*

W HAT shall we do for timber?
     The last of the woods is down,
Kilcash and the house of its glory
And the bell of the house are gone;
The spot where her lady waited
That shamed all women for grace
When earls came sailing to greet her
And Mass was said in that place.

My cross and my affliction
Your gates are taken away,
Your avenue needs attention,
Goats in the garden stray;
Your courtyard's filled with water
And the great earls where are they?
The earls, the lady, the people
Beaten into the clay.

Nor sound of duck or of geese there
Hawk's cry or eagle's call,
Nor humming of the bees there
That brought honey and wax for all,
Nor the sweet gentle song of the birds there
When the sun has gone down to the West
Nor a cuckoo atop of the boughs there
Singing the world to rest.

There 's a mist there tumbling from branches
Unstirred by night and by day,
And a darkness falling from heaven,
And our fortunes have ebbed away;

FRANK O'CONNOR

There 's no holly nor hazel nor ash there
But pastures of rock and stone,
The crown of the forest is withered
And the last of its game is gone.

I beseech of Mary and Jesus
That the great come home again
With long dances danced in the garden
Fiddle music and mirth among men,
That Kilcash the home of our fathers
Be lifted on high again
And from that to the deluge of waters
In bounty and peace remain.

(*From the Irish.*)

WILLIAM PLOMER

1903–

345   *The Scorpion*

LIMPOPO and Tugela churned
    In flood for brown and angry miles
Melons, maize, domestic thatch,
The trunks of trees and crocodiles;

The swollen estuaries were thick
With flotsam, in the sun one saw
The corpse of a young negress bruised
By rocks, and rolling on the shore,

Pushed by the waves of morning, rolled
Impersonally among shells,
With lolling breasts and bleeding eyes,
And round her neck were beads and bells.

That was the Africa we knew,
Where, wandering alone,
We saw, heraldic in the heat,
A scorpion on a stone.

346   *A Levantine*

A MOUTH like old silk soft with use,
   The weak chin of a dying race,
Eyes that know all and look at naught —
   Disease, depravity, disgrace
   Are all united in that face.

And yet the triumph of decay
Outbraves the pride of bouncing fools —
As an old craftsman smiles to hear
   His name respected in the schools
   And sees the rust upon his tools;

Through shades of truth and memory
He burrows, secret as a mole,
And smiles with loose and withered lips
   Because the workings of his soul
   Will, when he 's low, stay sound and whole.

With Socrates as ancestor,
And rich Byzantium in his veins,
What if this weakling does not work?
   He never takes the slightest pains
   To exercise his drowsy brains,

But drinks his coffee, smokes and yawns
While new-rich empires rise and fall:
His blood is bluer than their heaven,
  Poor, but no poorer than them all,
  He has no principles at all.

CECIL DAY LEWIS

1905–

347
Come up, Methuselah

COME up, Methuselah,
  You doddering superman!
Give me an instant realized
And I'll outdo your span.

In that one moment of evening
When roses are most red
I can fold back the firmament,
I can put time to bed.

Abraham, stint your tally
Of concubines and cattle!
Give place to me — capitalist
In more intrinsic metal.

I have a lover of flesh
And a lover that is a sprite:
To-day I lie down with finite,
To-morrow with infinite.

That one is a constant
And suffers no eclipse,
Though I feel sun and moon burning
Together on her lips.

This one is a constant,
But she's not kind at all;
She raddles her gown with my despairs
And paints her lip with gall.

My lover of flesh is wild,
And willing to kiss again;
She is the potency of earth
When woods exhale the rain.

My lover of air, like Artemis
Spectrally embraced,
Shuns the daylight that twists her smile
To mineral distaste.

Twin poles energic, they
Stand fast and generate
This spark that crackles in the void
As between fate and fate.

348   *Few Things can more inflame*

FEW things can more inflame
This far too combative heart
Than the intellectual Quixotes of the age
Prattling of abstract art.

No one would deny it —
But for a blind man's passion
Cassandra had been no more than a draggle-skirt,
Helen a ten-year fashion.
Yet had there not been one hostess
Ever whose arms waylaid
Like the tough bramble a princeling's journey, or
At the least no peasant maid

410

Redressing with rude heat
Nature's primeval wrong,
Epic had slumbered on beneath his blindness
And Helen lacked her song.

(So the antique balloon
Wobbles with no defence
Against the void but a grapnel that hops and ploughs
Through the landscape of sense.)

Phrase-making, dress-making —
Distinction 's hard to find;
For thought must play the mannequin, strut in phrase,
Or gape with the ruck: and mind,
Like body, from covering gets
Most adequate display.
Yet time trundles this one to the rag-and-bone man,
While that other may
Reverberate all along
Man's craggy circumstance —
Naked enough to keep its dignity
Though it eye God askance.

349 *Can the Mole take*

CAN the mole take
A census of the stars?
Our firmament will never
Give him headache.

The man who nuzzles
In a woman's lap
Burrows toward a night
Too deep for puzzles:

While he, whose prayer
Holds up the starry system
In a God's train, sees nothing
Difficult there.

So I, perhaps,
Am neither mole nor mantis;
I see the constellations,
But by their gaps.

350   *With me my Lover makes*

WITH me, my lover makes
The clock assert its chime:
But when she goes, she takes
The mainspring out of time.

Yet this time-wrecking charm
Were better than love dead
And its hollow alarum
Hammered out on lead.

Why should I fear that Time
Will superannuate
These workmen of my rhyme —
Love, despair and hate?

Fleeing the herd, I came
To a graveyard on a hill,
And felt its mould proclaim
The bone gregarious still.

Boredoms and agonies
Work out the rhythm of bone: —
No peace till creature his
Creator has outgrown.

Passion dies from the heart
   But to infect the marrow;
Holds dream and act apart
   Till the man discard his narrow

Sapience and folly
   Here, where the graves slumber
In a green melancholy
   Of overblown summer.

351   *Rest from Loving*

REST from loving and be living.
   Fallen is fallen past retrieving
The unique flyer dawn's dove
Arrowing down feathered with fire.

Cease denying, begin knowing.
Comes peace this way here comes renewing
With dower of bird and bud knocks
Loud on winter wall on death's door.

Here's no meaning but of morning.
Naught soon of night but stars remaining,
Sink lower, fade, as dark womb
Recedes creation will step clear.

352   *Tempt me no more*

TEMPT me no more; for I
   Have known the lightning's hour,
The poet's inward pride,
The certainty of power.

Bayonets are closing round.
I shrink; yet I must wring
A living from despair
And out of steel a song.

Though song, though breath be short,
I'll share not the disgrace
Of those that ran away
Or never left the base.

Comrades, my tongue can speak
No comfortable words,
Calls to a forlorn hope,
Gives work and not rewards.

Oh keep the sickle sharp
And follow still the plough:
Others may reap, though some
See not the winter through.

Father, who endest all,
Pity our broken sleep;
For we lie down with tears
And waken but to weep.

And if our blood alone
Will melt this iron earth,
Take it. It is well spent
Easing a saviour's birth.

353 *I've heard them lilting at Loom and Belting*

I'VE heard them lilting at loom and belting,
    Lasses lilting before dawn of day:
But now they are silent, not gamesome and gallant —
The flowers of the town are rotting away.

There was laughter and loving in the lanes at evening;
Handsome were the boys then, and girls were gay.
But lost in Flanders by medalled commanders
The lads of the village are vanished away.

Cursed be the promise that takes our men from us —
All will be champion if you choose to obey:
They fight against hunger but still it is stronger —
The prime of our land grows cold as the clay.

The women are weary, once lilted so merry,
Waiting to marry for a year and a day:
From wooing and winning, from owning or earning
The flowers of the town are all turned away.

354 *Come live with me and be my Love*

COME, live with me and be my love,
   And we will all the pleasures prove
Of peace and plenty, bed and board,
That chance employment may afford.

I'll handle dainties on the docks
And thou shalt read of summer frocks:
At evening by the sour canals
We'll hope to hear some madrigals.

Care on thy maiden brow shall put
A wreath of wrinkles, and thy foot
Be shod with pain: not silken dress
But toil shall tire thy loveliness.

Hunger shall make thy modest zone
And cheat fond death of all but bone —
If these delights thy mind may move,
Then live with me and be my love.

415

WILLIAM EMPSON

1906–

355   *Arachne*

'TWIXT devil and deep sea, man hacks his caves;
　　Birth, death; one, many; what is true, and seems;
Earth's vast hot iron, cold space's empty waves:

King spider, walks the velvet roof to streams:
Must bird and fish, must god and beast avoid:
Dance, like nine angels, on pin-point extremes.

His gleaming bubble between void and void,
Tribe-membrane, that by mutual tension stands,
Earth's surface film, is at a breath destroyed.

Bubbles gleam brightest with least depth of lands
But two is least can with full tension strain,
Two molecules; one, and the film disbands.

We two suffice.   But oh beware, whose vain
Hydroptic soap my meagre water saves.
Male spiders must not be too early slain.

MARGOT RUDDOCK

1907–

356   *The Child Compassion*

UNWELCOME child
　　Compassion come
Into my heart
As to the womb,

How heavily
It laboureth
In anguish to
Bring thee to birth,

416

O puny babe
With thy frail cry
Too weak to live
Too strong to die.

Unwilling mother
I confessed
Do suckle thee
Upon my breast.

357   ## *Spirit, Silken Thread*

SPIRIT, silken thread,
Lightly wind
Through the fingers
Of my soul
She is blind. . . .

358   ## *Take Away*

TAKE away, take away, all that
                I have seen,
Fold and wrap it away,
Lock and bar away all that I know. . . .

For I cannot drink
For the shrieking, blinding,
Tearing wrench of thought —

Cannot drink from the pool
That is waiting
Waiting. . . .
                Surging, sweetening, shaking,
                        Lapping.

359   *I take thee Life*

I TAKE thee, Life,
Because I need,
A wanton love
My flesh to feed.

But still my soul
Insatiate
Cries out, cries out
For its true mate.

360   *O Holy Water*

O HOLY water
Love, I learn
I may not take thee
Though I burn.

O frustrate passion,
Supple vine,
I tear thy tendrils
Waste thy wine.

O jagged path
Reality
I weep and bleed
To follow thee.

361   *Love Song*

THOUGH to think
Rejoiceth me,
Love I will
Not think of Thee,

MARGOT RUDDOCK

Though thy heart's
My resting place
Yet I will
Not seek embrace,

Not till soul
Has shed her pain
Will I come
To Thee again.

And then when
My heart is free
I will give
It back to Thee.

362   *Autumn, crystal Eye*

AUTUMN, crystal eye
  Look on me,
Passion chilled am I
Like to thee,

Seeking sterner truth,
Even now
Longing for the white
Frozen bough.

LOUIS MacNEICE

1907–

363   *The Individualist speaks*

WE with our Fair pitched among the feathery clover
  Are always cowardly and never sober
Drunk with steam-organs thigh-rub and cream-soda
— We cannot remember enemies in this valley.

LOUIS MacNEICE

As chestnut candles turn to conkers, so we
Knock our brains together extravagantly
Instead of planting them to make more trees
— Who have not as yet sampled God's malice.

But to us urchins playing with paint and filth
A prophet scanning the road on the hither hills
Might utter the old warning of the old sin
— Avenging youth threatening an old war.

Crawling down like lava or termites
Nothing seduces nothing dissolves nothing affrights
You who scale off masks and smash the purple lights
— But I will escape, with my dog, on the far side of the Fair.

364   *Circe*

'. . . *vitreamque Circen*'

SOMETHING of glass about her, of dead water,
Chills and holds us,
Far more fatal than painted flesh or the lodestone of live hair
This despair of crystal brilliance.
Narcissus' error
Enfolds and kills us —
Dazed with gazing on that unfertile beauty
Which is our own heart's thought.
Fled away to the beasts
One cannot stop thinking; Timon
Kept on finding gold.
In parrot-ridden forest or barren coast
A more importunate voice than bird or wave
Escutcheoned on the air with ice letters
Seeks and, of course, finds us
(Of course, being our echo).

Be brave, my ego, look into your glass
And realize that that never-to-be-touched
Vision is your mistress.

365   *Turf-stacks*

AMONG these turf-stacks graze no iron horses
    Such as stalk, such as champ in towns and the soul of
        crowds,
Here is no mass-production of neat thoughts
No canvas shrouds for the mind nor any black hearses:
The peasant shambles on his boots like hooves
Without thinking at all or wanting to run in grooves.

But those who lack the peasant's conspirators,
The tawny mountain, the unregarded buttress,
Will feel the need of a fortress against ideas and against the
Shuddering insidious shock of the theory-vendors,
The little sardine men crammed in a monster toy
Who tilt their aggregate beast against our crumbling Troy.

For we are obsolete who like the lesser things
Who play in corners with looking-glasses and beads;
It is better we should go quickly, go into Asia
Or any other tunnel where the world recedes,
Or turn blind wantons like the gulls who scream
And rip the edge off any ideal or dream.

366   *An Eclogue for Christmas*

A. I meet you in an evil time.
B.   The evil bells
    Put out of our heads, I think, the thought of everything
        else.

421

LOUIS MacNEICE

A. The jaded calendar revolves,
   Its nuts need oil, carbon chokes the valves,
   The excess sugar of a diabetic culture
   Rotting the nerve of life and literature;
   Therefore when we bring out the old tinsel and frills
   To announce that Christ is born among the barbarous hills
   I turn to you whom a morose routine
   Saves from the mad vertigo of being what has been.
B. Analogue of me, you are wrong to turn to me,
   My country will not yield you any sanctuary,
   There is no pinpoint in any of the ordnance maps
   To save you when your towns and town-bred thoughts
       collapse,
   It is better to die *in situ* as I shall,
   One place is as bad as another. Go back where your
       instincts call
   And listen to the crying of the town-cats and the taxis
       again,
   Or wind your gramophone and eavesdrop on great men.
A. Jazz-weary of years of drums and Hawaiian guitar,
   Pivoting on the parquet I seem to have moved far
   From bombs and mud and gas, have stuttered on my feet
   Clinched to the streamlined and butter-smooth trulls of
       the élite,
   The lights irritating and gyrating and rotating in gauze —
   Pomade-dazzle, a slick beauty of gewgaws —
   I who was Harlequin in the childhood of the century,
   Posed by Picasso beside an endless opaque sea,
   Have seen myself sifted and splintered in broken facets,
   Tentative pencillings, endless liabilities, no assets,
   Abstractions scalpelled with a palette-knife
   Without reference to this particular life.

LOUIS MacNEICE

And so it has gone on; I have not been allowed to be
Myself in flesh or face, but abstracting and dissecting
me
They have made of me pure form, a symbol or a
pastiche,
Stylized profile, anything but soul and flesh:
And that is why I turn this jaded music on
To forswear thought and become an automaton.

B. There are in the country also of whom I am afraid —
Men who put beer into a belly that is dead,
Women in the forties with terrier and setter who whistle
and swank
Over down and plough and Roman road and daisied bank,
Half-conscious that these barriers over which they stride
Are nothing to the barbed wire that has grown round
their pride.

A. And two there are, as I drive in the city, who suddenly
perturb —
The one sirening me to draw up by the kerb
The other, as I lean back, my right leg stretched
creating speed,
Making me catch and stamp, the brakes shrieking, pull
up dead:
She wears silk stockings taunting the winter wind,
He carries a white stick to mark that he is blind.

B. In the country they are still hunting, in the heavy shires
Greyness is on the fields and sunset like a line of pyres
Of barbarous heroes smoulders through the ancient air
Hazed with factory dust and, orange opposite, the
moon's glare,
Goggling yokel-stubborn through the iron trees,
Jeers at the end of us, our bland ancestral ease;

LOUIS MacNEICE

We shall go down like palaeolithic man
Before some new Ice Age or Genghiz Khan.

A. It is time for some new coinage, people have got so old,
 Hacked and handled and shiny from pocketing they
   have made bold
   To think that each is himself through these accidents,
     being blind
   To the fact that they are merely the counters of an un-
     known Mind.

B. A Mind that does not think, if such a thing can be,
 Mechanical Reason, capricious Identity.
   That I could be able to face this domination nor
     flinch —

A. The tin toys of the hawker move on the pavement inch
   by inch
 Not knowing that they are wound up; it is better to be so
 Than to be, like us, wound up and while running down
   to know —

B. But everywhere the pretence of individuality recurs —
A. Old faces frosted with powder and choked in furs.
B. The jutlipped farmer gazing over the humpbacked wall.
A. The commercial traveller joking in the urinal.
B. I think things draw to an end, the soil is stale.
A. And over-elaboration will nothing now avail,
 The street is up again, gas, electricity or drains,
 Ever-changing conveniences, nothing comfortable re-
   mains
 Un-improved, as flagging Rome improved villa and
   sewer
 (A sound-proof library and a stable temperature).
 Our street is up, red lights sullenly mark
 The long trench of pipes, iron guts in the dark,

424

And not till the Goths again come swarming down the
    hill
Will cease the clangour of the electric drill.
But yet there is beauty narcotic and deciduous
In this vast organism grown out of us:
On all the traffic-islands stand white globes like moons,
The city's haze is clouded amber that purrs and croons,
And tilting by the noble curve bus after tall bus comes
With an osculation of yellow light, with a glory like
    chrysanthemums.

B. The country gentry cannot change, they will die in their
    shoes
From angry circumstance and moral self-abuse,
Dying with a paltry fizzle they will prove their lives to be
An ever-diluted drug, a spiritual tautology.
They cannot live once their idols are turned out,
None of them can endure, for how could they, possibly,
    without
The flotsam of private property, pekingese and polyanthus,
The good things which in the end turn to poison and pus,
Without the bandy chairs and the sugar in the silver tongs
And the inter-ripple and resonance of years of dinner-
    gongs?
Or if they could find no more that cumulative proof
In the rain dripping off the conservatory roof?
What will happen when the only sanction the country-
    dweller has —

A. What will happen to us, planked and panelled with jazz?
Who go to the theatre where a black man dances like an
    eel,
Where pink thighs flash like the spokes of a wheel,
    where we feel

That we know in advance all the jogtrot and the cake-
    walk jokes,

All the bumfun and the gags of the comedians in boaters
    and toques,

All the tricks of the virtuosos who invert the usual —

B. What will happen to us when the State takes down the
    manor wall,

When there is no more private shooting or fishing, when
    the trees are all cut down,

When faces are all dials and cannot smile or frown —

A. What will happen when the sniggering machine-guns in
    the hands of the young men

Are trained on every flat and club and beauty parlour
    and Father's den?

What will happen when our civilization like a long pent
    balloon —

B. What will happen will happen; the whore and the buffoon

Will come off best; no dreamers, they cannot lose their
    dream

And are at least likely to be reinstated in the new régime.

But one thing is not likely —

A.   Do not gloat over yourself

Do not be your own vulture, high on some mountain shelf

Huddle the pitiless abstractions bald about the neck

Who will descend when you crumple in the plains a wreck.

Over the randy of the theatre and cinema I hear songs

Unlike anything —

B.   The lady of the house poises the silver tongs

And picks a lump of sugar, ' ne plus ultra ' she says

' I cannot do otherwise, even to prolong my days ' —

A. I cannot do otherwise either, to-night I will book my seat—

B. I will walk about the farm-yard which is replete

LOUIS MacNEICE

As with the smell of dung so with memories —

A. I will gorge myself to satiety with the oddities
Of every artiste, official or amateur,
Who has pleased me in my rôle of hero-worshipper
Who has pleased me in my rôle of individual man —

B. Let us lie once more, say ' What we think, we can '
The old idealist lie —

A.   And for me before I die
Let me go the round of the garish glare —

B.   And on the bare and high
Places of England, the Wiltshire Downs and the Long
  Mynd
Let the balls of my feet bounce on the turf, my face
  burn in the wind
My eyelashes stinging in the wind, and the sheep like
  grey stones
Humble my human pretensions —

A.   Let the saxophones and the xylophones
And the cult of every technical excellence, the miles of
  canvas in the galleries
And the canvas of the rich man's yacht snapping and
  tacking on the seas
And the perfection of a grilled steak —

B.   Let all these so ephemeral things
Be somehow permanent like the swallow's tangent
  wings:
Goodbye to you, this day remember is Christmas, this
  morn
They say, interpret it your own way, Christ is born.

1907–

367   *It's no use raising a Shout*

IT 'S no use raising a shout.
No, Honey, you can cut that right out.
I don't want any more hugs;
Make me some fresh tea, fetch me some rugs.
Here am I, here are you:
But what does it mean?   What are we going to do?

A long time ago I told my mother
I was leaving home to find another:
I never answered her letter
But I never found a better.
Here am I, here are you:
But what does it mean?   What are we going to do?

It wasn't always like this?
Perhaps it wasn't, but it is.
Put the car away; when life fails,
What 's the good of going to Wales?
Here am I, here are you:
But what does it mean?   What are we going to do?

In my spine there was a base;
And I knew the general's face:
But they've severed all the wires,
And I can't tell what the general desires.
Here am I, here are you:
But what does it mean?   What are we going to do?

In my veins there is a wish,
And a memory of fish:
When I lie crying on the floor,

It says, ' You've often done this before.'
Here am I, here are you:
But what does it mean?   What are we going to do?

A bird used to visit this shore:
It isn't going to come any more.
I've come a very long way to prove
No land, no water, and no love.
Here am I, here are you:
But what does it mean?   What are we going to do?

368   *This Lunar Beauty*

THIS lunar beauty
    Has no history
Is complete and early;
If beauty later
Bear any feature
It had a lover
And is another.

This like a dream
Keeps other time
And daytime is
The loss of this;
For time is inches
And the heart's changes
Where ghost has haunted
Lost and wanted.

But this was never
A ghost's endeavour
Nor finished this,
Was ghost at ease;
And till it pass
Love shall not near

WYSTAN HUGH AUDEN

The sweetness here
Nor sorrow take
His endless look.

Before this loved one
Was that one and that one
A family
And history
And ghost's adversity
Whose pleasing name
Was neighbourly shame.
Before this last one
Was much to be done,
Frontiers to cross
As clothes grew worse
And coins to pass
In a cheaper house
Before this last one
Before this loved one.

Face that the sun
Is supple on
May stir but here
Is no new year;
This gratitude for gifts is less
Than the old loss;
Touching is shaking hands
On mortgaged lands;
And smiling of
This gracious greeting
' Good day. Good luck '
Is no real meeting
But instinctive look
A backward love.

WYSTAN HUGH AUDEN

369   *The Silly Fool*

THE silly fool, the silly fool
      Was sillier in school
But beat the bully as a rule.

The youngest son, the youngest son
Was certainly no wise one
Yet could surprise one.

Or rather, or rather
To be posh, we gather,
One should have no father.

Simple to prove
That deeds indeed
In life succeed
But love in love
And tales in tales
Where no one fails.

JULIAN BELL

1908–

370   *The Redshanks*

DRIVE on, sharp wings, and cry above
      Not contemplating life or love
Or war or death: a winter flight
Impartial to our human plight.

I below shall still remain
On solid earth, with fear and pain,
Doubt, and act, and nervous strive,
As best I may, to keep alive.

JULIAN BELL

What useless dream, a hope to sail
Down the wide, transparent gale,
Until, insentient, I shall be
As gaseous a transparency.

What useless dream, a hope to wring
Comfort from a migrant wing:
Human or beast, before us set
The incommunicable net.

Parallel, yet separate,
The languages we mistranslate,
And knowledge seems no less absurd
If of a mistress, or a bird.

STEPHEN SPENDER

1909–

371   *The Shapes of Death*

SHAPES of death haunt life,
   Neurosis eclipsing each in special shadow:
Unrequited love not solving
One's need to become another's body
Wears black invisibility:
The greed for property
Heaps a skyscraper over the breathing ribs:
The speedlines of dictators
Cut their own stalks:
From afar, we watch the best of us —
Whose adored desire was to die for the world.

Ambition is my death. That flat thin flame
I feed, that plants my shadow. This prevents love
And offers love of being loved or loving.
The humorous self-forgetful drunkenness

432

It hates, demands the slavish pyramids
Be built. Who can prevent
His death's industry, which when he sleeps
Throws up its towers?   And conceals in slackness
The dreams of revolution, the birth of death?

Also the swallows by autumnal instinct
Comfort us with their effortless exhaustion
In great unguided flight to their complete South.
There on my fancied pyramids they lodge
But for delight, their whole compulsion.
Not teaching me to love, but soothing my eyes;
Not saving me from death, but saving me for speech.

372 *An ' I ' can never be Great Man*

AN ' I ' can never be great man.
This known great one has weakness
To friends is most remarkable for weakness
His ill-temper at meals, his dislike of being contradicted,
His only real pleasure fishing in ponds,
His only real desire — forgetting.

To advance from friends to the composite self
Central ' I ' is surrounded by ' I eating ',
' I loving ', ' I angry ', ' I excreting ',
And the ' great I ' planted in him
Has nothing to do with all these.

It can never claim its true place
Resting in the forehead, and secure in his gaze.
The ' great I ' is an unfortunate intruder
Quarrelling with ' I tiring ' and ' I sleeping '
And all those other ' I's who long for ' We dying '

433

CHARLES MADGE

373   *The Times*

TIME wasted and time spent
   Daytime with used up wit
Time to stand, time to sit
Or wait and see if it
Happens, happy event

For war is eating now.

Waking, shaking off death
Leaving the white sheets
And dull-head who repeats
The dream of his defeats
And drawing colder breath

For war is eating now.

Growing older, going
Where the water runs
Black as death, and guns
Explode the sinking suns,
Blowing like hell, snowing

For war is eating now.

374   *Solar Creation*

THE Sun, of whose terrain we creatures are,
   Is the director of all human love,
Unit of time, and circle round the earth,

434

CHARLES MADGE

And we are the commotion born of love
And slanted rays of that illustrious star,
Peregrine of the crowded fields of birth,

The crowded lane, the market and the tower.
Like sight in pictures, real at remove,
Such is our motion on dimensional earth.

Down by the river, where the ragged are,
Continuous the cries and noise of birth,
While to the muddy edge dark fishes move,

And over all, like death, or sloping hill,
Is nature, which is larger and more still.

GEORGE BARKER

1913–

375 *The Wraith-friend*

FOLLOWING forbidden streets
Towards unreal retreats,
Returning, lost again,
Encircling in vain:
No lunar eye, no star
Beckoning from the far
Wastes the trackless feet
Leading their beaten beat
Back on to the broad
And multitudinous road.
In what unearthly land
I fugitively stand,
Between what frenzied seas
Gaze, with my burning miseries
Miming the stars?

435

O angel in me hidden
Rise from the laden
Sorrow of this dark hand!
Companion and wraith-friend
From the rib's narrow prison
Step, in miraculous person!
Touch into these exhausted limbs
The alacrity of the birds
Which over the greatest ranges
Widely and eagerly range!

Though to wings those dark limbs
Spread, and that deep breast climbs
Eagerly the heights of the skies, or
Of the earliest lark's soar,
Until brushing against cold heaven
Like bluebirds in storms, even
Then that known flesh must fall.
Soon, within this prison's wider wall
Lie with those giant arms, that form,
For there is no upward egress from
This earthly, this unearthly land
Upon whose dust may stand
None, though heavenly high can fly,
But in whose dust all brighter dust must lie.

376   *The leaping Laughers*

WHEN will men again
Lift irresistible fists
Not bend from ends
But each man lift men
Nearer again.

436

Many men mean
Well: but tall walls
Impede, their hands bleed and
They fall, their seed the
Seed of the fallen.

See here the fallen
Stooping over stones, over their
Own bones: but all
Stooping doom beaten.

Whom the noonday washes
Whole, whom the heavens compel,
And to whom pass immaculate messages,
When will men again
Lift irresistible fists
Impede impediments
Leap mountains laugh at walls?

377   *The Crystal*

WITH burning fervour
    I am forever
Turning in my hand
The crystal, this moment

Whose spatial glitter
Travelling erratically
Forward

Touches with permanent
Disturbance the pavements
The faked walls the crevices
Of futurity.

Sooner than darken
This crystal miracle
With a hand's
Vagary

One would dissever
This wrist this hand,
Or remove the eyelid
To see the end.

378   *He comes among*

HE comes among
     The summer throngs of the young
Rose, and in his long
Hands flowers, fingers, carries;
Dreamed of like aviaries
In which many phoenixes sing,
Promising touch soon
In summer, never to come:

Or, the scarce falls
Of unearthly streams, calls
And recalls the call,
Tempting in echoes the aspatial
Glooms of the empty
Heart, till the senses, need inebriate,
Turning and burning through slow leaves of vague
Urge, shall, until age.

INDEX OF AUTHORS

References are to the numbers of the poems

INDEX OF AUTHORS

INDEX OF FIRST LINES

References are to pages

INDEX OF FIRST LINES

INDEX OF FIRST LINES

INDEX OF FIRST LINES

446

INDEX OF FIRST LINES

447

INDEX OF FIRST LINES

INDEX OF FIRST LINES

INDEX OF FIRST LINES

INDEX OF FIRST LINES

INDEX OF FIRST LINES

INDEX OF FIRST LINES

INDEX OF FIRST LINES